# Street by Street

C000171057

# CROYDON, SUTTON
# BECKENHAM, EPSOM,
# MITCHAM, PURLEY

**Banstead, Carshalton, Caterham, Chipstead, Coulsdon, Ewell, Merton, Morden, New Addington, Penge, Selsdon, Warlingham, Wimbledon, Woldingham**

**3rd edition September 2007**
© Automobile Association Developments Limited
2007

Original edition printed September 2002

 This product includes
map data licensed from
Ordnance Survey® with
the permission of the Controller of Her Majesty's
Stationery Office. © Crown copyright 2007.
All rights reserved. Licence number 100021153.

Published by AA Publishing (a trading name of
Automobile Association Developments Limited, whose
registered office is Fanum House, Basing View,
Basingstoke, Hampshire RG21 4EA. Registered
number 1878835).

Produced by the Mapping Services Department
of The Automobile Association. (A03278)

A CIP Catalogue record for this book is available from
the British Library.

Printed by Oriental Press in Dubai

Key to map pages — ii-iii

Key to map symbols — iv-1

Enlarged map pages — 2-3

Main map pages — 4-61

Index – towns & villages — 62

Index – streets — 63-77

Index – featured places — 77-80

Acknowledgements — 80

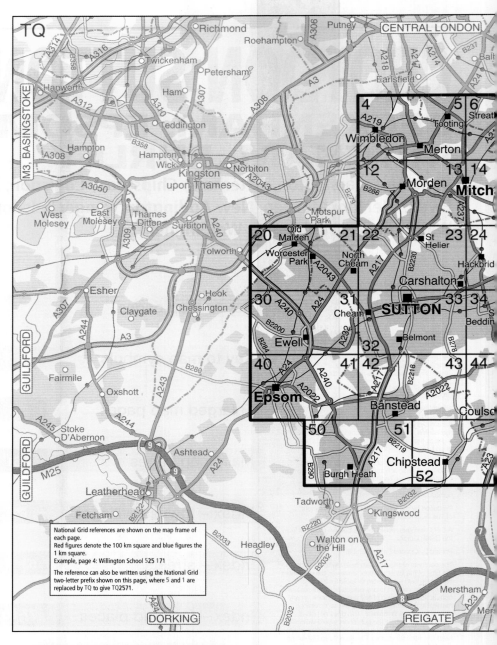

TQ

National Grid references are shown on the map frame of each page.
Red figures denote the 100 km square and blue figures the 1 km square.
Example: page 4: Willington School 525 171

The reference can also be written using the National Grid two-letter prefix shown on this page, where 5 and 1 are replaced by TQ to give TQ2571.

**Scale of enlarged map pages** 1:10,000 6.3 inches to 1 mile

0 ———— 1/4 ———— miles ———— 1/2

0 ———— 1/4 ———— 1/2 ———— kilometres ———— 3/4 ———— 1

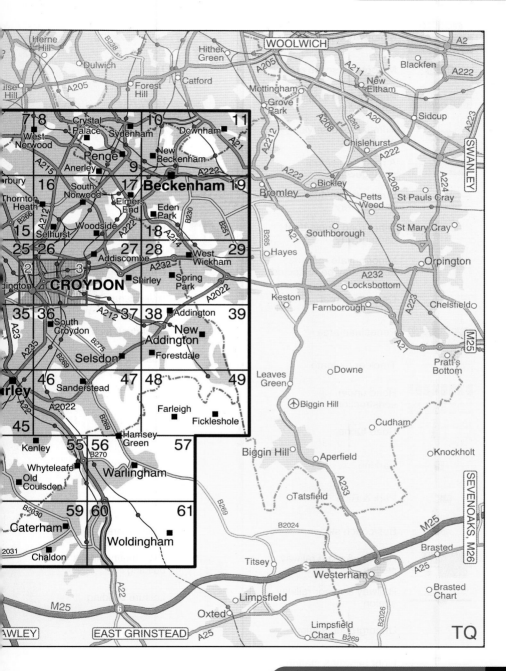

iv

|  |  |
|---|---|
| Junction 9 | Motorway & junction |
| Services | Motorway service area |
| | Primary road single/dual carriageway |
| Services | Primary road service area |
| | A road single/dual carriageway |
| | B road single/dual carriageway |
| | Other road single/dual carriageway |
| | Minor/private road, access may be restricted |
| ← ← | One-way street |
| | Pedestrian area |
| | Track or footpath |
| | Road under construction |
| | Road tunnel |
| P | Parking |
| P+ | Park & Ride |
| | Bus/coach station |
| | Railway & main railway station |
| | Railway & minor railway station |
| ⊖ | Underground station |
| ⊖ | Light railway & station |
| +++++++ | Preserved private railway |

|  |  |
|---|---|
| LC | Level crossing |
| •—•—•—• | Tramway |
| - - - - - | Ferry route |
| ........... | Airport runway |
| - · - · - | County, administrative boundary |
| ▼▼▼▼▼ | Mounds |
| 17 | Page continuation 1:15,000 |
| 3 | Page continuation to enlarged scale 1:10,000 |
| | River/canal, lake, pier |
| | Aqueduct, lock, weir |
| 465 ▲ Winter Hill | Peak (with height in metres) |
| | Beach |
| | Woodland |
| | Park |
| | Cemetery |
| | Built-up area |
| | Industrial/business building |
| | Leisure building |
| | Retail building |
| | Other building |
| IKEA | IKEA store |

| | | | | |
|---|---|---|---|---|
| ⊓⊓⊓⊓⊓⊓ | City wall | | 🏰 | Castle |
| A&E | Hospital with 24-hour A&E department | | 🏛 | Historic house or building |
| PO | Post Office | | Wakehurst Place NT | National Trust property |
| 📖 | Public library | | 🏛 | Museum or art gallery |
| 𝑖 | Tourist Information Centre | | 🐎 | Roman antiquity |
| 𝑖 | Seasonal Tourist Information Centre | | ⚊ | Ancient site, battlefield or monument |
| 🔋 🔋 | Petrol station, 24 hour<br>Major suppliers only | | 🏭 | Industrial interest |
| † | Church/chapel | | ✳ | Garden |
| 🚻 | Public toilets | | ◉ | Garden Centre<br>Garden Centre Association Member |
| ♿ | Toilet with disabled facilities | | 🌱 | Garden Centre<br>Wyevale Garden Centre |
| PH | Public house<br>AA recommended | | 🌳 | Arboretum |
| 🍴 | Restaurant<br>AA inspected | | 🛒 | Farm or animal centre |
| Madeira Hotel | Hotel<br>AA inspected | | 🦌 | Zoological or wildlife collection |
| 🎭 | Theatre or performing arts centre | | 🦜 | Bird collection |
| 🎥 | Cinema | | 🦆 | Nature reserve |
| 🚩 | Golf course | | 🐟 | Aquarium |
| ▲ | Camping<br>AA inspected | | V | Visitor or heritage centre |
| 🚐 | Caravan site<br>AA inspected | | ⛹ | Country park |
| ▲🚐 | Camping & caravan site<br>AA inspected | | ⊙ | Cave |
| 🎡 | Theme park | | 🌾 | Windmill |
| 🏰 | Abbey, cathedral or priory | | 🛢 | Distillery, brewery or vineyard |

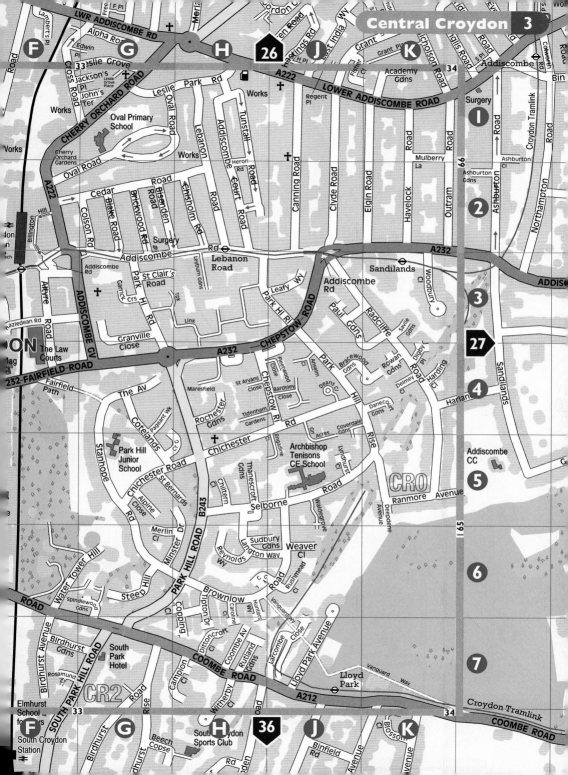

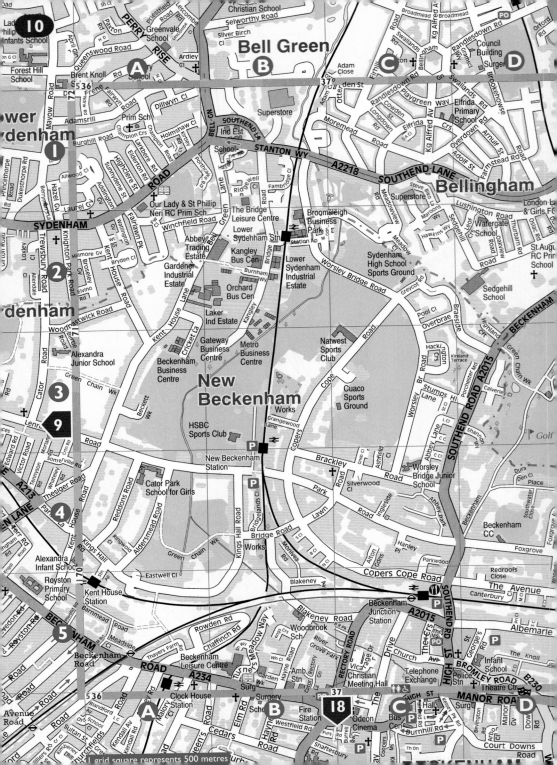

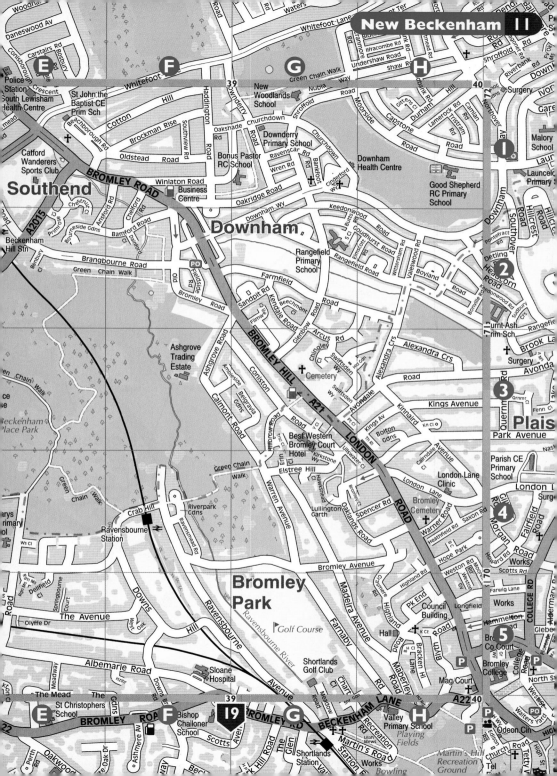

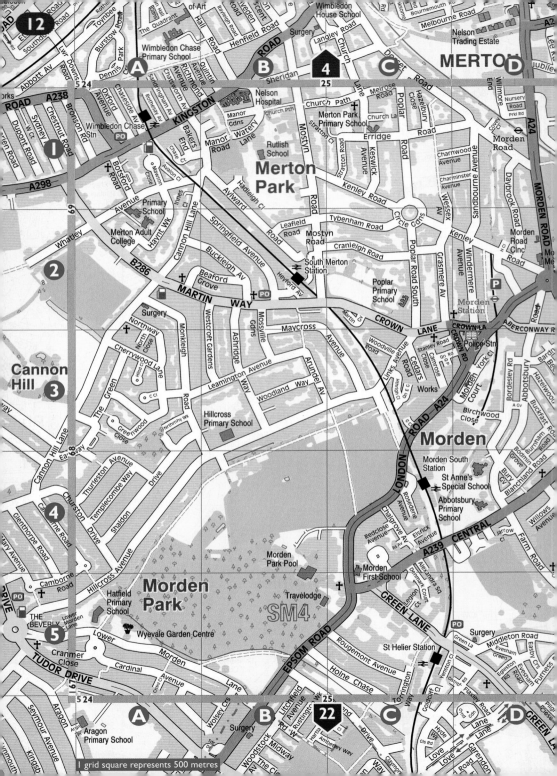

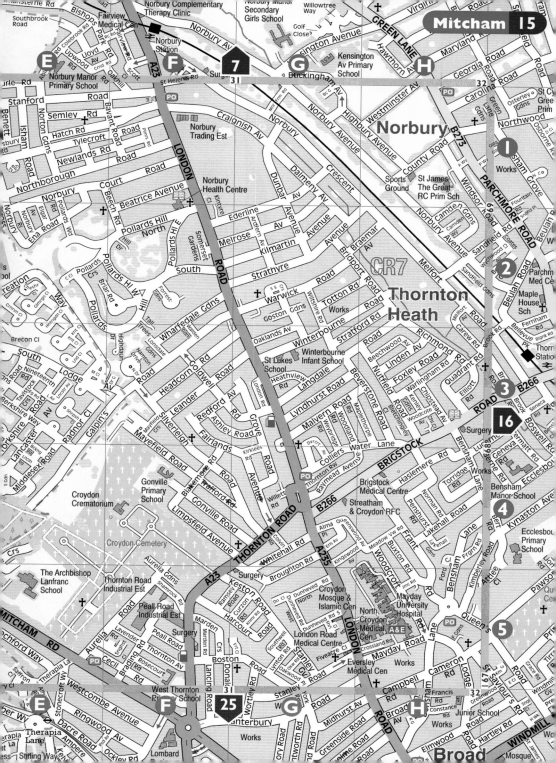

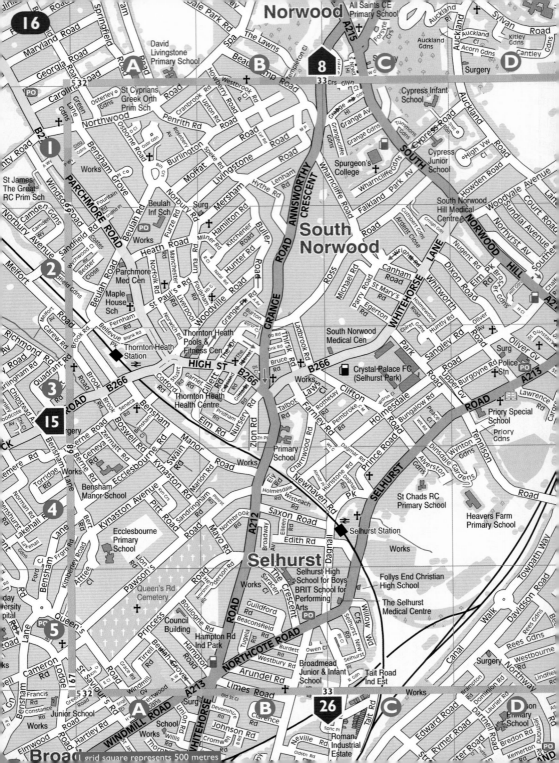

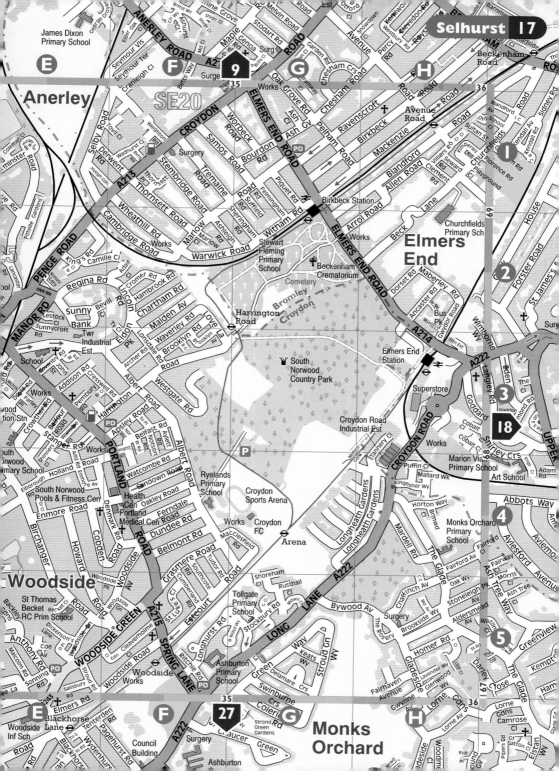

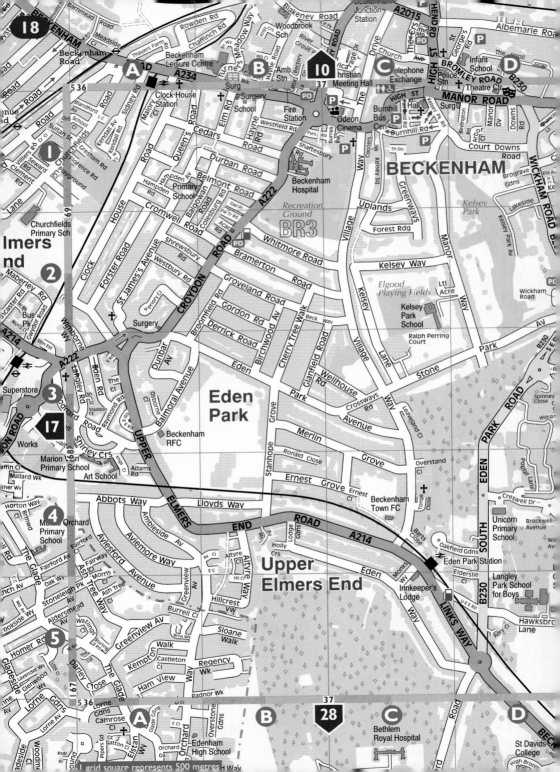

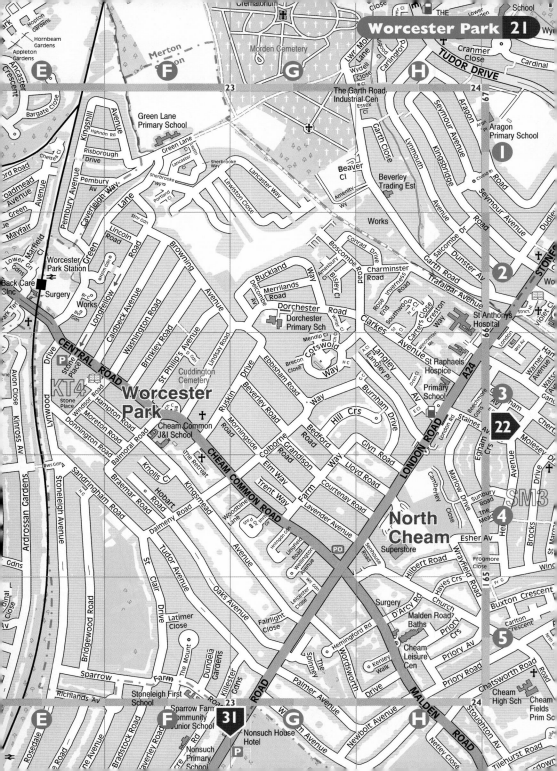

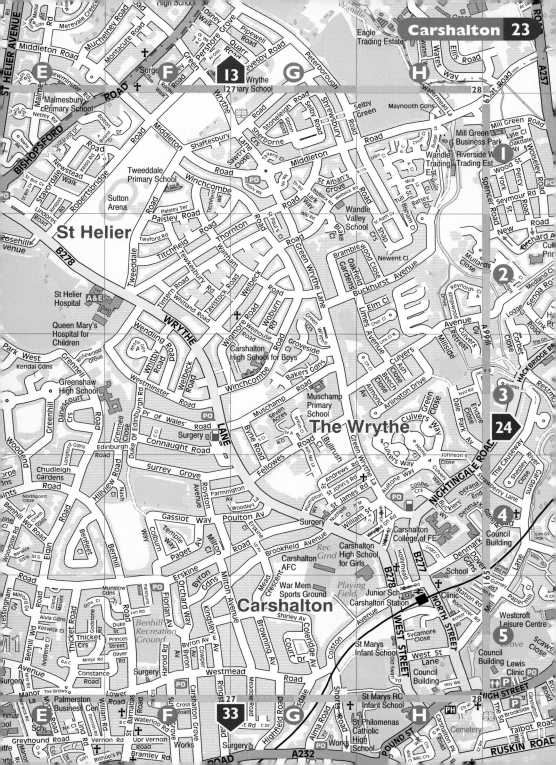

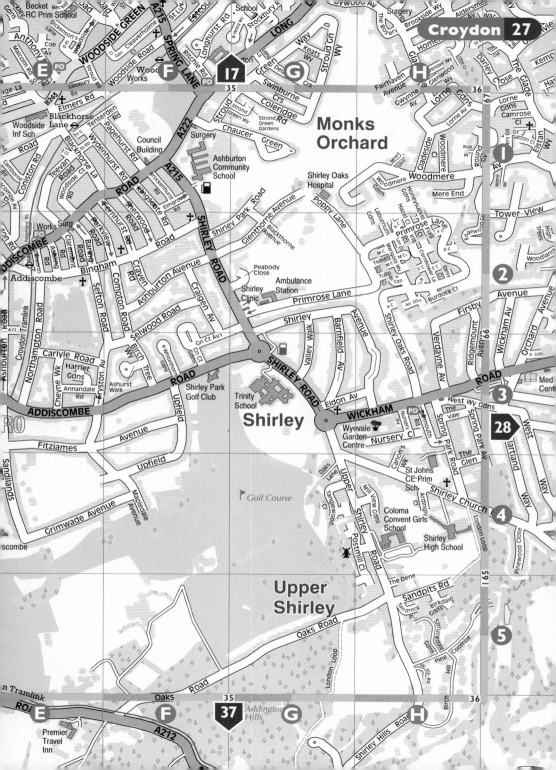

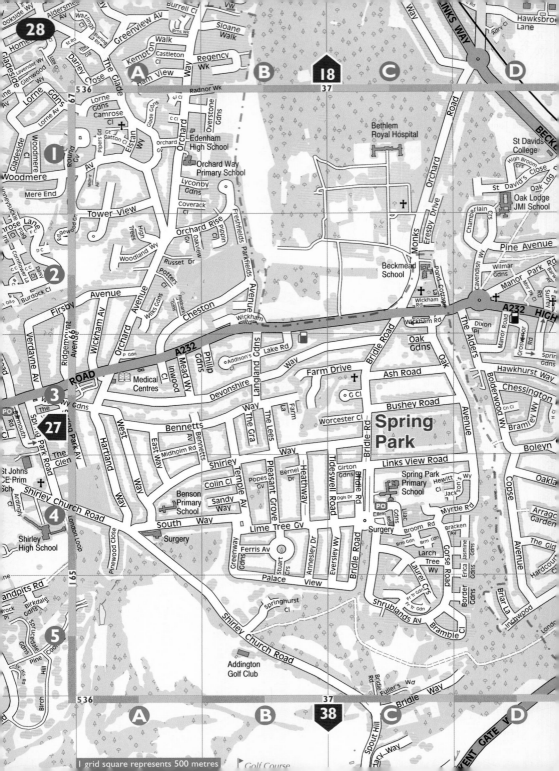

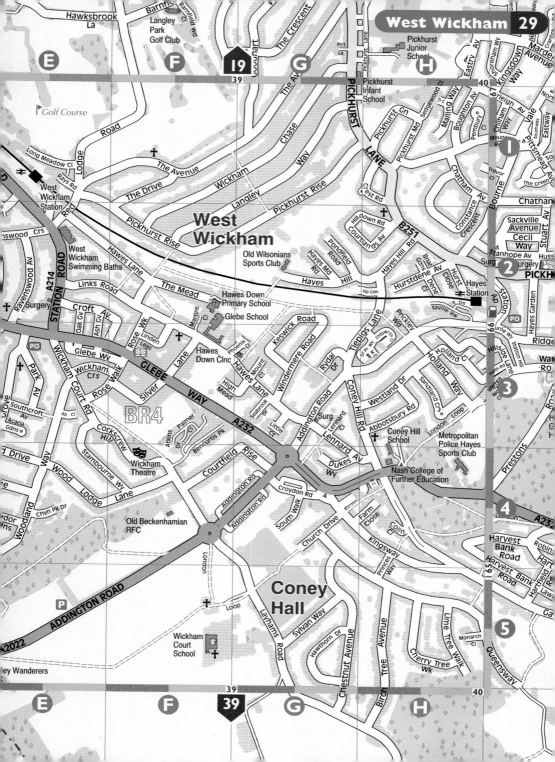

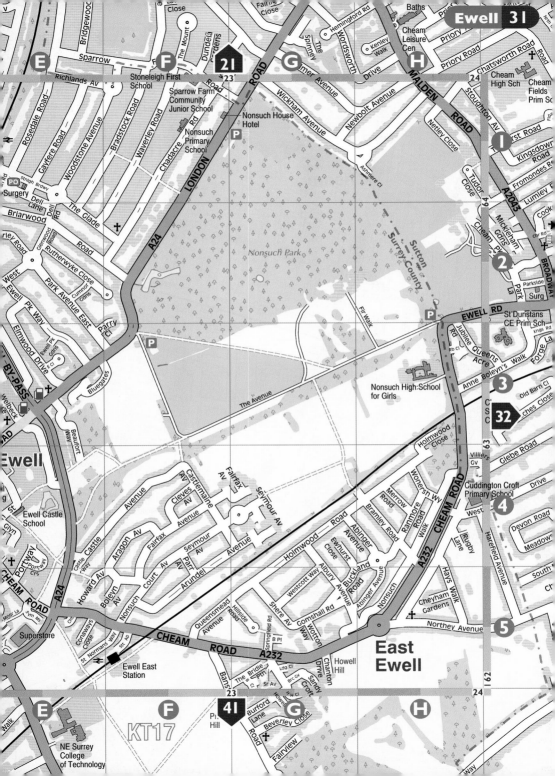

Benhill Recreation Ground

WEST STREET

Westcroft

Sycamore Close

Council Building

Lewis Clinic

St Marys Infant School

West St Lane

Old Swan

Thicket Rd

Godstone

Thicket Crs

Duke Av

Princes Street

Oliver Rd

Byron Av

Cowper Av

Shirley Av

Coleridge Av

Court Dr

Colston

Alvia Gdns

Keswick Cl

Benhill Rd

Ryde Cl

e A C

Mntpl Rd

Surgery

Constance Road

Bramley Rd

Vernon Rd

Upr Vernon Road

St Barnabas

Waterloo Rd

Cross Road

Carshalton Grove

Sutton Grove

Kingstead Road

Meadow Road

Highfield Road

Rossdale

Shorts Road

Alma Road

St Marys RC Infant School

St Philomenas Catholic High School

Carshalton Pk

Cemetery

**HIGH STREET**

Brookside

Talbot Road

ERSKIN ROAD

Carshalton Park

Carshalton War Memorial Hospital

Ashcombe Road

PARK HILL

POUND ST

BEYNON RD

Wales Av

Wales Av

Walnut Close

Sheridan Rd

SM5

Deroy Close

Cedar Cl

Blakehall Road

Carshalton

Gordon Road

Carshalton Beeches Station

Sussex Road

Stanley Park

Northwood Rd

Anglesey Gdns

Anglesey Ct

Woodfield

Grosvenor

Carshalton

**A232**

ROAD

Croft Rd

Surgery

Works

Alpine View

Fairview Road

Repton Close

Wales Rd

Oxford Road

Cambridge Road

Banstead Road

Beeches Close

Hill Road

The Warren

King's Lane

Welhurst Gdns

Gauntlett Road

Hawthorn Rd

Warren Park Road

Harrow Road

Downside Road

Waverley Way

Crichton Road

Stanley

Stanley Park Primary School

Fir Tree Grove

Windborough Road

Pine Ridge

Morland Rd

Albert Rd

Alfred Rd

Victoria Rd

Reading Rd

Eaton Road

Rutherford Cl

Cumnor Road

Hillcroome Road

Mayfield Road

Ridgway

Farm Road

The Ridgway

Upland Road

Prior Avenue

Kayemoor Rd

Willis Av

Farmdale Road

Central Way

Barrow Hedges Close

Barrow Hedges Way

Staplehurst Road

Barrow Hedges Primary School

Radcliffe Gdns

Ingleton Road

Fullerton Road

Woodmansterne Road

South Rise

The Close

Kings Av

Princes Av

East Drive

Fountain Drive

Gaynesford Rd

Balfour Rd

Oaks Way

Courtney Crs

Stanley Square

Cranfield Rd

East

Dingwall Road

Chelsea

Burns Cl

Bramble Banks

Damson Wy

Roman Rd

Fountain Dr

Lawson Wk

Kenny Cl

Cavendish Road

Cedar Gdns

Albion Road

Langley Park Road

Farndown Close

Montgomery

White Ldg

Mitre Cl

Christchurch Park

Devonshire Primary School

Devonshire Avenue

Chalgrove Road

Banstead

Harbury Road

Crossways

The Byway

Woodmansterne Walk

Beeches Walk

**Carshalton Beeches**

**Carshalton on t**

34

**Carshalton**

Downsway

The Gallop

The Causeway

The Highway

The Linkway

Cheylot Close

South West Way

The Warren

Wellfield Gdns

Oakhurst Rise

Seaton House School

Woodbury Drive

Banstead Road

Pine Walk

Bawtree Close

Royal Marsden Hospital

Itern Road

Furzedown Road

Fairway

Vincent Av

Annymede Av

Fairlawn Road

West Drive

West Walk

Pine Walk

**WOODMANSTERNE ROAD**

**B278**

Wellfield Gdns

Golf Course

Oaks Sports Centre

**Little**

23  27

E  F  G  H

I

2

3

4

5

E  F  43  G  H

27  28

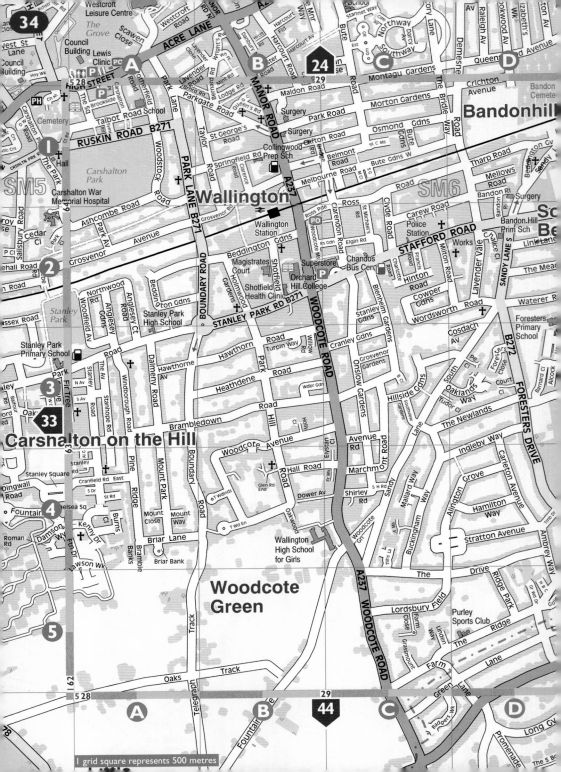

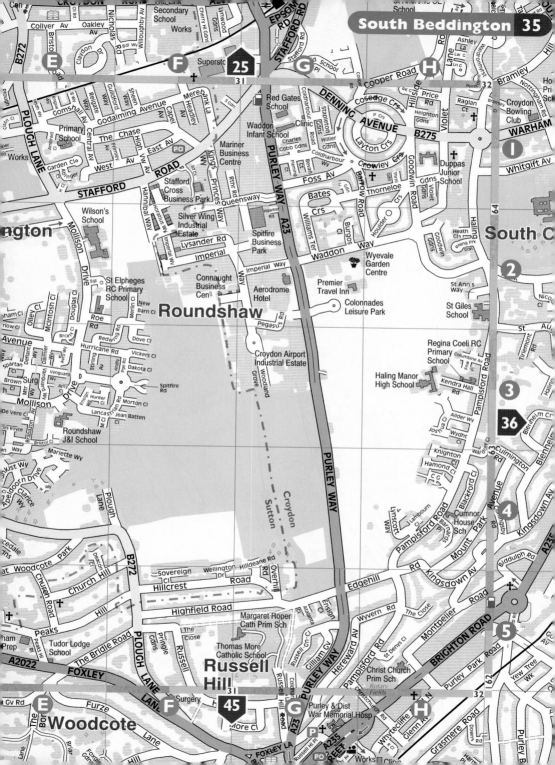

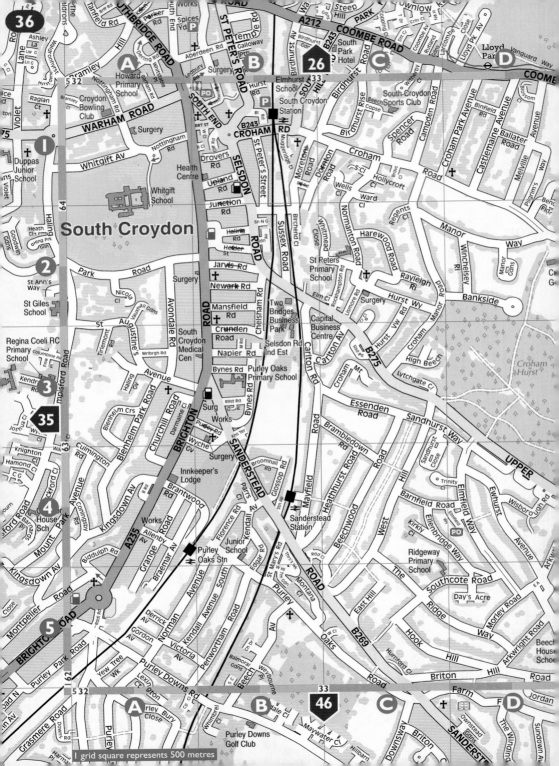

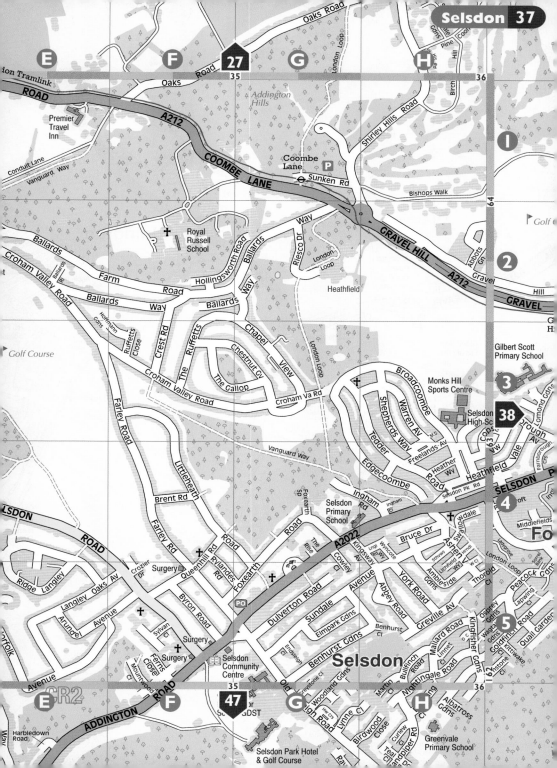

Greenvale Primary School

Forestdale

Addington

**38**

**28**

**48**

1 grid square represents 500 metres

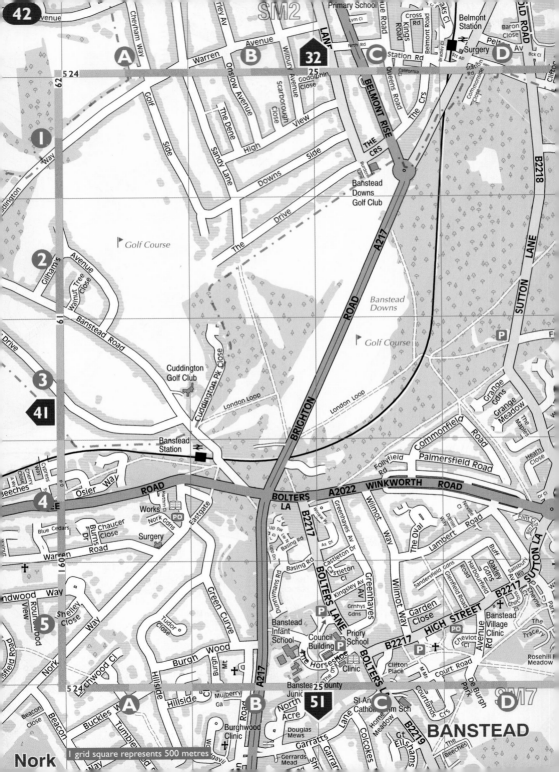

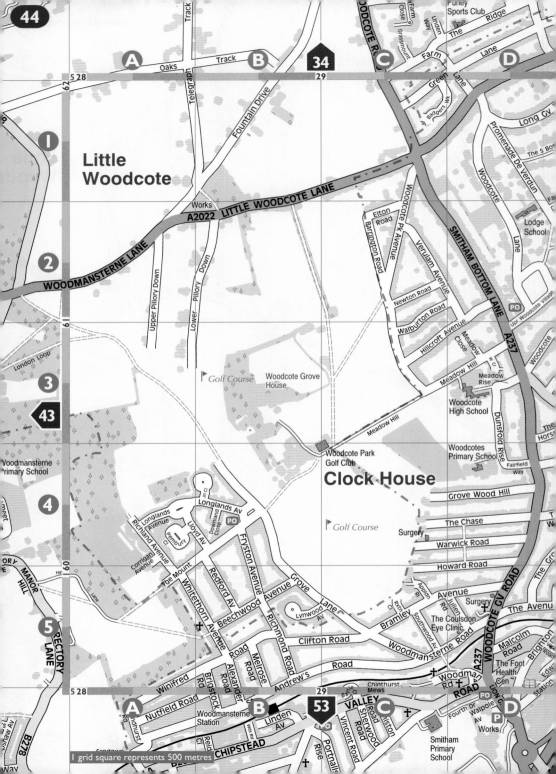

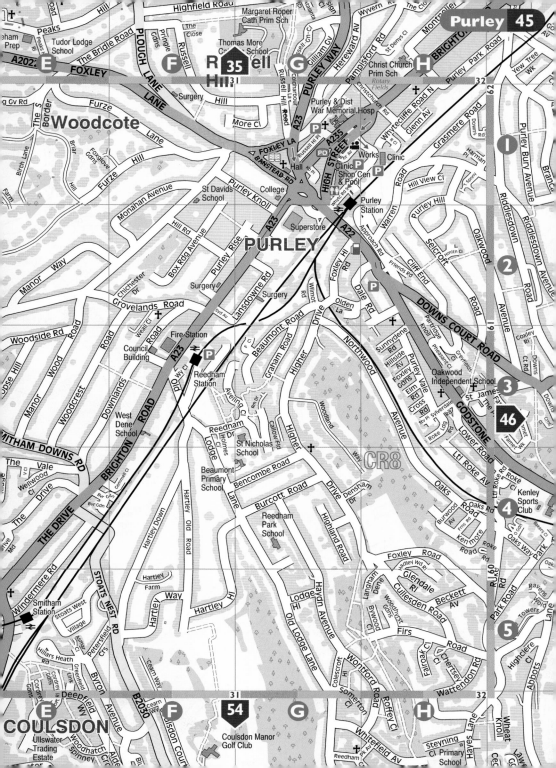

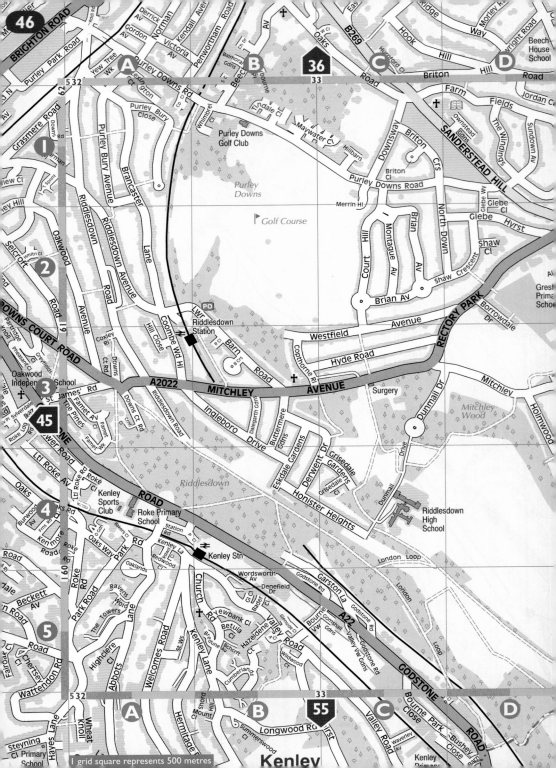

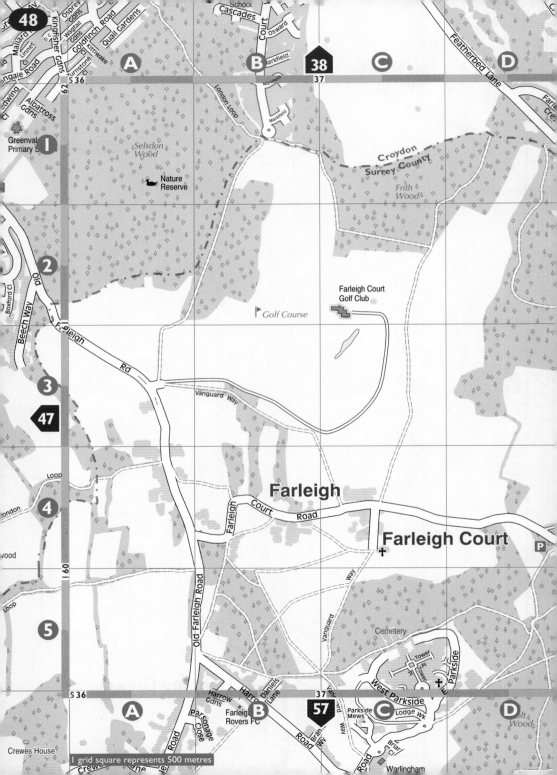

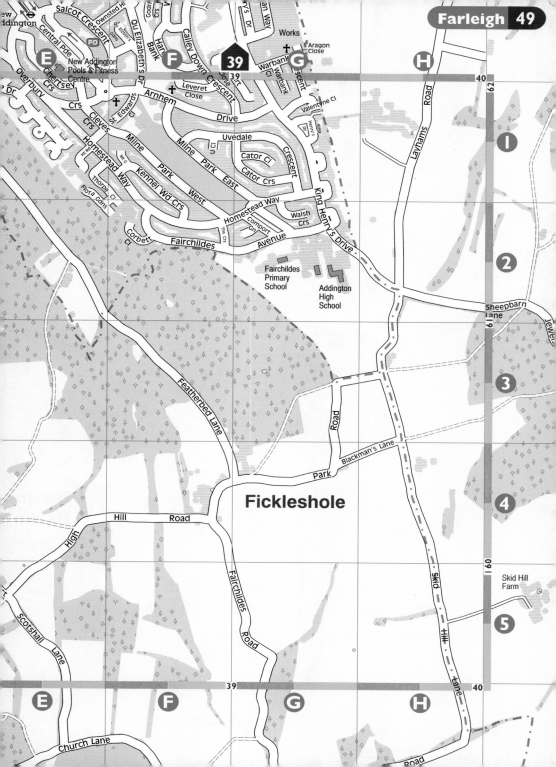

Salcot Crescent
Central Pde
PO
New Addington
Pools & Fitness
Centre
Chertsey
Crs
Overbury
Crs
Dr
Homestead Wy
Milne
Kennel Wd Crs
Park
Thorpe Cl
Flora Gdns
Corbett
Cl
St Edwards
Cleves
Crs
Arnhem
Drive
Milne Park East
Milne Park West
Homestead Way
Comport Gn
Fairchildes
Avenue
Qu Elizabeth's Dr
Hart
Bank
Leveret
Close
Calley Down Crescent
39
**39**
Uvedale
Cator Cl
Cator Crs
Crescent
King Henry's Drive
Walsh
Crs
Works
Warban
Warbank
Cl
Aragon
Close
Valentyne Cl
Henry's
Dr
King
Crescent

**40**

**62**

**I**

Lavhams
Road

**2**

Sheepbarn
Lane

Jewe

**3**

Featherbed Lane

Road

Blackman's Lane

Park

Fairchildes
Primary
School

Addington
High
School

**4**

**Fickleshole**

Hill
Road
High
Scotshall
Lane

Fairchildes
Road

Skid
Hill
Lane

**60**

Skid Hill
Farm

**5**

**39**

**40**

Church Lane

Road

E    F    G    H

E    F    G    H

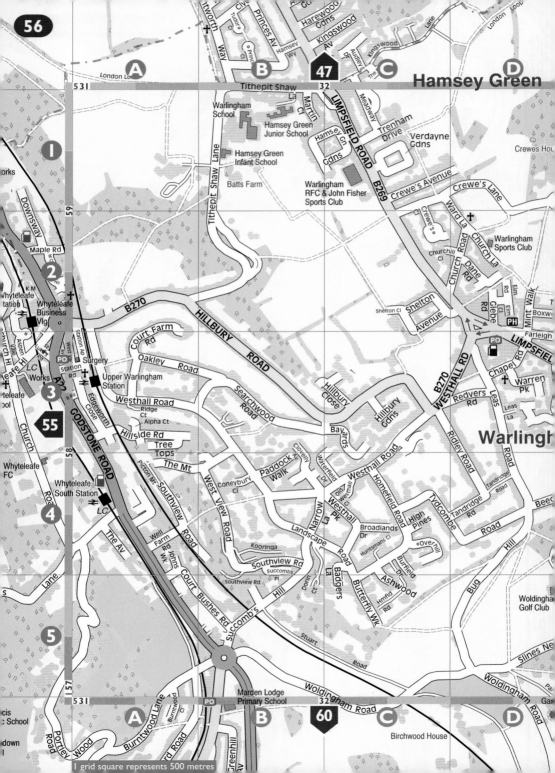

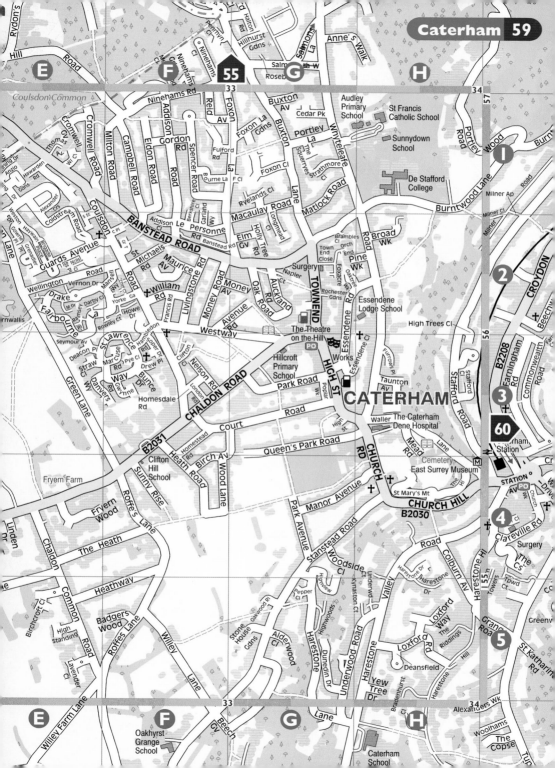

| | | | |
|---|---|---|---|
| Addington .....38 C2 | Clock House .....44 C4 | Lower Sydenham .....9 H1 | St Helier .....23 E2 | Upper Norwood .....8 |
| Addiscombe .....26 D1 | Collier's Wood .....5 F4 | Merton .....4 C5 | Sanderstead .....47 E1 | Upper Shirley .....27 |
| Anerley .....17 E1 | Coney Hall .....29 G5 | Merton Park .....12 B1 | Selhurst .....16 B4 | Upper Sydenham .....9 |
| Bandonhill .....34 D1 | Coulsdon .....54 A1 | Mitcham .....14 A2 | Selsdon .....37 G5 | Waddon .....25 |
| Banstead .....51 G1 | Croydon .....2 E4 | Monks Orchard .....27 G3 | Shirley .....27 G5 | Wallington .....34 |
| Beckenham .....18 C1 | Crystal Palace .....9 E3 | Morden .....12 C3 | Shortlands .....19 G2 | Wandle Park .....2 |
| Beddington .....25 E3 | Downham .....11 F2 | Morden Park .....12 A5 | South Beddington .....34 D2 | Warlingham .....56 |
| Beddington Corner .....24 A1 | East Ewell .....31 H5 | New Addington .....39 F3 | South Croydon .....35 H2 | West Ewell .....30 |
| Bellingham .....10 C1 | Eden Park .....18 B3 | New Beckenham .....10 A3 | South Wimbledon .....5 E2 | West Norwood .....9 |
| Belmont .....32 C4 | Elmers End .....17 H2 | Norbury .....15 H1 | Southend .....11 E1 | West Wickham .....29 |
| Benhilton .....22 D4 | Epsom .....40 A4 | Nork .....50 D1 | South Norwood .....16 B2 | Whyteleafe .....55 |
| Broad Green .....25 H1 | Ewell .....31 E4 | North Cheam .....21 H4 | Spring Park .....28 C3 | Wimbledon .....4 |
| Bromley Park .....11 G5 | Farleigh .....48 B4 | North Looe .....41 G3 | Stoneleigh .....30 D1 | Woldingham .....61 |
| Burgh Heath .....50 D4 | Farleigh Court .....48 C4 | Norwood New Town .....8 B3 | Streatham .....7 E2 | Woldingham Garden Village.....61 |
| Carshalton .....23 G5 | Fickleshole .....49 G4 | Old Coulsdon .....54 D5 | Streatham Park .....6 C1 | Woodcote .....45 |
| Carshalton Beeches .....33 G4 | Forestdale .....38 A4 | Old Malden .....20 B1 | Streatham Vale .....6 B4 | Woodcote Green .....34 |
| Carshalton on the Hill .....33 H3 | Furzedown .....6 B1 | Park Langley .....19 E5 | Sutton .....32 C1 | Woodmansterne .....43 |
| Caterham .....59 G3 | Great Burgh .....50 C2 | Penge .....9 G4 | Sydenham .....9 H2 | Woodside .....17 |
| Chaldon .....58 D4 | Hackbridge .....24 B3 | Purley .....45 G2 | Thornton Heath .....15 H2 | Worcester Park .....21 |
| Cheam .....32 A1 | Hamsey Green .....47 G5 | Rosehill .....22 D2 | Tooting .....5 H2 | The Wrythe .....23 |
| Chelsham .....57 G2 | Kenley .....55 F1 | Roundshaw .....35 F2 | Tooting Graveney .....5 F2 | |
| Chipstead .....53 E4 | Little Woodcote .....44 A1 | Russell Hill .....35 F5 | Upper Elmers End .....18 B4 | |

## USING THE STREET INDEX

Street names are listed alphabetically. Each street name is followed by its postal town or area locality, the Postcode District, the page number, and the reference to the square in which the name is found.

Standard index entries are shown as follows:

**Abbey Dr** *TOOT* SW17 .....**6** A2

Street names and selected addresses not shown on the map due to scale restrictions are shown in the index with an asterisk:

**Albemarle Pk** *BECK* BR3 * .....**10** D5

## GENERAL ABBREVIATIONS

| | | | | | | | |
|---|---|---|---|---|---|---|---|
| ACC .....ACCESS | CTYD .....COURTYARD | HLS .....HILLS | MWY .....MOTORWAY | SE .....SOUTH E. |
| ALY .....ALLEY | CUTT .....CUTTINGS | HO .....HOUSE | N .....NORTH | SER .....SERVICE A |
| AP .....APPROACH | CV .....COVE | HOL .....HOLLOW | NE .....NORTH EAST | SH .....SH( |
| AR .....ARCADE | CYN .....CANYON | HOSP .....HOSPITAL | NW .....NORTH WEST | SHOP .....SHOPP |
| ASS .....ASSOCIATION | DEPT .....DEPARTMENT | HRB .....HARBOUR | O/P .....OVERPASS | SKWY .....SKY\ |
| AV .....AVENUE | DL .....DALE | HTH .....HEATH | OFF .....OFFICE | SMT .....SUM |
| BCH .....BEACH | DM .....DAM | HTS .....HEIGHTS | ORCH .....ORCHARD | SOC .....SOCI |
| BLDS .....BUILDINGS | DR .....DRIVE | HVN .....HAVEN | OV .....OVAL | SP .....S\ |
| BND .....BEND | DRO .....DROVE | HWY .....HIGHWAY | PAL .....PALACE | SPR .....SPR |
| BNK .....BANK | DRY .....DRIVEWAY | IMP .....IMPERIAL | PAS .....PASSAGE | SQ .....SQU/ |
| BR .....BRIDGE | DWGS .....DWELLINGS | IN .....INLET | PAV .....PAVILION | ST .....STR |
| BRK .....BROOK | E .....EAST | IND EST .....INDUSTRIAL ESTATE | PDE .....PARADE | STN .....STAT |
| BTM .....BOTTOM | EMB .....EMBANKMENT | INF .....INFIRMARY | PH .....PUBLIC HOUSE | STR .....STRE |
| BUS .....BUSINESS | EMBY .....EMBASSY | INFO .....INFORMATION | PK .....PARK | STRD .....STRA |
| BVD .....BOULEVARD | ESP .....ESPLANADE | INT .....INTERCHANGE | PKWY .....PARKWAY | SW .....SOUTH W |
| BY .....BYPASS | EST .....ESTATE | IS .....ISLAND | PL .....PLACE | TDG .....TRAD |
| CATH .....CATHEDRAL | EX .....EXCHANGE | JCT .....JUNCTION | PLN .....PLAIN | TER .....TERR/ |
| CEM .....CEMETERY | EXPY .....EXPRESSWAY | JTY .....JETTY | PLNS .....PLAINS | THWY .....THROUGH\ |
| CEN .....CENTRE | EXT .....EXTENSION | KG .....KING | PLZ .....PLAZA | TNL .....TUNI |
| CFT .....CROFT | F/O .....FLYOVER | KNL .....KNOLL | POL .....POLICE STATION | TOLL .....TOLL\ |
| CH .....CHURCH | FC .....FOOTBALL CLUB | L .....LAKE | PR .....PRINCE | TPK .....TURNF |
| CHA .....CHASE | FK .....FORK | LA .....LANE | PREC .....PRECINCT | TR .....TR. |
| CHYD .....CHURCHYARD | FLD .....FIELD | LDG .....LODGE | PREP .....PREPARATORY | TRL .....TF |
| CIR .....CIRCLE | FLDS .....FIELDS | LGT .....LIGHT | PRIM .....PRIMARY | TWR .....TO\ |
| CIRC .....CIRCUS | FLS .....FALLS | LK .....LOCK | PROM .....PROMENADE | U/P .....UNDERF |
| CL .....CLOSE | FM .....FARM | LKS .....LAKES | PRS .....PRINCESS | UNI .....UNIVERS |
| CLFS .....CLIFFS | FORT .....FORT | LNDG .....LANDING | PRT .....PORT | UPR .....UPI |
| CMP .....CAMP | FTS .....FLATS | LTL .....LITTLE | PT .....POINT | V .....\ |
| CNR .....CORNER | FWY .....FREEWAY | LWR .....LOWER | PTH .....PATH | VA .....VAL |
| CO. .....COUNTY | FY .....FERRY | MAG .....MAGISTRATE | PZ .....PIAZZA | VIAD .....VIAD |
| COLL .....COLLEGE | GA .....GATE | MAN .....MANSIONS | QD .....QUADRANT | VIL .....V |
| COM .....COMMON | GAL .....GALLERY | MD .....MEAD | QU .....QUEEN | VIS .....V |
| COMM .....COMMISSION | GDN .....GARDEN | MDW .....MEADOWS | QY .....QUAY | VLG .....VILL |
| CON .....CONVENT | GDNS .....GARDENS | MEM .....MEMORIAL | R .....RIVER | VLS .....VIL |
| COT .....COTTAGE | GLD .....GLADE | MI .....MILL | RBT .....ROUNDABOUT | V .....\ |
| COTS .....COTTAGES | GLN .....GLEN | MKT .....MARKET | RD. .....ROAD | W .....W |
| CP .....CAPE | GN .....GREEN | MKTS .....MARKETS | RDG .....RIDGE | WD. .....WC |
| CPS .....COPSE | GND .....GROUND | ML .....MALL | REP .....REPUBLIC | WHF .....WH |
| CR. .....CREEK | GRA .....GRANGE | MNR .....MANOR | RES .....RESERVOIR | WK. .....W |
| CREM .....CREMATORIUM | GRG .....GARAGE | MS .....MEWS | RFC .....RUGBY FOOTBALL CLUB | WKS .....WA |
| CRS .....CRESCENT | GT .....GREAT | MSN .....MISSION | RI .....RISE | WLS .....WE |
| CSWY .....CAUSEWAY | GTWY .....GATEWAY | MT .....MOUNT | RP .....RAMP | WY .....\ |
| CT .....COURT | GV .....GROVE | MTN .....MOUNTAIN | ROW .....ROW | YD .....Y/ |
| CTRL .....CENTRAL | HGR .....HIGHER | MTS .....MOUNTAINS | S. .....SOUTH | YHA .....YOUTH HOS |
| CTS .....COURTS | HL .....HILL | MUS .....MUSEUM | SCH. .....SCHOOL | |

## POSTCODE TOWNS AND AREA ABBREVIATIONS

| | | | |
|---|---|---|---|
| BECK .....Beckenham | CROY/NA .....Croydon/ New Addington | KWD/TDW/WH .....Kingswood/ Tadworth/ | RYNPK .....Raynes Park | WARL .....Warling |
| BELMT .....Belmont | CTHM .....Caterham | Walton on the Hill | SAND/SEL .....Sanderstead/ | WIM/MER .....Wimbled |
| BMLY .....Bromley | DUL .....Dulwich | MRDN .....Morden | Selsdon | Me |
| BNSTD .....Banstead | EPSOM .....Epsom | MTCM .....Mitcham | SNWD .....South Norwood | WLGTN .....Wallin |
| BRYLDS .....Berrylands | EW .....Ewell | NRWD .....Norwood | STRHM/NOR .....Streatham/ | WNWD .....West Norw |
| CAR .....Carshalton | FSTH .....Forest Hill | NWMAL .....New Malden | Norbury | WPK .....Worcester |
| CAT .....Catford | HAYES .....Hayes | PGE/AN .....Penge/Anerley | SUT .....Sutton | WWKM .....West Wick |
| CHEAM .....Cheam | HOR/WEW .....Horton/ West Ewell | PUR/KEN .....Purley/Kenley | SYD .....Sydenham | |
| COUL/CHIP .....Coulsdon/ Chipstead | | REDH .....Redhill | THHTH .....Thornton Heath | |
| | | | TOOT .....Tooting | |

## A


ey Dr TOOT SW17 ... 6 A2
eyfield Cl MTCM CR4 ... 13 G1
ey La BECK BR3 ... 10 C4
ey Pk BECK BR3 ... 10 C4
ey Rd CROY/NA CR0 ... 2 B4
AND/SEL CR2 ... 37 H5
VIM/MER SW19 ... 5 E5
otsbury Rd MRDN SM4 ... 12 D3
VWKM BR4 ... 29 H3
ots Gn CROY/NA CR0 ... 37 H2
ots La PUR/KEN CR8 ... 55 E1
otsleigh Cl BELMT SM2 ... 32 D3
otsleigh Rd
TRHM/NOR SW16 ... 6 C2
ots Wk CTHM CR3 ... 60 B2
ots Wy BECK BR3 ... 18 A4
otts Rd CHEAM SM3 ... 22 A5
ITCM CR4 ... 14 C3
rcairn Rd
TRHM/NOR SW16 ... 6 C4
rconway Rd MRDN SM4 ... 12 D2
rcorn Cl SAND/SEL CR2 ... 47 H2
rdare Cl WWKM BR4 ... 29 E3
rdeen Rd CROY/NA CR0 ... 2 D7
rfoyle Rd
TRHM/NOR SW16 ... 6 D4
ngdon Cl WIM/MER SW19 ... 5 E3
ngdon Rd
TRHM/NOR SW16 ... 7 E5
nger Av BELMT SM2 ... 31 H5
nger Cl CROY/NA CR0 ... 39 E2
VLGTN SM6 ... 35 E1
nger Dr NRWD SE19 ... 8 A4
cia Dr BNSTD SM7 ... 41 H4
HEAM SM3 ... 22 B2
cia Gdns WWKM BR4 ... 29 E3
cia Rd BECK BR3 ... 18 B2
ITCM CR4 ... 14 A1
TRHM/NOR SW16 ... 7 E5
demy Gdns CROY/NA CR0 ... 3 K1
rn Gdns NRWD SE19 ... 8 D5
rn Wy BECK BR3 ... 19 E4
e La CAR SM5 ... 24 A5
e Rd WIM/MER SW19 ... 5 F3
es Gdns
WD/TDW/WH KT20 ... 50 C4
ir Cl SNWD SE25 ... 17 F2
ir Gdns CTHM CR3 ... 59 E1
m Cl CAT SE6 ... 10 B1
mson Wy BECK BR3 ... 19 E4
msrill Rd SYD SE26 ... 9 H1
ms Rd BECK BR3 ... 18 A4
ms Wy CROY/NA CR0 ... 16 D5
ington Gv SYD SE26 ... 10 A1
ington Rd CROY/NA CR0 ... 25 H2
AND/SEL CR2 ... 47 E1
VWKM BR4 ... 29 E5
ington Village Rd
ROY/NA CR0 ... 38 C2
iscombe Av
ROY/NA CR0 ... 27 E1
iscombe Court Rd
ROY/NA CR0 ... 3 H1
iscombe Gv CROY/NA CR0 ... 3 F3
iscombe Rd CROY/NA CR0 ... 3 G3
ROY/NA CR0 ... 27 E3
ison Cl CTHM CR3 ... 59 F2
ison Rd CTHM CR3 ... 59 F1
NWD SE25 ... 17 E3
ison's Cl CROY/NA CR0 ... 28 B3
lphi Rd EW KT17 ... 40 B3
lf St CAT SE6 ... 10 C1
ance Rd WNWD SE27 ... 8 A1
sworth Rd CROY/NA CR0 ... 2 B2
en Cl MTCM CR4 ... 23 H1
busi Cl CROY/NA CR0 ... 17 E5
Rd WIM/MER SW19 ... 4 A2
ny Ms SUT SM1 ... 32 D1
ny Rd WIM/MER SW19 ... 4 D2
atross Gdns
AND/SEL CR2 ... 47 H1
emarle Pk BECK BR3 * ... 10 D5
emarle Rd BECK BR3 ... 10 D5
erta Av SUT SM1 ... 22 A5
ert Carr Gdns
TRHM/NOR SW16 ... 7 E2
ertine Cl EW KT17 ... 50 B1
ert Rd EW KT17 ... 40 D3
ITCM CR4 ... 13 H2
PGE/AN SE20 ... 9 H4
NWD SE25 ... 17 F3
UT SM1 ... 33 F1
VARL CR6 ... 57 E2
ion Pl SNWD SE25 ... 17 E2
ion Rd BELMT SM2 ... 33 F2
ion St CROY/NA CR0 ... 2 A1
ury Av BELMT SM2 ... 31 G4
ester Rd WLGTN SM6 ... 24 B5
ock Cl WLGTN SM6 ... 34 D3
cks Cl
WD/TDW/WH KT20 ... 51 E5
cks La
WD/TDW/WH KT20 ... 51 E5
rn Cl CHEAM SM3 ... 22 C3
er Cft COUL/CHIP CR5 ... 54 A2
ersmead Av CROY/NA CR0 ... 17 H5
ersmead Rd BECK BR3 ... 10 A4
Alders
TRHM/NOR SW16 * ... 6 C1
VWKM BR4 ... 28 D2
erton Rd CROY/NA CR0 ... 26 D1
erwood Cl CTHM CR3 ... 59 G5
s Ms TOOT SW17 ... 5 G2
s St TOOT SW17 ... 5 G2
ich Crs CROY/NA CR0 ... 39 E4
ich Gdns CHEAM SM3 ... 22 B4
idge Ri NWMAL KT3 ... 20 C1
Aldrington Rd
STRHM/NOR SW16 ... 6 C2
Aldwick Rd CROY/NA CR0 ... 25 F4
Alexander Crs CTHM CR3 ... 59 E2
Alexander Rd
COUL/CHIP CR5 ... 44 B5
Alexandra Av SUT SM1 ... 22 C4
WARL CR6 ... 57 F2
Alexandra Crs BMLY BR1 ... 11 H3
Alexandra Dr NRWD SE19 ... 8 C2
Alexandra Gdns CAR SM5 ... 34 A4
Alexandra Pl CROY/NA CR0 ... 26 C2
SNWD SE25 ... 16 B4
Alexandra Rd CROY/NA CR0 ... 26 C2
EW KT17 ... 40 D3
MTCM CR4 ... 5 G4
PGE/AN SE20 ... 9 H3
WARL CR6 ... 57 E2
WIM/MER SW19 ... 4 C2
Alexandra Sq MRDN SM4 ... 12 C4
Alford Gn CROY/NA CR0 ... 39 F2
Alfred Rd SNWD SE25 ... 17 E4
SUT SM1 ... 33 E1
Alfriston Av CROY/NA CR0 ... 25 E1
Alington Gv WLGTN SM6 ... 34 D4
Alison Cl CROY/NA CR0 ... 27 H2
Allder Wy SAND/SEL CR2 ... 35 H3
Allenby Av SAND/SEL CR2 ... 36 A4
Allen Cl MTCM CR4 ... 6 B5
Allendale Cl SYD SE26 ... 9 H2
Allen Rd BECK BR3 ... 17 H1
CROY/NA CR0 ... 25 F1
Allerford Rd CAT SE6 ... 10 D1
Alleyn Pk DUL SE21 * ... 8 C1
All Saints Dr SAND/SEL CR2 ... 46 D2
All Saints Rd SUT SM1 ... 22 D4
WIM/MER SW19 ... 5 E4
Allwood Cl SYD SE26 ... 9 H1
Alma Crs SUT SM1 ... 32 A1
Alma Pl NRWD SE19 ... 8 D4
THHTH CR7 ... 15 G4
Alma Rd CAR SM5 ... 33 G1
Almond Av CAR SM5 ... 23 H3
Almond Rd HOR/WEW KT19 ... 40 B1
Almond Wy MTCM CR4 ... 14 D4
Alnwick Gv MRDN SM4 ... 12 D3
Alphabet Gdns CAR SM5 ... 13 F5
Alpha Ct CTHM CR3 ... 56 A3
Alpha Pl MRDN SM4 * ... 21 H1
Alpha Rd CROY/NA CR0 ... 26 C2
Alphea Cl WIM/MER SW19 ... 5 G4
Alpine Av BRYLDS KT5 ... 20 A3
Alpine Cl CROY/NA CR0 ... 3 G5
Alpine Vw CAR SM5 ... 33 G1
Alsom Av WPK KT4 ... 20 D5
Alston Rd TOOT SW17 ... 5 F1
Alt Gv WIM/MER SW19 ... 4 B4
Alton Gdns BECK BR3 ... 10 C4
Alton Rd CROY/NA CR0 ... 25 G5
Altyre Cl BECK BR3 ... 18 B4
Altyre Rd CROY/NA CR0 ... 3 F3
Altyre Wy BECK BR3 ... 18 B4
Alverston Gdns SNWD SE25 ... 16 C4
Alvia Gdns SUT SM1 ... 23 E5
Alway Av HOR/WEW KT19 ... 30 A1
Alwyn Cl CROY/NA CR0 ... 38 D3
Alwyne Rd WIM/MER SW19 ... 4 B3
Ambercroft Wy
COUL/CHIP CR5 ... 54 D4
Amberley Gdns
HOR/WEW KT19 ... 20 D5
Amberley Gv CROY/NA CR0 ... 26 D1
SYD SE26 ... 9 F1
Amberley Wy MRDN SM4 ... 22 C1
Amberwood Cl WLGTN SM6 ... 35 E1
Ambleside BMLY BR1 ... 11 F3
Ambleside Av BECK BR3 ... 18 A4
STRHM/NOR SW16 ... 6 D1
Ambleside Gdns BELMT SM2 ... 33 E2
SAND/SEL CR2 ... 37 H5
Ambrey Wy WLGTN SM6 ... 34 D4
Amen Cnr TOOT SW17 ... 6 A3
Amenity Wy MRDN SM4 ... 21 G1
Amersham Rd
CROY/NA CR0 ... 16 A5
Amesbury Cl WPK KT4 ... 21 G2
Ampere Wy CROY/NA CR0 ... 25 F2
Amy Cl WLGTN SM6 ... 35 E3
Ancaster Ms BECK BR3 ... 17 H2
Ancaster Rd BECK BR3 ... 17 H2
Anchorage Cl WIM/MER SW19 ... 4 C2
Anderson Cl CHEAM SM3 ... 22 C2
Andover Cl HOR/WEW KT19 ... 40 B1
Andrew's Cl EW KT17 ... 40 D4
WPK KT4 ... 21 H3
Anerley Gv NRWD SE19 ... 8 D4
Anerley Hl NRWD SE19 ... 8 D3
Anerley Pk PGE/AN SE20 ... 9 F4
Anerley Park Rd PGE/AN SE20 ... 9 F4
Anerley Rd PGE/AN SE20 ... 9 F5
Anerley Station Rd
PGE/AN SE20 ... 9 F5
Anerley V NRWD SE19 ... 8 D4
Angel Hl SUT SM1 ... 22 D4
Angel Hill Dr SUT SM1 ... 22 D4
Angelica Gdns CROY/NA CR0 ... 27 H2
Anglesey Court Rd CAR SM5 ... 34 A2
Anglesey Gdns CAR SM5 ... 34 A2
Angles Rd STRHM/NOR SW16 ... 7 E1
Annandale Rd CROY/NA CR0 ... 27 E3
Anne Boleyn's Wk
CHEAM SM3 ... 31 H3
Annesley Dr CROY/NA CR0 ... 28 B5
Anne's Wk CTHM CR3 ... 55 G5
Annsworthy Av THHTH CR7 ... 16 B2
Annsworthy Crs SNWD SE25 ... 16 B2
Ansell Gv CAR SM5 ... 23 H2
Anselm Cl CROY/NA CR0 ... 3 J4
Ansford Rd BMLY BR1 ... 11 E2
Ansley Cl SAND/SEL CR2 ... 47 F4
Anson Cl CTHM CR3 ... 55 F5
Anthony Rd SNWD SE25 ... 17 E5
Anton Crs SUT SM1 ... 22 C4
Antrobus Cl SUT SM1 ... 32 B1
Anvil Cl STRHM/NOR SW16 ... 6 C4
Anzio Gdns CTHM CR3 ... 59 E1
Aostle Wy THHTH CR7 ... 15 H1
Apeldoorn Dr WLGTN SM6 ... 35 E4
Apex Cl BECK BR3 ... 10 D5
Appledore Cl HAYES BR2 ... 19 H4
Appledown Ri
COUL/CHIP CR5 ... 44 C5
Applegarth CROY/NA CR0 ... 38 D3
Appletree Cl PGE/AN SE20 ... 9 F5
Approach Rd PUR/KEN CR8 ... 45 G2
Apsley Rd SNWD SE25 ... 17 F3
Aragon Av EW KT17 ... 31 F4
Aragon Cl CROY/NA CR0 ... 39 G5
Aragon Pl MRDN SM4 ... 21 H1
Aragon Rd MRDN SM4 ... 21 H1
Arbor Cl BECK BR3 ... 18 D1
Arcadia Cl CAR SM5 ... 24 A5
Archer Rd SNWD SE25 ... 17 F3
Archway Cl WIM/MER SW19 ... 4 D1
WLGTN SM6 * ... 25 E4
Arcus Rd BMLY BR1 ... 11 G3
Ardent Cl SNWD SE25 ... 16 C2
Ardfern Av
STRHM/NOR SW16 ... 15 G2
Ardingly Cl CROY/NA CR0 ... 27 H4
Ardleigh Gdns CHEAM SM3 ... 22 C2
Ardrossan Gdns WPK KT4 ... 21 E4
Arkell Gv NRWD SE19 ... 7 H4
Arkwright Rd SAND/SEL CR2 ... 36 D5
Arlington Cl SUT SM1 ... 22 C3
Arlington Dr CAR SM5 ... 23 H3
Armfield Crs MTCM CR4 ... 13 H1
Armistice Gdns SNWD SE25 ... 17 E2
Arney's La MTCM CR4 ... 14 A5
Arnhem Dr CROY/NA CR0 ... 49 F1
Arnold Rd TOOT SW17 ... 5 H4
Arnulf St CAT SE6 ... 10 D1
Arnull's Rd STRHM/NOR SW16 ... 7 H3
Arragon Gdns
STRHM/NOR SW16 ... 7 E4
WWKM BR4 ... 28 D4
Arran Cl WLGTN SM6 ... 24 C5
Arras Av MRDN SM4 ... 13 E4
Arrol Rd BECK BR3 ... 17 G2
Arthur Rd WIM/MER SW19 ... 4 C1
Arundel Av EW KT17 ... 31 F5
MRDN SM4 ... 12 B3
SAND/SEL CR2 ... 37 E5
Arundel Cl CROY/NA CR0 ... 2 A5
Arundel Rd BELMT SM2 ... 32 B3
CROY/NA CR0 ... 16 B5
Aschurch Rd CROY/NA CR0 ... 26 D1
Ascot Ms WLGTN SM6 ... 34 C4
Ascot Rd TOOT SW17 ... 6 A3
Ashbourne Cl COUL/CHIP CR5 ... 53 G3
Ashbourne Rd MTCM CR4 ... 6 A3
Ashbourne Ter
WIM/MER SW19 ... 4 C4
Ashburton Av CROY/NA CR0 ... 27 F2
Ashburton Cl CROY/NA CR0 ... 27 E2
Ashburton Gdns
CROY/NA CR0 ... 27 E3
Ashburton Rd CROY/NA CR0 ... 27 E3
Ashbury Pl WIM/MER SW19 ... 5 E3
Ashby Wk CROY/NA CR0 ... 16 A5
Ash Cl CAR SM5 ... 23 H3
PGE/AN SE20 ... 17 G1
WIM/MER SW19 ... 4 C2
Ashcombe Rd CAR SM5 ... 34 A2
Ashcombe Ter
KWD/TDW/WH KT20 ... 50 B5
Ash Ct HOR/WEW KT19 ... 20 A5
Ashcroft Ri COUL/CHIP CR5 ... 54 A1
Ashdown Cl BECK BR3 ... 18 D1
Ashdown Gdns
SAND/SEL CR2 ... 47 F5
Ashdown Rd EW KT17 ... 40 D3
Ashen V SAND/SEL CR2 ... 37 H4
Ashfield Cl BECK BR3 ... 10 C4
Ash Gv PGE/AN SE20 ... 17 G1
WWKM BR4 ... 29 E3
Ashgrove Rd BMLY BR1 ... 11 F3
Ashlake Rd STRHM/NOR SW16 ... 7 E2
Ashleigh Gdns SUT SM1 ... 22 D3
Ashleigh Rd PGE/AN SE20 ... 17 F2
Ashley Av EPSOM KT18 ... 40 B3
MRDN SM4 ... 12 C4
Ashley Ct EPSOM KT18 ... 40 B3
Ashley Dr BNSTD SM7 ... 42 C4
Ashley La CROY/NA CR0 ... 2 B7
Ashley Rd HOR/WEW KT19 ... 40 B3
THHTH CR7 ... 15 F3
WIM/MER SW19 ... 4 D3
Ashling Rd CROY/NA CR0 ... 27 E2
Ashmere Av BECK BR3 ... 19 F1
Ashmere Cl CHEAM SM3 ... 31 H1
Ash Ms EPSOM KT18 ... 40 C4
Ashridge Wy MRDN SM4 ... 12 B3
Ash Rd CHEAM SM3 ... 22 A2
CROY/NA CR0 ... 28 C3
Ashton Cl SUT SM1 ... 22 C5
Ashtree Av MTCM CR4 ... 13 F1
Ash Tree Cl CROY/NA CR0 ... 18 A5
Ash Tree Wy CROY/NA CR0 ... 18 A4
Ashurst Cl PGE/AN SE20 ... 9 F5
PUR/KEN CR8 ... 46 B5
Ashurst Wk CROY/NA CR0 ... 27 F3
Ashvale Rd TOOT SW17 ... 5 H2
Ashwick Cl CTHM CR3 ... 60 A5
Ashwood WARL CR6 ... 56 C5
Ashwood Gdns CROY/NA CR0 ... 38 D2
Asmar Cl COUL/CHIP CR5 ... 45 E5
Aspen Gdns MTCM CR4 ... 14 A4
Aspen V CTHM CR3 ... 55 H3
Aspen Wy BNSTD SM7 ... 41 H4
Asprey Gv CTHM CR3 ... 60 A4
Asprey Ms BECK BR3 ... 18 B4
Assembly Wk CAR SM5 ... 23 G1
Astonplace STRHM/NOR SW16 ... 7 H3
Atalanta Cl PUR/KEN CR8 ... 35 G5
Atkins Dr WWKM BR4 ... 29 F4
Attlee Cl THHTH CR7 ... 16 A5
Attwood Cl SAND/SEL CR2 ... 47 F4
Aubyn Hl WNWD SE27 ... 8 A1
Auckland Cl NRWD SE19 ... 8 D5
Auckland Gdns NRWD SE19 ... 8 C5
Auckland Hl WNWD SE27 ... 8 A1
Auckland Ri NRWD SE19 ... 8 C5
Auckland Rd CTHM CR3 ... 59 G2
NRWD SE19 ... 8 D5
Auden Pl
CHEAM SM3 * ... 21 G5
Audley Dr WARL CR6 ... 47 G5
Audley Pl BELMT SM2 ... 32 D3
Audrey Cl BECK BR3 ... 18 D5
Aultone Wy SUT SM1 ... 22 D3
Aurelia Gdns CROY/NA CR0 ... 15 F4
Aurelia Rd CROY/NA CR0 ... 15 E5
Auriol Cl WPK KT4 ... 20 C4
Auriol Park Rd WPK KT4 ... 20 C4
Austin Cl COUL/CHIP CR5 ... 54 D3
Autumn Cl WIM/MER SW19 ... 5 E3
Autumn Dr BELMT SM2 ... 32 D4
Avalon Cl RYNPK SW20 ... 12 A1
Avarn Rd TOOT SW17 ... 5 H3
Avebury Rd WIM/MER SW19 ... 4 B5
Aveling Cl PUR/KEN CR8 ... 45 G3
Avenue Gdns SNWD SE25 ... 17 E2
Avenue Rd BELMT SM2 ... 32 C5
BNSTD SM7 ... 42 D5
CTHM CR3 ... 59 F2
EPSOM KT18 ... 40 B4
PGE/AN SE20 ... 9 G5
SNWD SE25 ... 17 E2
STRHM/NOR SW16 ... 14 D1
WLGTN SM6 ... 34 C3
The Avenue BECK BR3 ... 10 D5
BELMT SM2 ... 32 B4
CAR SM5 ... 34 A3
COUL/CHIP CR5 ... 44 D5
CROY/NA CR0 ... 3 G4
CTHM CR3 ... 56 A4
EW KT17 ... 31 G3
WPK KT4 ... 20 D3
WWKM BR4 ... 29 F1
Averil Gv STRHM/NOR SW16 ... 7 H3
Aviemore Cl BECK BR3 ... 18 B4
Aviemore Wy BECK BR3 ... 18 A4
Avington Gv PGE/AN SE20 ... 9 G4
Avoca Rd TOOT SW17 ... 6 A1
Avon Cl SUT SM1 ... 23 E5
WPK KT4 ... 21 E3
Avondale Av WPK KT4 ... 20 D2
Avondale Rd BMLY BR1 ... 11 H3
SAND/SEL CR2 ... 36 A2
WIM/MER SW19 ... 4 D2
Avro Wy WLGTN SM6 ... 35 E3
Axwood EPSOM KT18 ... 40 A5
Aylesford Av BECK BR3 ... 18 A4
Aylett Rd SNWD SE25 ... 17 F3
Aylward Rd RYNPK SW20 ... 12 B1


## B


Babington Rd
STRHM/NOR SW16 ... 6 D2
Backley Gdns CROY/NA CR0 ... 17 E5
Bader Cl PUR/KEN CR8 ... 46 B5
Badgers Copse WPK KT4 ... 20 D3
Badgers Ct
WPK KT4 * ... 20 D3
Badgers La WARL CR6 ... 56 C4
Badgers Wk CTHM CR3 ... 55 H3
PUR/KEN CR8 ... 44 C1
Badgers Wd CTHM CR3 ... 59 E5
Bahram Rd HOR/WEW KT19 ... 30 B5
Bailey Pl SYD SE26 ... 9 G3
Baines Cl SAND/SEL CR2 ... 36 B1
Baird Gdns NRWD SE19 ... 8 C1
Baker La MTCM CR4 ... 14 A1
Bakers Cl PUR/KEN CR8 ... 46 A4
Bakers End RYNPK SW20 ... 12 A1
Bakers Gdns CAR SM5 ... 23 G3
Baldry Gdns
STRHM/NOR SW16 ... 7 E3
Balfont Cl SAND/SEL CR2 ... 47 E3
Balfour Rd CAR SM5 ... 33 H3
SNWD SE25 ... 17 E3
WIM/MER SW19 ... 4 D4
Balgowan Rd BECK BR3 ... 18 B2
Ballards Farm Rd
CROY/NA CR0 ... 37 F2
Ballards Gn
KWD/TDW/WH KT20 ... 51 E4
Ballards Ri SAND/SEL CR2 ... 37 E2
Ballards Wy SAND/SEL CR2 ... 37 E2
Ballater Rd SAND/SEL CR2 ... 36 D1
Balmoral Av BECK BR3 ... 18 A3
Balmoral Gdns
SAND/SEL CR2 ... 36 B5
Balmoral Rd WPK KT4 ... 21 F4
Balmoral Wy BELMT SM2 ... 32 C5
Baltic Cl WIM/MER SW19 ... 5 F4
Bamford Rd BMLY BR1 ... 11 F2
Bampfylde Cl WLGTN SM6 ... 24 C4
Banavie Gdns BECK BR3 ... 10 D5
Banbury Ct
BELMT SM2 * ... 32 C3
Bandon Ri WLGTN SM6 ... 34 D2
Bank Av MTCM CR4 ... 13 F1
Bankfoot Rd BMLY BR1 ... 11 G1
Bank Ms SUT SM1 ... 32 D2
Bankside SAND/SEL CR2 ... 36 D2
Bankside Cl CAR SM5 ... 33 G1
Bannow Cl HOR/WEW KT19 ... 20 C5
Banstead Rd BNSTD SM7 ... 42 A3
CAR SM5 ... 33 G2
CTHM CR3 ... 59 F2
EW KT17 ... 31 F5
PUR/KEN CR8 ... 45 G1
Banstead Rd South
BELMT SM2 ... 33 E5
Banstead Wy WLGTN SM6 ... 35 E1
Barclay Rd CROY/NA CR0 ... 2 E4
Bardney Rd MRDN SM4 ... 12 D3
Bardolph Av CROY/NA CR0 ... 38 B4
Bardsley Cl CROY/NA CR0 ... 3 J4
Barfreston Wy PGE/AN SE20 ... 9 F5
Bargate Cl NWMAL KT3 ... 21 E1
Bargrove Cl PGE/AN SE20 ... 9 E4
Barham Rd SAND/SEL CR2 ... 2 D7
Baring Rd CROY/NA CR0 ... 27 E2
Barlow Cl WLGTN SM6 ... 35 E2
Barmouth Rd CROY/NA CR0 ... 27 H3
Barnard Cl WLGTN SM6 ... 34 D3
Barnard Pl EW KT17 ... 31 G5
Barnard Rd MTCM CR4 ... 14 A2
WARL CR6 ... 57 H4
Barnards Pl SAND/SEL CR2 ... 35 H4
Barn Cl BNSTD SM7 ... 43 F5
Barn Crs PUR/KEN CR8 ... 46 B3
Barn Fld BNSTD SM7 ... 42 D4
Barnfield Av CROY/NA CR0 ... 27 G3
MTCM CR4 ... 14 B3
Barnfield Cl COUL/CHIP CR5 ... 55 E4
Barnfield Rd SAND/SEL CR2 ... 36 C4
Barnfield Wood Cl BECK BR3 ... 19 F5
Barnfield Wood Rd BECK BR3 ... 19 G4
Barnmead Rd BECK BR3 ... 9 H5
Barnsbury Crs BRYLDS KT5 ... 20 A2
Barnsbury La BRYLDS KT5 ... 20 A2
Baron Cl BELMT SM2 ... 32 D5
Baron Gv MTCM CR4 ... 13 G3
Baron's Wk CROY/NA CR0 ... 18 A5
Barrie Cl COUL/CHIP CR5 ... 53 G1
Barringer Sq TOOT SW17 ... 6 A1
Barrington Rd CHEAM SM3 ... 22 C2
PUR/KEN CR8 ... 44 C2
Barrington Wk NRWD SE19 * ... 8 C3
Barrow Av CAR SM5 ... 33 H3
Barrow Hedges Cl CAR SM5 ... 33 G3
Barrow Hedges Wy CAR SM5 ... 33 G3
Barrow Hl WPK KT4 ... 20 C3
Barrow Hill Cl WPK KT4 ... 20 C3
Barrow Rd CROY/NA CR0 ... 35 G1
STRHM/NOR SW16 ... 6 D3
Barsons Cl PGE/AN SE20 ... 9 G4
Bartlett St SAND/SEL CR2 ... 36 B1
Barts Cl BECK BR3 ... 18 C4
Barwood Av WWKM BR4 ... 28 D2
Basildon Cl BELMT SM2 ... 32 D4
Basil Gdns CROY/NA CR0 ... 27 H2
WNWD SE27 ... 8 A2
Basinghall Gdns BELMT SM2 ... 32 D4
Basing Rd BNSTD SM7 ... 42 B5
Bassett Cl BELMT SM2 ... 32 D4
Bates Crs CROY/NA CR0 ... 35 G2
STRHM/NOR SW16 ... 6 C4
Bath House Rd CROY/NA CR0 ... 25 E2
Bathurst Av WIM/MER SW19 ... 4 D5
Batley Cl CAR SM5 ... 23 H1
Batsworth Rd MTCM CR4 ... 13 F2
Battle Cl WIM/MER SW19 ... 5 E3
Bavant Rd STRHM/NOR SW16 ... 15 E1
Bawtree Cl BELMT SM2 ... 33 E5
Bayards WARL CR6 ... 56 C3
Bayham Rd MRDN SM4 ... 12 D3
Bays Cl SYD SE26 ... 9 G2
Beachborough Rd BMLY BR1 ... 11 E1
Beacon Cl BNSTD SM7 ... 50 D1
Beacon Pl CROY/NA CR0 ... 25 E4
Beaconsfield Pl EW KT17 ... 40 C2
Beaconsfield Rd
CROY/NA CR0 ... 16 B5
Beacon Wy BNSTD SM7 ... 50 D1
Beadlow Cl CAR SM5 ... 13 F5
Beadman Pl WNWD SE27 * ... 7 H1
Beadman St WNWD SE27 ... 7 H1
Beaford Gv RYNPK SW20 ... 12 A2
Beardell St NRWD SE19 ... 8 D3
Bearstead Ter BECK BR3 * ... 10 C5
Beatrice Av
STRHM/NOR SW16 ... 15 F2
Beauchamp Rd NRWD SE19 ... 8 B5
SUT SM1 ... 32 C1
Beaufort Gdns
STRHM/NOR SW16 ... 7 F4
Beaufort Wy EW KT17 ... 31 E3
Beaulieu Av SYD SE26 ... 9 F1
Beaulieu Cl MTCM CR4 ... 6 A5
Beaumont Rd NRWD SE19 ... 8 A3
PUR/KEN CR8 ... 45 G3
Beaver Cl MRDN SM4 ... 21 G1
PGE/AN SE20 * ... 9 E4
Beckenham Gv HAYES BR2 ... 19 F1
Beckenham Hill Rd BECK BR3 ... 10 D3
Beckenham La HAYES BR2 ... 19 G1
Beckenham Place Pk
BECK BR3 ... 10 D4
Beckenham Rd BECK BR3 ... 9 H5
BECK BR3 ... 28 D1
Beckenshaw Gdns
BNSTD SM7 ... 43 G5
Becket Cl SNWD SE25 ... 17 E5
WIM/MER SW19 * ... 4 D5
Beckett Av PUR/KEN CR8 ... 45 H5
Beckett Wk BECK BR3 ... 10 A3
Beckford Rd CROY/NA CR0 ... 16 D5
Beck La BECK BR3 ... 17 H2
Beck River Pk BECK BR3 ... 10 B5
Beck Wy BECK BR3 ... 18 B2
Beckway Rd
STRHM/NOR SW16 ... 14 D1
Beclands Rd TOOT SW17 ... 6 A3
Becmead Av
STRHM/NOR SW16 ... 6 D1

Becondale Rd NRWD SE19 8 C2
Beddington Cross
CROY/NA CR0 24 D2
Beddington Farm Rd
CROY/NA CR0 25 F3
Beddington Gdns CAR SM5 34 A2
Beddington Gv WLGTN SM6 34 D1
Beddington La CROY/NA CR0 24 D2
Beddington Ter
CROY/NA CR0 * 25 F1
Bedfont Cl MTCM CR4 14 A1
Bedford Pk CROY/NA CR0 2 D1
Bedford Pl CROY/NA CR0 2 E1
Bedford Rd WPK KT4 21 G3
Bedlow Wy CROY/NA CR0 25 F5
Bedser Cl THHTH CR7 16 A2
Bedwardine Rd NRWD SE19 8 C4
Beech Av SAND/SEL CR2 46 B1
Beech Cl CAR SM5 23 H3
Beech Copse SAND/SEL CR2 36 C1
Beechcroft Av
PUR/KEN CR8 46 B5
Beechcroft Cl
STRHM/NOR SW16 7 F2
Beeches Av CAR SM5 33 G3
Beeches Cl PGE/AN SE20 9 G5
Beeches Rd CHEAM SM3 22 A2
The Beeches BNSTD SM7 51 H1
Beeches Wk BELMT SM2 33 F4
Beechfield BNSTD SM7 42 D3
Beech Gv EPSOM KT18 50 B2
MTCM CR4 14 D4
Beech House Rd
CROY/NA CR0 2 E5
Beechmont Cl BMLY BR1 11 G2
Beechmore Gdns
CHEAM SM3 21 H3
Beecholme BNSTD SM7 * 42 A4
Beecholme Av MTCM CR4 6 B5
Beech Rd EW KT17 40 D5
STRHM/NOR SW16 15 E1
Beech Tree Pl SUT SM1 32 D1
Beech Wk EW KT17 41 E1
Beech Wy EW KT17 40 D5
SAND/SEL CR2 47 H3
Beechwood Av
COUL/CHIP CR5 44 B5
THHTH CR7 15 H3
Beechwood Gdns CTHM CR3 60 A2
Beechwood La WARL CR6 56 D4
Beechwood Rd CTHM CR3 60 A2
SAND/SEL CR2 36 C4
Beeleigh Rd MRDN SM4 12 D3
Beggar's Roost La SUT SM1 32 C2
Belcroft Cl BMLY BR1 11 H4
Belfast Rd SNWD SE25 17 F3
Belfield Rd HOR/WEW KT19 30 B4
Belgrave Rd MTCM CR4 13 F2
SNWD SE25 16 D3
Belgrave Wk MTCM CR4 13 F2
Belgravia Gdns BMLY BR1 11 G3
Bellevue Pk THHTH CR7 16 A3
Bellfield CROY/NA CR0 38 A4
Bell Gn SYD SE26 10 B1
Bell Green La SYD SE26 10 B2
Bell Meadow NRWD SE19 8 C1
Bell Pde WWKM BR4 * 29 E3
Belltrees Gv
STRHM/NOR SW16 7 F2
Belmont Ri BELMT SM2 42 C1
Belmont Rd BECK BR3 18 A1
BELMT SM2 32 C5
SNWD SE25 17 F4
WLGTN SM6 34 C1
Belsize Gdns SUT SM1 22 D5
Belvedere Av WIM/MER SW19 4 A2
Belvedere Dr WIM/MER SW19 4 A2
Belvedere Gv WIM/MER SW19 4 A2
Belvedere Rd NRWD SE19 8 D4
Belvedere Sq WIM/MER SW19 4 A2
Benbury Cl BMLY BR1 11 E2
Bench Fld SAND/SEL CR2 36 D2
Bencombe Rd PUR/KEN CR8 45 G4
Bencroft Rd
STRHM/NOR SW16 6 C4
Bencurtis Pk WWKM BR4 29 F4
Benedict Rd MTCM CR4 13 F2
Benedict Whf MTCM CR4 13 G2
Benett Gdns
STRHM/NOR SW16 15 E1
Benfleet Cl SUT SM1 23 E4
Benham Cl COUL/CHIP CR5 54 D3
Benhill Av SUT SM1 22 D5
Benhill Rd SUT SM1 23 F4
Benhill Wood Rd SUT SM1 23 E5
Benhilton Gdns SUT SM1 22 D4
Benhurst Cl SAND/SEL CR2 37 H5
Benhurst Gdns
SAND/SEL CR2 37 G5
Benhurst La
STRHM/NOR SW16 7 G2
Bennetts Av CROY/NA CR0 28 A3
Bennetts Cl MTCM CR4 6 B5
Bennetts Wy CROY/NA CR0 28 A3
Bensham Cl THHTH CR7 16 A3
Bensham Gv THHTH CR7 16 A1
Bensham La CROY/NA CR0 25 H1
THHTH CR7 15 H5
Bensham Manor Rd
THHTH CR7 16 B4
Benson Rd CROY/NA CR0 25 G4
Benthall Gdns PUR/KEN CR8 55 E1
Bentley Cl WIM/MER SW19 4 C1
Benton's La WNWD SE27 8 A1
Benton's Ri WNWD SE27 8 B2
Benwood Ct SUT SM1 23 E4
Beresford Rd BELMT SM2 32 B3
Berkeley Ct WLGTN SM6 24 C4
Berkeley Pl EPSOM KT18 40 B5
The Berkeleys
SNWD SE25 * 17 E3
Berkshire Cl CTHM CR3 59 F2
Berkshire Wy MTCM CR4 15 E3
Bernard Gdns WIM/MER SW19 4 B2
Bernard Rd WLGTN SM6 34 B1
Bernel Dr CROY/NA CR0 28 B4
Berne Rd THHTH CR7 15 H4
Berney Rd CROY/NA CR0 26 B1
Berridge Rd NRWD SE19 8 B2
Berry La DUL SE21 8 B1
Berryman's La SYD SE26 9 H1
Bertal Rd TOOT SW17 5 F1
Bertie Rd SYD SE26 9 H3
Bert Rd THHTH CR7 16 A4
Berwick Gdns SUT SM1 23 E4
Besley St STRHM/NOR SW16 6 C3
Betchworth Cl SUT SM1 33 F1
Betchworth Wy
CROY/NA CR0 39 E4
Bethersden Cl BECK BR3 10 B4
Betjeman Cl COUL/CHIP CR5 54 B2
Betony Cl CROY/NA CR0 27 H2
Betts Cl BECK BR3 18 A1
Betts Wy PGE/AN SE20 17 F1
Betula Cl PUR/KEN CR8 46 B5
Beulah Av
THHTH CR7 * 16 A1
Beulah Crs THHTH CR7 16 A1
Beulah Gv CROY/NA CR0 16 A5
Beulah Hl NRWD SE19 7 H3
Beulah Rd SUT SM1 22 C5
THHTH CR7 16 A2
WIM/MER SW19 4 B4
Beulah Wk CTHM CR3 57 E5
Bevan Ct CROY/NA CR0 35 G1
Bevan Pk EW KT17 40 D1
Beverley Cl EW KT17 41 G1
Beverley Gdns WPK KT4 21 E2
Beverley Rd CTHM CR3 55 G2
MTCM CR4 14 D3
PGE/AN SE20 17 F1
WPK KT4 21 G3
Beverstone Rd THHTH CR7 15 G3
Bevill Allen Cl TOOT SW17 5 H3
Bevill Cl SNWD SE25 17 E2
Bevington Rd BECK BR3 18 D1
Bewley St WIM/MER SW19 5 F3
Bewlys Rd WNWD SE27 7 H2
Beynon Rd CAR SM5 33 H1
Bickersteth Rd TOOT SW17 5 H3
Bickley St TOOT SW17 5 H2
Bicknoller Cl BELMT SM2 32 D5
Bidborough Cl HAYES BR2 19 H4
Biddulph Rd SAND/SEL CR2 36 A4
Biggin Av MTCM CR4 5 H5
Biggin Hl NRWD SE19 7 H4
Biggin Wy NRWD SE19 7 H4
Bigginwood Rd
STRHM/NOR SW16 7 H4
Billington Hl CROY/NA CR0 3 F2
Binfield Rd SAND/SEL CR2 36 D1
Bingham Rd CROY/NA CR0 27 E2
Birchanger Rd SNWD SE25 17 E4
Birch Av CTHM CR3 59 F4
Birch Ct WLGTN SM6 24 B5
Birchcroft Cl CTHM CR3 59 E5
Birchend Cl SAND/SEL CR2 36 B2
Birches Cl EPSOM KT18 40 C5
MTCM CR4 13 H2
Birchfield Cl COUL/CHIP CR5 54 B1
Birchfield Gv EW KT17 31 G5
Birch Hl CROY/NA CR0 37 H1
Birch La PUR/KEN CR8 45 E1
Birch Tree Av WWKM BR4 39 H1
Birch Tree Wy CROY/NA CR0 27 F3
Birch Wk MTCM CR4 6 B5
Birch Wy WARL CR6 57 E3
Birchwood Av BECK BR3 18 B3
WLGTN SM6 24 A4
Birchwood Cl MRDN SM4 12 D3
Birchwood La CTHM CR3 58 D5
Birchwood Rd TOOT SW17 6 B2
Birdhurst Av SAND/SEL CR2 3 F7
Birdhurst Gdns SAND/SEL CR2 3 F7
Birdhurst Ri SAND/SEL CR2 36 C1
Birdhurst Rd SAND/SEL CR2 36 C1
WIM/MER SW19 5 G3
Birdwood Cl SAND/SEL CR2 47 H1
Birkbeck Rd BECK BR3 17 H1
WIM/MER SW19 4 D3
Birkdale Gdns CROY/NA CR0 27 H5
Bisenden Rd CROY/NA CR0 3 G2
Bisham Cl CAR SM5 23 H2
Bishop's Cl COUL/CHIP CR5 54 C3
SUT SM1 22 C4
Bishopsford Rd MRDN SM4 23 E1
Bishopsmead Cl
HOR/WEW KT19 30 B5
Bishops Park Rd
STRHM/NOR SW16 7 E5
Bishop's Pl SUT SM1 33 E1
Bishop's Rd CROY/NA CR0 25 H1
Bishopsthorpe Rd SYD SE26 9 G1
Bishops Wk CROY/NA CR0 37 H1
Bisley Cl WPK KT4 21 G2
Blackbush Cl BELMT SM2 32 D3
Blackenham Rd TOOT SW17 5 H1
Blackford Cl SAND/SEL CR2 35 H4
Blackhorse La CROY/NA CR0 27 E1
Blacklands Rd CAT SE6 11 E1
Blackman's La WARL CR6 49 G4
Blackshaw Rd TOOT SW17 5 F2
Blacksmiths Hl
SAND/SEL CR2 47 F3
Blackthorne Av
CROY/NA CR0 27 G2
Blake Cl CAR SM5 23 G2
Blakehall Rd CAR SM5 33 H2
Blakemore Rd THHTH CR7 15 F4
Blakeney Av BECK BR3 10 B5
Blakeney Cl HOR/WEW KT19 40 B1
Blakeney Rd BECK BR3 10 B5
Blake Rd CROY/NA CR0 3 G2
MTCM CR4 13 G2
Blake's Gn WWKM BR4 29 E2
Blanchland Rd MRDN SM4 12 D4
Blanchman's Rd WARL CR6 57 E3
Blandford Av BECK BR3 18 A1
Blandford Cl CROY/NA CR0 25 E4
Blandford Rd BECK BR3 17 H1
Blean Gv PGE/AN SE20 9 G4
Blegborough Rd
STRHM/NOR SW16 6 C3
Blenheim Cl WLGTN SM6 34 C3
Blenheim Crs SAND/SEL CR2 36 A3
Blenheim Gdns
SAND/SEL CR2 47 E2
WLGTN SM6 34 C2
Blenheim Park Rd
SAND/SEL CR2 36 A4
Blenheim Rd HOR/WEW KT19 40 B1
PGE/AN SE20 9 G4
SUT SM1 22 D4
Bletchingley Cl THHTH CR7 15 H3
Bloomhall Rd NRWD SE19 8 B2
Bloomsbury Cl
HOR/WEW KT19 30 B5
Blossom Cl SAND/SEL CR2 36 D1
Bloxworth Cl WLGTN SM6 24 C4
Bluebell Cl SYD SE26 8 D1
WLGTN SM6 24 B2
Blueberry Gdns
COUL/CHIP CR5 54 B1
Blue Cedars BNSTD SM7 41 H4
Bluegates EW KT17 31 E3
Blue Riband Est
CROY/NA CR0 * 2 A2
Blunt Rd SAND/SEL CR2 36 B1
Blytheswood Pl
STRHM/NOR SW16 7 F1
Blyth Rd BMLY BR1 11 H5
Bodiam Rd STRHM/NOR SW16 6 D5
Bodmin Gv MRDN SM4 12 D4
Bolderwood Wy WWKM BR4 28 D3
Boleyn Av EW KT17 31 F5
Boleyn Gdns WWKM BR4 28 D3
Bolstead Rd MTCM CR4 6 B5
Bolters La BNSTD SM7 51 G1
Bolton Dr MRDN SM4 23 F1
Bolton Gdns BMLY BR1 11 H3
Bonchurch Cl BELMT SM2 32 D3
Bond Gdns WLGTN SM6 24 C5
Bond Rd MTCM CR4 13 H1
WARL CR6 56 D3
Bonville Rd BMLY BR1 11 H2
Booth Rd CROY/NA CR0 2 B3
Border Crs SYD SE26 9 F2
Border Gdns CROY/NA CR0 28 D5
Border Ga MTCM CR4 5 G5
Border Rd SYD SE26 9 G2
Bordesley Rd MRDN SM4 12 D3
Borough Hl CROY/NA CR0 2 A5
Borough Rd MTCM CR4 13 G1
Borrowdale Cl SAND/SEL CR2 46 D3
Borrowdale Dr
SAND/SEL CR2 46 D2
Boscombe Rd TOOT SW17 6 A3
WIM/MER SW19 4 C5
WPK KT4 21 G2
Boston Rd CROY/NA CR0 15 F5
Boswell Rd THHTH CR7 16 A3
Bothwell Rd CROY/NA CR0 39 E5
Botsford Rd RYNPK SW20 12 A1
Boughton Av HAYES BR2 29 H1
Boulogne Rd CROY/NA CR0 16 B5
Boundary Business Ct
MTCM CR4 13 F2
Boundary Rd CAR SM5 34 A4
WIM/MER SW19 5 F3
Boundary Wy CROY/NA CR0 38 C1
Bourdon Rd PGE/AN SE20 17 G1
Bourke Hl COUL/CHIP CR5 52 D3
Bourne Dr MTCM CR4 13 F1
Bournefield Rd CTHM CR3 55 H3
Bourne La CTHM CR3 59 F1
Bournemouth Rd
WIM/MER SW19 4 C5
Bourne Park Cl PUR/KEN CR8 55 G1
Bourneside Gdns CAT SE6 11 E2
Bourne St CROY/NA CR0 2 B3
Bournevale Rd
STRHM/NOR SW16 7 E1
Bourne Vw PUR/KEN CR8 46 B5
Bourne Wy HOR/WEW KT19 20 A5
SUT SM1 32 B1
Bouverie Gdns PUR/KEN CR8 45 E4
Bouverie Rd COUL/CHIP CR5 53 E3
Bowenswood CROY/NA CR0 38 B4
Bowens Wd CROY/NA CR0 * 38 B4
Bowley Cl NRWD SE19 8 D3
Bowley La NRWD SE19 8 D2
Bowman's Meadow
WLGTN SM6 24 B4
Boxford Cl SAND/SEL CR2 47 H2
Boxley Rd MRDN SM4 13 E3
Box Ridge Av PUR/KEN CR8 45 F2
Boxwood Wy WARL CR6 56 D2
Boyd Rd WIM/MER SW19 5 F3
Boyland Rd BMLY BR1 11 H2
Brabazon Av WLGTN SM6 35 E3
Brabourne Cl NRWD SE19 8 C2
Brabourne Ri BECK BR3 19 F4
Bracewood Gdns
CROY/NA CR0 3 J4
Bracken Av CROY/NA CR0 28 C4
Bracken Hill Cl BMLY BR1 11 H5
Bracken Hill La BMLY BR1 11 H5
Brackley Cl WLGTN SM6 35 E3
Brackley Rd BECK BR3 10 B4
Bradford Cl SYD SE26 9 F1
Bradford Dr HOR/WEW KT19 30 D2
Brading Rd CROY/NA CR0 15 F5
Bradley Cl BELMT SM2 32 D5
Bradley Rd NRWD SE19 8 A3
Bradmore Wy
COUL/CHIP CR5 54 A3
Bradshaw Cl WIM/MER SW19 4 C3
Bradshaws Cl SNWD SE25 17 E2
Bradstock Rd EW KT17 31 F1
Braemar Av SAND/SEL CR2 36 A5
THHTH CR7 15 H2
Braemar Gdns WWKM BR4 29 E2
Braemar Rd WPK KT4 21 F4
Braeside BECK BR3 10 C2
Braeside Av RYNPK SW20 4 A5
Braeside Rd
STRHM/NOR SW16 6 C4
Brafferton Rd CROY/NA CR0 2 C6
Brailsford Cl WIM/MER SW19 5 G4
Bramber Wy WARL CR6 57 F1
Bramble Acres Cl BELMT SM2 32 C3
Bramble Banks CAR SM5 34 A4
Bramble Cl BECK BR3 19 E4
CROY/NA CR0 28 C5
Brambledown Cl WWKM BR4 19 G5
Brambledown Rd CAR SM5 34 A3
SAND/SEL CR2 36 C4
Brambles Cl CTHM CR3 59 G2
The Brambles SUT SM1 23 F3
WIM/MER SW19 * 4 B2
Bramblewood Cl CAR SM5 23 G2
Bramcote Av MTCM CR4 13 H3
Bramerton Rd BECK BR3 18 B2
Bramley Av COUL/CHIP CR5 44 C5
Bramley Cl SAND/SEL CR2 35 H1
Bramley Hl SAND/SEL CR2 2 C7
Bramley Hyrst
SAND/SEL CR2 * 36 A1
Bramley Rd BELMT SM2 31 H4
SUT SM1 33 F1
Bramley Wy WWKM BR4 28 D3
Brampton Rd CROY/NA CR0 26 D1
Bramston Rd MTCM CR4 5 H4
Brancaster La PUR/KEN CR8 46 A1
Brandon Rd SUT SM1 22 D5
The Brandries WLGTN SM6 24 D4
Brandy Wy BELMT SM2 32 C3
Brangbourne Rd BMLY BR1 11 E2
Brangwyn Crs
WIM/MER SW19 13 F1
Branksome Rd
WIM/MER SW19 4 C5
Brantwood Rd
SAND/SEL CR2 36 A4
Brasted Cl BELMT SM2 32 C5
SYD SE26 9 G1
Braxted Pk STRHM/NOR SW16 7 F3
Braybrooke Gdns NRWD SE19 8 C4
Brazil Cl CROY/NA CR0 25 E1
Breakfield COUL/CHIP CR5 54 A1
Brecon Cl MTCM CR4 15 E3
WPK KT4 21 G3
Bredhurst Cl PGE/AN SE20 9 G3
Bredon Rd CROY/NA CR0 26 D1
Bredune PUR/KEN CR8 46 B5
Brenchley Cl HAYES BR2 19 H4
Brenley Cl MTCM CR4 14 A2
Brent Rd SAND/SEL CR2 37 F4
Brettgrave HOR/WEW KT19 30 A5
Brian Av SAND/SEL CR2 46 C2
Briane Rd HOR/WEW KT19 30 A5
Briar Av STRHM/NOR SW16 7 F4
Briar Bank CAR SM5 34 A4
Briar Cl WARL CR6 57 G1
Briar Gdns HAYES BR2 29 H2
Briar Gv SAND/SEL CR2 47 E3
Briar Hl PUR/KEN CR8 45 E1
Briar La CAR SM5 34 A4
CROY/NA CR0 28 D5
Briar Rd STRHM/NOR SW16 15 E2
Briarwood Ct WPK KT4 * 21 E2
Briarwood Rd EW KT17 31 E2
Brickfield Rd THHTH CR7 7 H5
WIM/MER SW19 4 D1
Brickfield Vls CAR SM5 * 23 G4
Brickwood Rd CROY/NA CR0 3 G2
Bridgefield Cl BNSTD SM7 41 G5
Bridgefield Rd SUT SM1 32 C2
Bridgelands Cl BECK BR3 10 B4
Bridge Pde
STRHM/NOR SW16 * 7 E2
Bridge Pl CROY/NA CR0 26 B2
Bridge Rd BECK BR3 10 B4
EW KT17 40 D2
SUT SM1 32 D2
WLGTN SM6 34 B1
Bridge Rw CROY/NA CR0 * 26 B2
Bridges La CROY/NA CR0 25 E5
Bridges Road Ms
WIM/MER SW19 4 D3
Bridgetown Cl NRWD SE19 8 C2
Bridge Vls
WIM/MER SW19 * 4 C2
Bridge Wy COUL/CHIP CR5 52 C4
Bridgewood Cl PGE/AN SE20 9 F4
Bridgewood Rd
STRHM/NOR SW16 6 D4
WPK KT4 21 E5
Bridle Cl HOR/WEW KT19 20 A5
Bridle Pth CROY/NA CR0 25 E4
The Bridle Pth EW KT17 31 G5
Bridle Rd CROY/NA CR0 28 C5
EW KT17 40 D3
The Bridle Rd PUR/KEN CR8 35 E5
Bridle Wy CROY/NA CR0 38 C1
Bridleway Cl EW KT17 31 G5
The Bridle Wy WLGTN SM6 24 C5
Bridport Rd THHTH CR7 15 G2
Brierley CROY/NA CR0 38 D2
Brierley Cl SNWD SE25 17 E3
Brier Rd KWD/TDW/WH KT20 50 B4
Brigade Pl CTHM CR3 59 E2
Briggs Cl MTCM CR4 6 B5
Brighton Rd BELMT SM2 32 D5
BNSTD SM7 42 B4
COUL/CHIP CR5 53 G3
KWD/TDW/WH KT20 51 E3
PUR/KEN CR8 45 E4
SAND/SEL CR2 36
Brightwell Cl CROY/NA CR0 25
Brightwell Crs TOOT SW17 5
Brigstock Rd COUL/CHIP CR5 44
THHTH CR7 15
The Brindles BNSTD SM7 51
Brinkley Rd WPK KT4 21
Brisbane Av WIM/MER SW19 4
Briscoe Rd WIM/MER SW19 5
Bristol Cl WLGTN SM6 35
Bristol Rd MRDN SM4 13
Bristow Rd CROY/NA CR0 25
NRWD SE19 8
Briton Cl SAND/SEL CR2 46
Briton Crs SAND/SEL CR2 46
Briton Hill Rd SAND/SEL CR2 36
Broadcoombe SAND/SEL CR2 37
Broadeaves Cl SAND/SEL CR2 36
Broadfield Cl
KWD/TDW/WH KT20 50
Broad Green Av
CROY/NA CR0 25
Broadlands Dr WARL CR6 56
Broadmead Av WPK KT4 21
Broad Oaks Wy HAYES BR2 19
Broadview Rd
STRHM/NOR SW16 6
Broad Wk CTHM CR3 59
EPSOM KT18 50
Broadwater Rd TOOT SW17 5
Broadway Av CROY/NA CR0 16
Broadway Cl SAND/SEL CR2 47
Broadway Ct WIM/MER SW19 4
Broadway Gdns MTCM CR4 13
The Broadway CHEAM SM3 32
SUT SM1 23
WIM/MER SW19 4
Brockenhurst Av WPK KT4 20
Brockenhurst Rd
CROY/NA CR0 27
Brockenhurst Wy
STRHM/NOR SW16 14
Brockham Cl WIM/MER SW19 4
Brockham Crs CROY/NA CR0 39
Brocklesby Rd SNWD SE25 17
Brockman Ri BMLY BR1 11
Brocks Dr CHEAM SM3 22
Brockwell Av BECK BR3 18
Brograve Gdns BECK BR3 18
Bromley Av BMLY BR1 11
Bromley Ct BMLY BR1 11
Bromley Crs HAYES BR2 19
Bromley Gdns HAYES BR2 19
Bromley Gv HAYES BR2 19
Bromley Hl BMLY BR1 11
Bromley Rd BECK BR3 10
BECK BR3 19
CAT SE6 11
Brook Cl HOR/WEW KT19 30
Brook Ct BECK BR3 * 10
Brookfield Av SUT SM1 23
Brookfields Av MTCM CR4 13
Brooklyn Av SNWD SE25 17
Brooklyn Cl CAR SM5 23
Brooklyn Gv SNWD SE25 17
Brooklyn Rd SNWD SE25 17
Brookmead CROY/NA CR0 14
Brook Md HOR/WEW KT19 30
Brookmead Rd CROY/NA CR0 14
Brook Rd THHTH CR7 16
Brookscroft CROY/NA CR0 38
Brookside CAR SM5 34
Brookside Crs WPK KT4 21
Brookside Wy CROY/NA CR0 17
Brookview Rd
STRHM/NOR SW16 6
Brookwood Cl HAYES BR2 19
Broomfield Rd BECK BR3 18
Broom Gdns CROY/NA CR0 28
Broomhall Rd SAND/SEL CR2 36
Broomloan La SUT SM1 22
Broom Rd CROY/NA CR0 28
Broomwood Cl CROY/NA CR0 17
Broseley Gv SYD SE26 9
Broster Gdns SNWD SE25 16
Broughton Rd THHTH CR7 15
Brown Cl WLGTN SM6 34
Browning Av SUT SM1 23
WPK KT4 21
Brownlow Rd CROY/NA CR0 3
Bruce Dr SAND/SEL CR2 37
Bruce Rd MTCM CR4 6
SNWD SE25 16
Brumfield Rd HOR/WEW KT19 30
Brunel Cl NRWD SE19 8
Brunswick Ms
STRHM/NOR SW16 6
Brunswick Pl NRWD SE19 9
Brunswick Rd SUT SM1 22
Bruton Rd MRDN SM4 13
Bryden Cl SYD SE26 10
Buckfast Rd MRDN SM4 12
Buckhurst Av CAR SM5 23
Buckingham Av THHTH CR7 7
Buckingham Ct BELMT SM2 * 32
Buckingham Gdns
THHTH CR7 15
Buckingham Rd MTCM CR4 15
Buckingham Wy WLGTN SM6 34
Buckland Rd BELMT SM2 31
Buckland Wk MRDN SM4 13
Buckland Wy WPK KT4 21
Buckleigh Av RYNPK SW20 12
Buckleigh Rd
STRHM/NOR SW16 6
Buckleigh Wy NRWD SE19 8
Bucklers' Wy CAR SM5 23
Buckles Wy BNSTD SM7 51
Bucknall Wy BECK BR3 18
Bucknills Cl EPSOM KT18 40
Budge La MTCM CR4 23
Buff Av BNSTD SM7 42

g Hl WARL CR6 56 D5
ganak Rd THHTH CR7 16 A3
ler Rd THHTH CR7 16 B2
finch Rd SAND/SEL CR2 37 H5
rush Cl CAR SM5 23 G3
CROY/NA CR0 16 C5
bury Wy EW KT17 50 B1
ce Dr CTHM CR3 59 F3
galow Rd SNWD SE25 16 C3
Bungalows
STRHM/NOR SW16 6 B4
ting Cl MTCM CR4 13 H4
cott Rd PUR/KEN CR8 45 G4
dett Rd CROY/NA CR0 16 B5
dock Cl CROY/NA CR0 27 H2
don La BELMT SM2 32 B4
don Pk BELMT SM2 32 B4
field Cl TOOT SW17 5 E1
field Dr WARL CR6 56 C4
ford La EW KT17 41 G1
ford Rd SUT SM1 22 C3
WPK KT4 21 E1
ford Wy CROY/NA CR0 39 E3
gess Ms WIM/MER SW19 4 D3
gess Rd SUT SM1 22 D5
ghfield EW KT17 40 D5
gh Heath Rd EW KT17 40 D5
ghill Rd SYD SE26 9 H1
ghley Pl MTCM CR4 13 H3
ghley Rd WIM/MER SW19 4 A1
gh Mt BNSTD SM7 42 B5
gh Wd BNSTD SM7 42 A5
gos Cl CROY/NA CR0 35 G2
goyne Rd SNWD SE25 16 D3
ham Cl PGE/AN SE20 9 G4
leigh Av WLGTN SM6 24 A4
leigh Rd CHEAM SM3 22 A2
ley Cl STRHM/NOR SW16 14 D1
lington Rd THHTH CR7 16 A1
ma Ter NRWD SE19 * 8 C2
nell Rd SUT SM1 22 D5
net Gv HOR/WEW KT19 40 A3
nham Dr WPK KT4 21 H3
nham Gdns CROY/NA CR0 26 D1
nham Rd MRDN SM4 12 D4
nham Wy SYD SE26 10 B2
nhill Rd BECK BR3 18 C1
ns Cl CAR SM5 34 A4
WIM/MER SW19 5 F3
ns Dr BNSTD SM7 42 A4
ntwood Cl CTHM CR3 60 A1
ntwood La CTHM CR3 60 A1
ntwood Vw NRWD SE19 * 8 D2
rell Cl CROY/NA CR0 18 A5
rell Rw BECK BR3 18 C1
stow Rd RYNPK SW20 4 A5
ton Cl THHTH CR7 16 B2
well La DUL SE21 8 B1
wood Av PUR/KEN CR8 45 H4
Gv MRDN SM4 12 D4
hey Cl PUR/KEN CR8 55 H1
hey La SUT SM1 22 C4
hey Rd CROY/NA CR0 28 C3
UT SM1 22 D5
hey Wy BECK BR3 19 F5
e Gdns WLGTN SM6 34 C1
e Gdns West WLGTN SM6 34 C1
e Rd CROY/NA CR0 25 G2
VLGTN SM6 24 C5
ers Dene Rd CTHM CR3 57 G5
terfly Wk WARL CR6 56 C5
ter Hl CAR SM5 24 A4
termere Gdns
UR/KEN CR8 46 B4
ts Rd BMLY BR1 11 G2
ton Av CTHM CR3 59 G1
ton Crs CHEAM SM3 22 A5
ton La CTHM CR3 59 G1
ton Rd THHTH CR7 15 H4
rds Cft STRHM/NOR SW16 6 D5
roft St PGE/AN SE20 9 H4
rove CROY/NA CR0 38 D2
rove Rd WIM/MER SW19 5 F3
nd Cl CAR SM5 23 F1
e Rd CAR SM5 23 G3
YD SE26 9 G3
es Rd SAND/SEL CR2 36 B3
on Av COUL/CHIP CR5 45 E5
UT SM1 23 F5
on Av East SUT SM1 23 F5
on Cl PGE/AN SE20 * 17 F2
TRHM/NOR SW16 7 E3
YD SE26 * 10 A1
on Gdns SUT SM1 23 F5
on Rd SAND/SEL CR2 37 F5
on Rd TOOT SW17 5 H3
Byway BELMT SM2 33 F4
OR/WEW KT19 20 D5
ood Av CROY/NA CR0 17 G5
ood Cl PUR/KEN CR8 45 H5

C

gan Ct BELMT SM2 32 D2
gan Pl PUR/KEN CR8 55 E2
narvon Cl MTCM CR4 15 E2
ars Wk MTCM CR4 13 H4
ndale Cl BMLY BR1 11 H4
New Rd CROY/NA CR0 2 B3
nness Dr EPSOM KT18 40 B4
nness Rd MTCM CR4 6 B4
beck Av WPK KT4 21 F3
er Rd MRDN SM4 13 E4
don Rd WLGTN SM6 24 A5
ornia Cl BELMT SM2 32 C5
y Down Crs
ROY/NA CR0 39 F5
w Fld PUR/KEN CR8 45 G3
ont Rd BMLY BR1 11 F3

Calthorpe Gdns SUT SM1 23 E4
Calverley Cl BECK BR3 10 D3
Calverley Rd EW KT17 31 E2
Camberley Cl CHEAM SM3 21 H4
Camborne Rd BELMT SM2 32 C3
CROY/NA CR0 27 E1
Cambridge Gv PGE/AN SE20 * 9 F5
Cambridge Rd CAR SM5 33 G2
MTCM CR4 14 C2
PGE/AN SE20 17 E2
Camden Gdns SUT SM1 32 D1
THHTH CR7 15 H2
Camden Hill Rd NRWD SE19 8 C3
Camden Rd CAR SM5 23 H5
SUT SM1 32 D1
Camden Wy THHTH CR7 15 H2
Camelot Cl WIM/MER SW19 4 B1
Cameron Rd CROY/NA CR0 15 H5
Cameron Sq MTCM CR4 5 G5
Camille Cl SNWD SE25 17 E2
Camlan Rd BMLY BR1 11 H1
Camomile Av MTCM CR4 5 H5
Campbell Cl
STRHM/NOR SW16 * 6 D2
Campbell Cottages
MTCM CR4 * 14 A1
Campbell Rd CROY/NA CR0 25 H1
CTHM CR3 59 F1
Campden Rd SAND/SEL CR2 36 C1
Campion Cl CROY/NA CR0 3 H7
Campion Dr
KWD/TDW/WH KT20 50 B5
Camp Rd CTHM CR3 61 E1
Camrose Cl CROY/NA CR0 28 A1
MRDN SM4 12 C3
Canal Wk CROY/NA CR0 16 C5
Canham Rd SNWD SE25 16 C2
Can Hatch
KWD/TDW/WH KT20 51 E3
Canmore Gdns
STRHM/NOR SW16 6 C4
Canning Rd CROY/NA CR0 3 J2
Canon's Hl COUL/CHIP CR5 54 C3
Canons La
KWD/TDW/WH KT20 51 E4
Canon's Wk CROY/NA CR0 27 H4
Canterbury Cl BECK BR3 10 D5
Canterbury Rd CROY/NA CR0 25 F1
MRDN SM4 13 E5
Cantley Gdns NRWD SE19 8 D5
Capel Av WLGTN SM6 35 F1
Capri Rd CROY/NA CR0 26 D1
Capstone Rd BMLY BR1 11 H1
Caraway Pl WLGTN SM6 24 B4
Carberry Rd NRWD SE19 8 C3
Cardigan Rd WIM/MER SW19 5 E3
Cardinal Av MRDN SM4 12 A5
Cardinal Cl MRDN SM4 12 A5
SAND/SEL CR2 47 E3
WPK KT4 21 E5
Carew Cl COUL/CHIP CR5 54 D4
Carew Rd MTCM CR4 14 A1
THHTH CR7 15 H2
WLGTN SM6 34 C2
Cargreen Rd SNWD SE25 16 D3
Carisbrooke Rd MTCM CR4 15 E3
Carleton Av WLGTN SM6 34 D4
Carlisle Rd SUT SM1 32 B2
Carlisle Wy TOOT SW17 6 A2
Carlton Av SAND/SEL CR2 36 B3
Carlton Crs CHEAM SM3 22 A5
Carlton Dene EW KT17 * 31 F1
Carlton Rd SAND/SEL CR2 36 B3
Carlton Ter SYD SE26 9 G1
Carlwell St TOOT SW17 5 G2
Carlyle Rd CROY/NA CR0 27 E3
Carlys Cl BECK BR3 17 H1
Carmichael Rd SNWD SE25 17 E4
Carnac St WNWD SE27 8 B1
Carnforth Rd
STRHM/NOR SW16 6 D4
Carolina Rd THHTH CR7 15 H1
Caroline Cl CROY/NA CR0 3 H6
Caroline Rd WIM/MER SW19 4 B4
Carpenter Cl EW KT17 30 D4
Carrington Cl CROY/NA CR0 28 A1
Carshalton Gv SUT SM1 23 F5
Carshalton Park Rd CAR SM5 33 H2
Carshalton Pl CAR SM5 34 A1
Carshalton Rd BNSTD SM7 43 H3
MTCM CR4 14 A4
SUT SM1 33 E1
Carter Cl WLGTN SM6 34 D3
Carter Rd WIM/MER SW19 5 F3
Carters Cl WPK KT4 21 H3
Carter's Rd EW KT17 40 D5
Cartmel Gdns MRDN SM4 13 E4
Cascades CROY/NA CR0 38 B5
Casewick Rd WNWD SE27 7 H2
Cassland Rd THHTH CR7 16 B3
Castle Av EW KT17 31 E4
Castle Cl HAYES BR2 19 G2
Castle Ct SYD SE26 10 A1
Castledine Rd PGE/AN SE20 9 F4
Castle Hill Av CROY/NA CR0 38 D4
Castlemaine Av EW KT17 31 F4
SAND/SEL CR2 36 D1
Castle Ms TOOT SW17 5 G1
Castle Pde EW KT17 * 31 E3
Castle Rd COUL/CHIP CR5 52 C5
Castleton Cl BNSTD SM7 42 C5
CROY/NA CR0 18 A5
Castleton Dr BNSTD SM7 42 C5
Castleton Rd MTCM CR4 14 D3
Castle Wy EW KT17 31 E5
Caterham-By-Pass
CTHM CR3 60 B2
Caterham Dr COUL/CHIP CR5 54 D4
Cator Cl CROY/NA CR0 49 G1
Cator Crs CROY/NA CR0 49 G1
Cator La BECK BR3 18 B1
Cator Rd CAR SM5 33 H1

SYD SE26 9 H3
The Causeway BELMT SM2 33 E4
CAR SM5 24 A4
Cavendish Rd BELMT SM2 33 E3
CROY/NA CR0 25 H2
WIM/MER SW19 5 G4
Cavendish Wy WWKM BR4 28 D2
Caverleigh Wy WPK KT4 21 E2
Caversham Av CHEAM SM3 22 A3
Cawnpore St NRWD SE19 8 C2
Caxton Rd WIM/MER SW19 5 E2
Caygill Cl HAYES BR2 19 H3
Cearn Wy COUL/CHIP CR5 54 B1
Cecil Pl MTCM CR4 13 H4
Cecil Rd CROY/NA CR0 15 E5
SUT SM1 32 B2
WIM/MER SW19 4 D4
Cedar Cl CAR SM5 33 H2
EW KT17 40 D4
WARL CR6 57 E4
Cedar Gdns BELMT SM2 33 E2
Cedar Hl EPSOM KT18 40 A5
Cedarhurst BMLY BR1 * 11 G4
Cedar Pk CTHM CR3 59 G1
Cedar Rd BELMT SM2 33 E2
CROY/NA CR0 3 G2
Cedars BNSTD SM7 43 H4
Cedars Av MTCM CR4 14 A3
Cedars Rd BECK BR3 18 A1
CROY/NA CR0 25 E4
MRDN SM4 12 C3
Cedar Tree Gv WNWD SE27 7 H2
Cedarville Gdns
STRHM/NOR SW16 7 F3
Cedar Wk PUR/KEN CR8 55 E1
Celtic Av HAYES BR2 19 G2
Central Av WLGTN SM6 35 E1
Central Hl NRWD SE19 8 A2
Central Pde CROY/NA CR0 39 E5
PGE/AN SE20 * 9 H4
STRHM/NOR SW16 * 7 E1
Central Pl SNWD SE25 * 17 E3
Central Rd MRDN SM4 12 D4
WPK KT4 21 E3
Central Ter BECK BR3 * 17 H2
Central Wy CAR SM5 33 G3
Centurion Ct WLGTN SM6 * 24 B3
Cerne Rd MRDN SM4 13 E5
Chadacre Rd EW KT17 31 F1
Chadwick Av WIM/MER SW19 4 C3
Chaffinch Av CROY/NA CR0 17 H5
Chaffinch Cl CROY/NA CR0 17 H4
Chaffinch Rd BECK BR3 10 A5
Chalcot Cl BELMT SM2 32 C3
Chaldon Common Rd
CTHM CR3 59 E4
Chaldon Rd CTHM CR3 59 F3
Chaldon Wy COUL/CHIP CR5 54 A2
Chalfont Rd SNWD SE25 16 D2
Chalford Rd DUL SE21 8 B1
Chalgrove Av MRDN SM4 12 C4
Chalgrove Rd BELMT SM2 33 F3
Chalice Cl WLGTN SM6 34 D2
Chalkenden Cl PGE/AN SE20 9 F4
Chalkley Cl MTCM CR4 13 H1
Chalk Paddock EPSOM KT18 40 B5
Chalk Pit Rd BNSTD SM7 51 G2
SUT SM1 33 E1
Challin St PGE/AN SE20 9 G5
Chalmers Rd BNSTD SM7 43 E5
Chamberlain Crs WWKM BR4 28 D2
Chambers Pl SAND/SEL CR2 36 B3
Champion Crs SYD SE26 10 A1
Champion Rd SYD SE26 10 A1
Champness Cl WNWD SE27 8 B1
Champneys Cl BELMT SM2 32 B3
Chancellor Gdns
SAND/SEL CR2 35 H4
Chancery La BECK BR3 18 D1
Chanctonbury Gdns
BELMT SM2 32 D3
Chandos Gdns
COUL/CHIP CR5 54 D4
Chanton Dr BELMT SM2 31 G5
Chantry Hurst EPSOM KT18 40 B5
Chantry Wy MTCM CR4 13 F2
Chapel Gv EPSOM KT18 50 C4
Chapel Rd WARL CR6 56 D3
WNWD SE27 7 H1
Chapel Vw SAND/SEL CR2 37 G3
Chapel Wy EPSOM KT18 50 C4
Chapman Rd CROY/NA CR0 25 G2
Chapter Wy WIM/MER SW19 5 F5
Charles Cobb Gdns
CROY/NA CR0 35 G1
Charles Dickens Ter
PGE/AN SE20 * 9 G4
Charles Rd WIM/MER SW19 4 C5
Charles St CROY/NA CR0 2 C4
Charleville Circ SYD SE26 9 E2
Charlmont Rd TOOT SW17 5 G3
Charlotte Rd WLGTN SM6 34 C2
Charlton Gdns
COUL/CHIP CR5 53 G3
Charlwood CROY/NA CR0 38 B4
Charminster Av
WIM/MER SW19 12 C1
Charminster Rd WPK KT4 21 H2
Charnwood Av
WIM/MER SW19 12 C1
Charnwood Rd SNWD SE25 16 B4
Charrington Rd CROY/NA CR0 2 C3
Chart Cl CROY/NA CR0 17 G5
HAYES BR2 11 G5
MTCM CR4 13 H3
Charters Cl NRWD SE19 8 C2
Chartham Rd SNWD SE25 17 F2
Chartwell Cl CROY/NA CR0 26 B2
Chartwell Gdns CHEAM SM3 22 A4
Chartwell Pl CHEAM SM3 22 A5
EPSOM KT18 40 C4
Chartwell Wy PGE/AN SE20 9 F5

Charwood STRHM/NOR SW16 7 G1
Chase Ct RYNPK SW20 12 A1
Chase End HOR/WEW KT19 40 B2
Chasefield Rd TOOT SW17 5 H1
Chaseley Dr SAND/SEL CR2 36 B5
Chasemore Cl MTCM CR4 23 H1
Chasemore Gdns
CROY/NA CR0 35 G1
Chase Rd HOR/WEW KT19 40 B2
Chaseside Av RYNPK SW20 4 A5
The Chase COUL/CHIP CR5 44 C4
STRHM/NOR SW16 7 F4
WLGTN SM6 35 E1
Chatfield Ct CTHM CR3 59 F2
Chatfield Rd CROY/NA CR0 25 H2
Chatham Av HAYES BR2 29 H1
Chatham Cl CHEAM SM3 22 B1
Chatsfield EW KT17 31 E5
Chatsworth Av RYNPK SW20 4 A5
Chatsworth Cl WWKM BR4 29 H3
Chatsworth Pl MTCM CR4 13 H2
Chatsworth Rd CHEAM SM3 21 H5
CROY/NA CR0 3 F6
Chaucer Cl BNSTD SM7 42 A4
Chaucer Gdns SUT SM1 22 C5
Chaucer Gn CROY/NA CR0 27 G1
Chaucer Rd SUT SM1 22 C5
Chaucer Wy WIM/MER SW19 5 F3
Chave Cft EPSOM KT18 * 50 C4
Chavecroft Ter
EPSOM KT18 * 50 C4
Cheam Common Rd
WPK KT4 21 F3
Cheam Man CHEAM SM3 * 32 A2
Cheam Park Wy CHEAM SM3 31 H2
Cheam Rd EW KT17 31 F5
SUT SM1 32 B2
Chelford Rd BMLY BR1 11 F2
Chelmsford Cl BELMT SM2 32 C4
Chelsea Cl WPK KT4 21 E1
Chelsea Gdns CHEAM SM3 22 A5
Chelsea Sq CAR SM5 33 H4
Chelsham Common Rd
WARL CR6 57 G2
Chelsham Rd SAND/SEL CR2 36 B3
Chelwood Cl COUL/CHIP CR5 53 G4
EW KT17 40 D2
Chepstow Ri CROY/NA CR0 3 H4
Chepstow Rd CROY/NA CR0 3 J3
Cherry Cl BNSTD SM7 41 H4
CAR SM5 23 H3
MRDN SM4 12 A3
Cherry Hill Gdns
CROY/NA CR0 25 F5
Cherry Orchard Gdns
CROY/NA CR0 3 F1
Cherry Orchard Rd
CROY/NA CR0 3 F1
Cherry Tree Ct
COUL/CHIP CR5 54 B3
Cherry Tree Gn
SAND/SEL CR2 47 F4
Cherry Tree Wk BECK BR3 18 B3
WWKM BR4 29 H5
Cherry Wy HOR/WEW KT19 30 B2
Cherrywood La RYNPK SW20 12 A3
Chertsey Cl PUR/KEN CR8 45 H5
Chertsey Crs CROY/NA CR0 49 E1
Chertsey Dr CHEAM SM3 22 A3
Chertsey St TOOT SW17 6 A2
Cherwell Ct HOR/WEW KT19 20 A5
Chesham Cl BELMT SM2 32 A5
Chesham Crs PGE/AN SE20 9 G5
Chesham Rd PGE/AN SE20 17 G1
WARL CR6 57 G1
WIM/MER SW19 5 F3
Cheshire Cl MTCM CR4 15 E2
Chesney Crs CROY/NA CR0 39 E3
Chessell Cl THHTH CR7 15 H3
Chessington Cl
HOR/WEW KT19 30 A2
Chessington Rd
HOR/WEW KT19 30 A2
Chessington Wy WWKM BR4 28 D3
Chester Cl SUT SM1 22 C3
Chesterfield Rd
HOR/WEW KT19 30 B3
Chester Gdns MRDN SM4 13 E4
Chestnut Av HOR/WEW KT19 20 C5
WWKM BR4 39 G1
Chestnut Cl CAR SM5 23 H2
CAT SE6 11 E1
STRHM/NOR SW16 7 G1
Chestnut Gv MTCM CR4 14 D4
SAND/SEL CR2 37 F3
Chestnut Pl NRWD SE19 8 D1
The Chestnuts BECK BR3 * 17 H2
Chestnut Ter SUT SM1 * 22 D5
Cheston Av CROY/NA CR0 28 A2
Chetwode Dr EPSOM KT18 50 D3
Chetwode Rd EPSOM KT18 50 C4
Chevening Rd NRWD SE19 8 B4
Cheviot Cl BELMT SM2 33 F4
BNSTD SM7 42 D5
Cheviot Rd WNWD SE27 7 H2
Cheyham Gdns BELMT SM2 31 H5
Cheyham Wy BELMT SM2 32 A5
Cheyne Ct BNSTD SM7 42 D5
Cheyne Park Dr WWKM BR4 29 E4
Cheyne Wk CROY/NA CR0 27 E3
Chichele Gdns CROY/NA CR0 3 H6
Chichester Ct EW KT17 * 30 D4
Chichester Dr PUR/KEN CR8 45 F2
Chichester Rd CROY/NA CR0 3 H5
Chiddingstone Cl BELMT SM2 32 C5
Childs La NRWD SE19 * 8 C3
Chillerton Rd TOOT SW17 6 A2
Chilmark Rd
STRHM/NOR SW16 14 D1
Chiltern Cl CROY/NA CR0 3 H5
WPK KT4 21 G3
Chiltern Gdns HAYES BR2 19 H3

Chiltern Rd BELMT SM2 33 E5
The Chilterns BELMT SM2 * 32 D4
Chiltons Cl BNSTD SM7 42 D5
Chilworth Gdns SUT SM1 23 E4
Chingley Cl BMLY BR1 11 G3
Chinthurst Ms
COUL/CHIP CR5 44 C5
Chipstead Av THHTH CR7 15 H3
Chipstead Cl BELMT SM2 32 D4
COUL/CHIP CR5 53 E2
NRWD SE19 8 D4
Chipstead Rd BNSTD SM7 51 F2
Chipstead Station Pde
COUL/CHIP CR5 52 D3
Chipstead Valley Rd
COUL/CHIP CR5 53 F1
Chipstead Wy BNSTD SM7 52 D2
Chisholm Rd CROY/NA CR0 3 H2
Chislet Cl BECK BR3 10 C4
Chiswick Cl CROY/NA CR0 25 F4
Christchurch Cl
WIM/MER SW19 5 F4
Christchurch Pk BELMT SM2 33 E3
Christ Church Rd
BECK BR3 * 18 C1
Christchurch Rd
PUR/KEN CR8 35 G5
WIM/MER SW19 5 F5
Christian Flds
STRHM/NOR SW16 7 G4
Christie Dr CROY/NA CR0 17 E4
Christie Wk COUL/CHIP CR5 54 D4
Chudleigh Gdns SUT SM1 23 E4
Chulsa Rd SYD SE26 9 F2
Church Av BECK BR3 10 C5
Church Cl EW KT17 * 40 C3
Churchdown BMLY BR1 11 G1
Church Dr WWKM BR4 29 G4
Church Farm La CHEAM SM3 32 A2
Churchfields Rd BECK BR3 17 H1
Church Hl CAR SM5 33 H1
CTHM CR3 59 H4
PUR/KEN CR8 35 E5
WIM/MER SW19 4 B2
Church Hill Rd CHEAM SM3 21 H5
Churchill Cl WARL CR6 56 C2
Churchill Rd SAND/SEL CR2 36 A4
Church La CTHM CR3 58 C3
KWD/TDW/WH KT20 50 D2
TOOT SW17 5 H2
WARL CR6 56 D2
WIM/MER SW19 4 C5
WIM/MER SW19 12 C1
WLGTN SM6 24 D4
Churchley Rd SYD SE26 9 F1
Churchmore Rd
STRHM/NOR SW16 6 C5
Church Paddock Ct
WLGTN SM6 24 D4
Church Pth COUL/CHIP CR5 54 C3
MTCM CR4 13 G2
RYNPK SW20 12 B1
Church Pl MTCM CR4 13 G2
Church Rd CHEAM SM3 32 A2
CROY/NA CR0 2 C5
CTHM CR3 55 H3
CTHM CR3 59 H3
CTHM CR3 60 D1
EW KT17 40 C3
HAYES BR2 19 G2
HOR/WEW KT19 30 B3
MTCM CR4 13 G2
NRWD SE19 8 C4
PUR/KEN CR8 35 E5
PUR/KEN CR8 46 B5
WARL CR6 56 D2
WIM/MER SW19 13 F1
WLGTN SM6 24 C4
WPK KT4 20 C2
Church St CROY/NA CR0 2 B4
EW KT17 31 E4
EW KT17 40 C3
Church Wk CTHM CR3 60 A4
STRHM/NOR SW16 14 C1
Church Wy SAND/SEL CR2 36 D5
Chuters Gv EW KT17 40 D2
Cinderford Wy BMLY BR1 11 G1
Cinnamon Cl CROY/NA CR0 * 25 E1
Cintra Pk NRWD SE19 8 D4
Circle Gdns WIM/MER SW19 12 C2
Clairview Rd
STRHM/NOR SW16 6 B2
Clandon Cl EW KT17 30 D2
Clare Ct CTHM CR3 61 G3
Claremont Cl SAND/SEL CR2 47 F5
Claremont Rd CROY/NA CR0 27 E2
Claremount Cl EPSOM KT18 50 C2
Claremount Gdns
EPSOM KT18 50 D2
Clarence Rd CROY/NA CR0 26 B1
SUT SM1 22 D5
WIM/MER SW19 4 D3
WLGTN SM6 34 B1
Clarendon Gv MTCM CR4 13 H2
Clarendon Rd CROY/NA CR0 2 B2
WIM/MER SW19 5 G4
WLGTN SM6 34 C2
The Clares CTHM CR3 60 A4
Claret Gdns SNWD SE25 16 C3
Clareville Rd CTHM CR3 60 A4
Clarice Wy WLGTN SM6 35 E4
Clarkes Av WPK KT4 21 H2
Clay Av MTCM CR4 14 B1
Claydon Dr CROY/NA CR0 25 E5
Claygate Crs CROY/NA CR0 39 F2
Claymore Cl MRDN SM4 22 C1
Clayton Rd EW KT17 40 C2
Cleave Prior
COUL/CHIP CR5 52 C4
Cleaverholme Cl SNWD SE25 17 F5
Cleeve Wy SUT SM1 22 D2
Clement Cl PUR/KEN CR8 54 D1

Clement Rd BECK BR3 17 H1
WIM/MER SW19 4 A2
Clensham Ct SUT SM1 22 C3
Clensham La SUT SM1 22 C3
Clevedon Rd PGE/AN SE20 9 H5
Cleveland Gdns WPK KT4 20 C3
Cleveland Ri MRDN SM4 21 H1
Cleveland Rd WPK KT4 20 C3
Cleves Av EW KT17 31 F4
Cleves Crs CROY/NA CR0 49 E1
Cliff End PUR/KEN CR8 45 H2
Cliffe Rd SAND/SEL CR2 36 B1
Clifford Av WLGTN SM6 24 C5
Clifford Rd SNWD SE25 17 E3
Clifton Av BELMT SM2 42 D1
Clifton Cl CTHM CR3 59 F3
Clifton Ct BECK BR3 * 10 D5
Clifton Ms SNWD SE25 16 C3
Clifton Pl BNSTD SM7 42 C5
Clifton Rd COUL/CHIP CR5 44 B5
SNWD SE25 16 C3
WLGTN SM6 34 B1
Clinton Ter SUT SM1 * 23 E5
Cliveden Rd WIM/MER SW19 4 B5
Clive Rd WIM/MER SW19 5 G3
Clock House Rd BECK BR3 18 A2
Cloister Gdns SNWD SE25 17 F5
The Close BECK BR3 18 A3
CAR SM5 33 G4
CHEAM SM3 22 B1
MTCM CR4 13 H3
PUR/KEN CR8 35 F5
SNWD SE25 * 17 E5
Clouston Cl WLGTN SM6 35 E1
Clovelly Av WARL CR6 56 B4
Clover Wy WLGTN SM6 24 B2
Clowser Cl SUT SM1 33 E1
Clyde Av SAND/SEL CR2 47 F5
Clyde Rd CROY/NA CR0 3 J2
SUT SM1 32 C1
WLGTN SM6 34 C1
Coates Cl THHTH CR7 16 A2
Cobalt Cl BECK BR3 17 H3
Cobblestone Pl CROY/NA CR0 2 C1
Cobden Ms SYD SE26 9 F2
Cobden Rd SNWD SE25 17 E4
Cobham Cl WLGTN SM6 35 E2
Cochrane Rd WIM/MER SW19 4 A4
Cody Cl WLGTN SM6 34 D3
Coe Av SNWD SE25 17 E5
Colborne Wy WPK KT4 21 G4
Colburn Av CTHM CR3 59 H4
Colburn Wy SUT SM1 23 F4
Colby Rd NRWD SE19 8 C2
Colcokes Rd BNSTD SM7 51 G1
Coldharbour La
PUR/KEN CR8 45 G1
Coldharbour Rd
CROY/NA CR0 35 G1
Coldharbour Wy
CROY/NA CR0 35 G1
Coldstream Rd CTHM CR3 59 E2
Colebrook Ri HAYES BR2 19 G1
Colebrook Rd
STRHM/NOR SW16 7 E5
Coleman Cl SNWD SE25 17 E1
Coleridge Av SUT SM1 23 G5
Coleridge Rd CROY/NA CR0 27 G1
Colesburg Rd BECK BR3 18 B2
Colescroft Hl PUR/KEN CR8 45 G5
Colin Cl CROY/NA CR0 28 B4
WWKM BR4 29 H4
Colin Rd CTHM CR3 60 A3
Collard Cl PUR/KEN CR8 55 F5
College Av EW KT17 40 D4
College Gn NRWD SE19 8 C4
College Rd CROY/NA CR0 2 E3
EW KT17 40 D4
NRWD SE19 8 D2
WIM/MER SW19 5 F3
The College EW KT17 * 40 E5
Colliers CTHM CR3 60 A5
Colliers Water La THHTH CR7 15 H3
Collingtree Rd SYD SE26 9 G1
Collingwood Av BRYLDS KT5 20 A2
Colling Wood Cl PGE/AN SE20 9 F5
Collingwood Rd MTCM CR4 13 G1
SUT SM1 22 C5
Collyer Av CROY/NA CR0 25 E5
Collyer Rd CROY/NA CR0 25 E5
Colman Cl EPSOM KT18 50 C2
Colmer Rd STRHM/NOR SW16 7 E4
Colne Ct HOR/WEW KT19 20 A5
Colson Rd CROY/NA CR0 3 G2
Colson Wy STRHM/NOR SW16 6 C1
Colston Av CAR SM5 23 G5
Columbia Av WPK KT4 20 D1
Columbine Av SAND/SEL CR2 35 H3
Colvin Cl SYD SE26 9 G2
Colvin Rd THHTH CR7 15 G4
Colwood Gdns
WIM/MER SW19 5 G4
Colworth Rd CROY/NA CR0 27 E2
Colwyn Cl STRHM/NOR SW16 6 C2
Colyton La STRHM/NOR SW16 7 G2
Combermere Rd MRDN SM4 12 D5
Commerce Wy CROY/NA CR0 25 F4
Commodore Pde
STRHM/NOR SW16 * 7 F4
Commonfield Rd BNSTD SM7 42 C4
Commonside Cl BELMT SM2 42 D1
COUL/CHIP CR5 54 D5
Commonside East
MTCM CR4 14 A2
Commonside West
MTCM CR4 14 A2
Commonwealth Rd
CTHM CR3 60 A3
Comport Gn CROY/NA CR0 49 G2
Compton Rd CROY/NA CR0 27 F2
WIM/MER SW19 4 B3
Conaways Cl EW KT17 31 E5
Conduit La SAND/SEL CR2 37 E1
Coneybury Cl WARL CR6 56 B4
Coney Hall Pde WWKM BR4 * 29 G4
Coney Hill Rd WWKM BR4 29 G3
Conifer Gdns SUT SM1 22 D3
Conifer Pk EW KT17 40 C1
Coningsby Rd SAND/SEL CR2 36 A4
Coniston Gdns BELMT SM2 * 33 F2
Coniston Rd BMLY BR1 11 G3
COUL/CHIP CR5 53 G1
CROY/NA CR0 27 E1
Connaught Cl SUT SM1 23 F3
Connaught Gdns MRDN SM4 13 E4
Connaught Rd SUT SM1 23 F3
Conrad Dr WPK KT4 21 G2
Constance Crs HAYES BR2 29 H2
Constance Rd CROY/NA CR0 25 H1
SUT SM1 23 E5
Convent Cl BECK BR3 11 E4
Convent Hl NRWD SE19 8 A3
Conway Dr BELMT SM2 32 D3
Conway Gdns MTCM CR4 14 D3
Conyers Rd
STRHM/NOR SW16 6 D2
Cookes La CHEAM SM3 32 A2
Coombe Av CROY/NA CR0 3 H7
Coombe La CROY/NA CR0 37 F1
Coombe Rd CROY/NA CR0 2 E6
SYD SE26 9 F1
Coomber Wy CROY/NA CR0 24 D1
Coombe Wood Hl
PUR/KEN CR8 46 A2
Cooper Crs CAR SM5 23 H4
Cooper Rd CROY/NA CR0 2 A7
Coopers Ms BECK BR3 18 C1
Cooper's Yd NRWD SE19 8 C3
Copeman Cl SYD SE26 9 G2
Copers Cope Rd BECK BR3 10 C5
Copgate Pth
STRHM/NOR SW16 7 F3
Copleigh Dr
KWD/TDW/WH KT20 51 E5
Copley Pk STRHM/NOR SW16 7 F3
Copley Wy
KWD/TDW/WH KT20 50 D5
Copper Cl NRWD SE19 8 D4
Copperfield Cl SAND/SEL CR2 46 A1
Copper Mill La TOOT SW17 5 E1
Coppice Cl BECK BR3 18 D3
Copping Cl CROY/NA CR0 3 H6
The Coppins CROY/NA CR0 38 D2
Copse Av WWKM BR4 28 D4
Copse Edge Av EW KT17 40 D4
Copse Hl BELMT SM2 32 D3
PUR/KEN CR8 45 E3
Copse Vw SAND/SEL CR2 37 H3
Copt Hill La
KWD/TDW/WH KT20 51 F5
Copthorne Ri SAND/SEL CR2 46 B3
Corbet Cl WLGTN SM6 24 A3
Corbet Rd EW KT17 30 C5
Corbett Cl CROY/NA CR0 49 F2
Cordrey Gdns
COUL/CHIP CR5 45 E5
Corkscrew Hl WWKM BR4 29 E3
Cornflower La CROY/NA CR0 27 H2
Cornish Gv PGE/AN SE20 9 F5
Cornwall Gdns SNWD SE25 * 16 D3
Cornwallis Cl CTHM CR3 59 E2
Cornwall Rd BELMT SM2 32 B3
CROY/NA CR0 2 A3
Corrib Dr SUT SM1 33 G1
Corrigan Av COUL/CHIP CR5 44 A5
Corsehill St STRHM/NOR SW16 6 C3
Cosdach Av WLGTN SM6 34 D3
Cosedge Crs CROY/NA CR0 35 G1
Coteford St TOOT SW17 5 H1
Cotelands CROY/NA CR0 3 G4
Cotford Rd THHTH CR7 16 A3
Cotherstone HOR/WEW KT19 30 B4
Cotswold Rd BELMT SM2 32 D5
Cotswold St WNWD SE27 7 H1
Cotswold Wy WPK KT4 21 G3
Cottage Rd HOR/WEW KT19 30 B3
Cottingham Rd PGE/AN SE20 9 H4
Cottongrass Cl CROY/NA CR0 27 H2
Cotton Hl BMLY BR1 11 F1
Coulsdon Court Rd
COUL/CHIP CR5 54 B1
Coulsdon La COUL/CHIP CR5 53 E4
Coulsdon Pl CTHM CR3 59 F2
Coulsdon Ri COUL/CHIP CR5 54 A2
Coulsdon Rd COUL/CHIP CR5 54 B3
CTHM CR3 59 E1
County Rd THHTH CR7 15 H1
Court Av COUL/CHIP CR5 54 C3
Court Bushes Rd CTHM CR3 56 B5
Court Cl WLGTN SM6 34 D3
Court Downs Rd BECK BR3 18 D1
Court Dr CROY/NA CR0 25 F5
SUT SM1 23 G5
Courtenay Av BELMT SM2 32 C4
Courtenay Dr BECK BR3 19 F1
Courtenay Rd PGE/AN SE20 9 H4
WPK KT4 21 G4
Court Farm Av
HOR/WEW KT19 30 C1
Court Farm Gdns
HOR/WEW KT19 * 40 B1
Court Farm Pk WARL CR6 * 56 A1
Court Farm Rd WARL CR6 56 A3
Courtfield Ri WWKM BR4 29 F4
Court Haw BNSTD SM7 43 G5
Court Hl SAND/SEL CR2 46 C2
Courthope Rd
WIM/MER SW19 4 A2
Courthope Vls
WIM/MER SW19 4 A4
Courtland Av
STRHM/NOR SW16 7 F4
Courtlands Av HAYES BR2 29 G2
Courtlands Cl SAND/SEL CR2 36 D5
Courtlands Crs BNSTD SM7 51 G1
Courtlands Dr
HOR/WEW KT19 30 C2
Court La HOR/WEW KT19 40 A3
Courtney Cl NRWD SE19 8 C3
Courtney Crs CAR SM5 33 H3
Courtney Pl CROY/NA CR0 25 G4
Courtney Rd CROY/NA CR0 25 G4
WIM/MER SW19 5 G4
Court Rd BNSTD SM7 42 C5
CTHM CR3 59 F3
SNWD SE25 16 D1
The Courts STRHM/NOR SW16 7 E4
The Court WARL CR6 57 E3
Court Wood La CROY/NA CR0 38 B5
Coventry Rd SNWD SE25 17 E3
Coverack Cl CROY/NA CR0 28 A2
Coverdale Gdns CROY/NA CR0 3 J4
Coverton Rd TOOT SW17 5 G1
The Covert NRWD SE19 * 8 D4
Covey Cl WIM/MER SW19 12 D1
Covington Gdns
STRHM/NOR SW16 7 H4
Covington Wy
STRHM/NOR SW16 7 H4
Cowden St CAT SE6 10 C1
Cowdrey Rd WIM/MER SW19 4 D3
Cowick Rd TOOT SW17 5 H1
Cowley Cl SAND/SEL CR2 37 G5
Cowper Av SUT SM1 23 F5
Cowper Gdns WLGTN SM6 34 C2
Cowper Rd WIM/MER SW19 5 E3
Coxdean EPSOM KT18 50 C4
Cox La HOR/WEW KT19 30 A1
Coxley Ri PUR/KEN CR8 46 A3
Coxs Cottages WARL CR6 * 49 G4
Coxwell Rd NRWD SE19 8 C4
Crab Hl BECK BR3 11 F4
Craigen Av CROY/NA CR0 27 F2
Craignish Av
STRHM/NOR SW16 15 F1
Crampton Rd PGE/AN SE20 9 G3
Cranbourne Cl
STRHM/NOR SW16 15 E2
Cranbrook Rd THHTH CR7 16 B1
WIM/MER SW19 4 A4
Cranfield Rd East CAR SM5 34 A4
Cranfield Rd West CAR SM5 * 33 H4
Cranford Cl PUR/KEN CR8 46 A3
Cranleigh Cl PGE/AN SE20 17 F1
SAND/SEL CR2 47 E2
Cranleigh Gdns
SAND/SEL CR2 47 E2
SNWD SE25 16 C2
SUT SM1 22 D3
Cranleigh Rd WIM/MER SW19 12 C2
Cranley Gdns WLGTN SM6 34 C3
Cranmer Cl WARL CR6 57 E2
Cranmer Farm Cl MTCM CR4 13 H3
Cranmer Gdns WARL CR6 57 E2
Cranmer Rd CROY/NA CR0 2 B4
MTCM CR4 13 H3
Cranmer Ter TOOT SW17 5 F2
Craven Gdns WIM/MER SW19 4 D2
Craven Rd CROY/NA CR0 27 F2
Credenhill St
STRHM/NOR SW16 6 C3
Cremorne Gdns
HOR/WEW KT19 30 B4
Crescent Gv MTCM CR4 13 G3
Crescent Rd BECK BR3 18 D1
CTHM CR3 60 A4
The Crescent BECK BR3 10 C5
BELMT SM2 42 C1
CROY/NA CR0 16 B5
CTHM CR3 61 G3
SUT SM1 33 F1
WWKM BR4 19 G5
Crescent Wy
STRHM/NOR SW16 7 F4
Cressingham Gv SUT SM1 23 E5
The Cressinghams
EPSOM KT18 40 B3
Cresswell Rd SNWD SE25 17 F3
Creston Wy WPK KT4 21 H2
Crest Rd HAYES BR2 29 H1
SAND/SEL CR2 37 F3
Creswell Dr BECK BR3 18 D4
Crewe's Av WARL CR6 56 C1
Crewe's Cl WARL CR6 56 C1
Crewe's Farm La WARL CR6 56 D1
Crewe's La WARL CR6 56 D1
Crichton Av WLGTN SM6 34 D1
Crichton Rd CAR SM5 33 H3
Cricketers Wk SYD SE26 9 G2
Cricket Gn MTCM CR4 13 H3
Cricket La BECK BR3 10 A3
Crispin Crs CROY/NA CR0 24 D4
Crocus Cl CROY/NA CR0 27 H2
Croft Av WWKM BR4 29 E2
Croft Ct SUT SM1 * 23 F3
Crofters Md CROY/NA CR0 * 38 B4
Croftleigh Av PUR/KEN CR8 54 C1
Croft Rd CTHM CR3 61 F2
STRHM/NOR SW16 7 G4
SUT SM1 33 F1
WIM/MER SW19 5 E4
Croham Cl SAND/SEL CR2 36 C3
Croham Manor Rd
SAND/SEL CR2 36 C3
Croham Mt SAND/SEL CR2 36 C3
Croham Park Av
SAND/SEL CR2 36 D1
Croham Rd SAND/SEL CR2 36 C1
Croham Valley Rd
SAND/SEL CR2 37 E2
Croindene Rd
STRHM/NOR SW16 7 E5
Cromer Hyde MRDN SM4 * 12 D4
Cromer Rd SNWD SE25 17 F2
TOOT SW17 6 A3
Cromwell Gv CTHM CR3 59 E1
Cromwell Rd BECK BR3 18 A1
CROY/NA CR0 26 B1
CTHM CR3 59 E1
WIM/MER SW19 4 C2
WPK KT4 20 B4
Crossland Rd THHTH CR7 15 H5
Crosslands Rd
HOR/WEW KT19 30 B2
Cross Rd BELMT SM2 32 C5
CROY/NA CR0 26 B2
PUR/KEN CR8 45 H3
SUT SM1 33 F1
WIM/MER SW19 4 C4
Crossways BELMT SM2 33 F4
SAND/SEL CR2 38 B3
Crossways Rd BECK BR3 18 C3
MTCM CR4 14 B2
The Crossways
COUL/CHIP CR5 54 B4
Crouch Cl BECK BR3 10 C3
Crowborough Cl WARL CR6 57 E3
Crowborough Dr WARL CR6 57 E3
Crowborough Rd TOOT SW17 6 A2
Crowland Rd THHTH CR7 * 16 B3
Crowland Wk MRDN SM4 12 D5
Crowley Crs CROY/NA CR0 35 G1
Crownbourne Ct SUT SM1 * 22 D5
Crown Dl NRWD SE19 8 A3
Crown Hl CROY/NA CR0 2 D3
Crown La MRDN SM4 12 C3
STRHM/NOR SW16 7 G2
Crown Lane Gdns
STRHM/NOR SW16 * 7 G2
Crown Pde MRDN SM4 * 12 D3
Crown Rd MRDN SM4 12 D3
SUT SM1 22 D5
Crowther Rd SNWD SE25 17 E3
Croxden Wk MRDN SM4 13 E5
The Croydon F/O
CROY/NA CR0 2 C6
Croydon Gv CROY/NA CR0 25 H2
Croydon La BNSTD SM7 43 F3
Croydon La South
BNSTD SM7 42 D4
Croydon Rd CROY/NA CR0 25 E5
CTHM CR3 60 A2
MTCM CR4 14 B4
PGE/AN SE20 17 F1
WLGTN SM6 24 B5
WWKM BR4 29 G4
Crozier Dr SAND/SEL CR2 37 F5
Crunden Rd SAND/SEL CR2 36 B3
Crusader Gdns CROY/NA CR0 3 H5
Crusoe Rd MTCM CR4 5 H4
Crystal Palace NRWD SE19 * 9 E4
Crystal Palace Pde
NRWD SE19 8 D3
Crystal Palace Park Rd
SYD SE26 9 F2
Crystal Palace Station Rd
NRWD SE19 9 E3
Crystal Ter NRWD SE19 8 B3
Cuda's Cl HOR/WEW KT19 20 D5
Cuddington Av WPK KT4 20 D4
Cuddington Cl
KWD/TDW/WH KT20 50 C5
Cuddington Park Cl
BNSTD SM7 42 B3
Cuddington Wy BELMT SM2 41 H2
Cudham Cl BELMT SM2 32 C5
Cudham Dr CROY/NA CR0 38 D5
Cullerne Cl EW KT17 30 D5
Cullesden Rd PUR/KEN CR8 45 H5
Culmington Rd
SAND/SEL CR2 36 A4
Culverhouse Gdns
STRHM/NOR SW16 7 F1
Culvers Av CAR SM5 23 H3
Culvers Retreat CAR SM5 23 H2
Culverstone Cl HAYES BR2 19 H5
Culvers Wy CAR SM5 23 H4
Cumberland Cl
HOR/WEW KT19 30 C5
Cumberland Rd HAYES BR2 19 G3
SNWD SE25 17 F5
Cumberlands PUR/KEN CR8 46 B5
Cumberland Ter
PGE/AN SE20 * 9 F4
Cumberlow Av SNWD SE25 17 E2
Cumnor Gdns EW KT17 31 E2
Cumnor Ri PUR/KEN CR8 55 E2
Cumnor Rd BELMT SM2 33 E2
Cunliffe Rd HOR/WEW KT19 20 D5
Cunliffe St STRHM/NOR SW16 6 C3
Cunningham Cl WWKM BR4 28 D3
Cunningham Rd BNSTD SM7 43 F5
Curlew Cl SAND/SEL CR2 47 H1
Curling Cl COUL/CHIP CR5 54 B5
Curnick's La WNWD SE27 8 A1
Curran Av WLGTN SM6 24 A4
Currie Hill Cl WIM/MER SW19 4 B1
Curtis Field Rd
STRHM/NOR SW16 7 F1
Curtis Rd HOR/WEW KT19 20 A5
Curvan Cl EW KT17 30 D5
Curzon Rd THHTH CR7 15 G5
Cuthbert Gdns SNWD SE25 16 C2
Cuthbert Rd CROY/NA CR0 2 B3
Cyclamen Wy
HOR/WEW KT19 30 A1
Cypress Rd SNWD SE25 16 C1
Cypress Wy BNSTD SM7 41 H4


## D


Dacre Rd CROY/NA CR0 25 E1
Daffodil Cl CROY/NA CR0 27 H2
Dagmar Rd SNWD SE25 16 C3
Dagnall Pk SNWD SE25 16 C4
Dagnall Rd SNWD SE25 16
Dahlia Gdns MTCM CR4 14
Dahomey Rd
STRHM/NOR SW16 6
Daimler Wy WLGTN SM6 35
Dainford Cl BMLY BR1 11
Dairy Cl THHTH CR7 16
Daisy Cl CROY/NA CR0 27
Dakota Cl WLGTN SM6 35
Dalegarth Gdns
PUR/KEN CR8 46
Dale Park Av CAR SM5 23
Dale Park Rd NRWD SE19 8
Dale Rd PUR/KEN CR8 45
SUT SM1 22
Daleside Rd HOR/WEW KT19 30
STRHM/NOR SW16 6
Dalewood Gdns WPK KT4 21
Dallas Rd CHEAM SM3 32
SYD SE26 9
Dalmally Rd CROY/NA CR0 26
Dalmeny Av
STRHM/NOR SW16 15
Dalmeny Rd CAR SM5 34
WPK KT4 21
Dalton Av MTCM CR4 13
Damson Wy CAR SM5 33
Danbrook Rd
STRHM/NOR SW16 7
Danbury Ms WLGTN SM6 24
Danebury CROY/NA CR0 38
Danecourt Gdns CROY/NA CR0 3
Dane Rd WARL CR6 56
WIM/MER SW19 5
Danescourt Crs SUT SM1 23
Danetree Cl HOR/WEW KT19 30
Danetree Rd HOR/WEW KT19 30
Daniel Cl TOOT SW17 5
Daniell Wy CROY/NA CR0 25
Daniels La WARL CR6 57
Daniel Wy BNSTD SM7 42
Danvers Wy CTHM CR3 59
Darby Cl CTHM CR3 59
Darcy Av WLGTN SM6 24
Darcy Cl COUL/CHIP CR5 54
D'Arcy Rd CHEAM SM3 21
Darcy Rd STRHM/NOR SW16 15
Dargate Cl NRWD SE19 8
Darley Cl CROY/NA CR0 17
Darley Gdns MRDN SM4 12
Darlington Rd WNWD SE27 7
Darmaine Cl SAND/SEL CR2 36
Dartnell Rd CROY/NA CR0 26
Dassett Rd WNWD SE27 7
Davidson Rd CROY/NA CR0 26
Davies Cl CROY/NA CR0 16
Daybrook Rd
WIM/MER SW19 12
Day's Acre SAND/SEL CR2 36
Deacon Cl PUR/KEN CR8 35
Deacon Pl CTHM CR3 59
Deal Rd TOOT SW17 6
Deanfield Gdns
CROY/NA CR0 * 2
Dean La REDH RH1 58
Dean Rd CROY/NA CR0 2
Deans Cl CROY/NA CR0 3
Deansfield CTHM CR3 59
Deans Rd SUT SM1 22
Deans Wk COUL/CHIP CR5 54
De'Arn Gdns MTCM CR4 13
De Burgh Gdns
KWD/TDW/WH KT20 50
De Burgh Pk BNSTD SM7 51
Deburgh Rd WIM/MER SW19 5
Decimus Cl THHTH CR7 16
Deepdale Av HAYES BR2 19
Deepdene Av CROY/NA CR0 3
Deepfield Wy
COUL/CHIP CR5 54
Deerhurst Rd
STRHM/NOR SW16 7
Deer Park Gdns MTCM CR4 * 13
Deer Park Rd
WIM/MER SW19 12
Deer Park Wy WWKM BR4 29
Deerswood Cl CTHM CR3 60
Dee Wy HOR/WEW KT19 30
Defiant Wy WLGTN SM6 35
Defoe Cl TOOT SW17 5
Defoe Pl TOOT SW17 5
De Frene Rd SYD SE26 9
Delamare Crs CROY/NA CR0 17
Delaporte Cl EW KT17 40
Delcombe Av WPK KT4 21
Dell Cl WLGTN SM6 24
Dellfield Cl BECK BR3 11
Dell La EW KT17 31
Dell Rd EW KT17 31
The Dell BECK BR3 * 10
NRWD SE19 8
Delmey Cl CROY/NA CR0 3
Delta Cl WPK KT4 20
Delta Rd WPK KT4 20
Demesne Rd WLGTN SM6 24
Denbigh Cl SUT SM1 32
Den Cl BECK BR3 19
Dene Cl COUL/CHIP CR5 52
HAYES BR2 29
WPK KT4 20
Denefield Dr PUR/KEN CR8 46
The Dene BELMT SM2 42
CROY/NA CR0 27
Denewood EW KT17 * 40
Denham Crs MTCM CR4 13
Denham Rd EW KT17 40
Denison Rd WIM/MER SW19 5
Denmark Av WIM/MER SW19 4
Denmark Ct MRDN SM4 12
Denmark Gdns CAR SM5 23
Denmark Rd CAR SM5 23
SNWD SE25 17

mead Rd CROY/NA CR0.....25 H2
sham Dr PUR/KEN CR8.....45 G4
side CI BECK BR3 *......10 A5
vale Trade Pk MTCM CR4..13 F3
lot Rd EW KT17..........10 A5
by CI EPSOM KT18........50 B4
...y CI CR0..............2 B1
...UT SM1...............32 B2
...ng PI CROY/NA CR0.....4 C4
...k Av WLGTN SM6.......24 B4
...ng PI CROY/NA CR0.....2 C7
...ng Rd CROY/NA CR0.....2 D7
...ng Rd TOOT SW17......6 A1
...by CI CAR SM5........33 H2
...ick Av SAND/SEL CR2..36 A5
...ick Rd BECK BR3......18 E2
...y Rd CROY/NA CR0.....25 E4
...vent Dr PUR/KEN CR8..46 B4
...vent Rd PGE/AN SE20..17 E1
...ana End CAR SM5......23 H4
...eraux CI BECK BR3....19 E4
...ere CI WLGTN SM6.....35 E3
...on CI PUR/KEN CR8....55 E1
...on Rd BELMT SM2......32 A4
...wall Rd CAR SM5......33 H4
...ROY/NA CR0...........2 E2
...dale Gdns SNWD SE25..16 C4
...ene CI WIM/MER SW19...5 F1
...ene Gdns EW KT17.....40 C2
...ene Gv EW KT17.......40 C2
...ies La COUL/CHIP CR5..53 H2
...ncroft CI CROY/NA CR0..24 C1
...n PI PGE/AN SE20 *....9 F5
...n Rd SNWD SE25.......16 C2
...ors CI SYD SE26......9 G2
...ors La CTHM CR3......58 C4
...CI WIM/MER SW19.......5 F1
...hurst La COUL/CHIP CR5..52 D5
...e Hill Pk SYD SE26...5 F5
...nion Rd CROY/NA CR0..26 D1
...ld Rd CROY/NA CR0....2 D3
...e PI MTCM CR4........14 B3
...ington Rd WPK KT4....21 E3
...ybrook Rd
  STRHM/NOR SW16.......6 D4
...van CI HOR/WEW KT19..30 B3
...d Wy CAR SM5.........33 H1
...Rd WIM/MER SW19.......4 C2
...hester Rd MRDN SM4...22 D1
...PK KT4...............21 G2
...Gdns MRDN SM4........22 D1
...n Ct WARL CR6........56 B4
...r Dr KWD/TDW/WH KT20..51 F1
...CI WARL CR6..........56 B4
...ng CI WPK KT4........21 H5
...et Rd BECK BR3.......17 H2
...LMT SM2..............32 C5
...CM CR4...............13 G1
...ford Gdns
  ...UL/CHIP CR5........55 E4
...et Rd SAND/SEL CR2...36 C1
...ngton Wy BECK BR3....18 C5
...la Gdns MTCM CR4.....15 F3
...ale St MTCM CR4......5 H4
...rcourt Av THHTH CR7..15 G3
...rcourt La SUT SM1....23 H4
...r Gdns CAR SM5.......23 H4
...e Rd NRWD SE19.......8 B5
...ton Rd SAND/SEL CR2..47 H1
...GTN SM6..............35 F5
...r Av WLGTN SM6.......34 B4
...ham Wy WIM/MER SW19..4 D5
...ham Rd MTCM CR4......13 H1
...afield WPK KT4.......20 D2
...ham Wy BMLY BR1......11 G2
...nland CI COUL/CHIP CR5..44 B4
...SOM KT18.............40 A5
...nland Gdns EPSOM KT18..50 B3
...lands Rd PUR/KEN CR8..45 E3
...land Wy EPSOM KT18...40 D5
...s Av EPSOM KT18......40 D5
...s Bridge Rd BECK BR3..11 F5
...s Court Rd
  ...K/KEN CR8..........45 H3
...s HI BECK BR3 *......10 C5
...s Hill Rd EPSOM KT18 *..40 C5
...side BECK BR3 *......10 C5

EPSOM KT18..............40 C4
Downside CI WIM/MER SW19..5 E3
Downside Rd BELMT SM2...33 F2
Downs Lodge CI EW KT17 *..40 C4
Downs Rd BECK BR3.......18 D1
  BELMT SM2.............42 D1
  COUL/CHIP CR5.........53 H5
  EPSOM KT18............40 C5
  PUR/KEN CR8...........45 H1
  THHTH CR7.............8 A5
Downs Side BELMT SM2....42 B1
Downsview Gdns NRWD SE19..8 A4
Downsview Rd NRWD SE19..8 A4
Downsway CTHM CR3.......55 H1
  SAND/SEL CR2..........46 C1
The Downsway BELMT SM2..33 E4
Downsway Rd EPSOM KT18..50 B2
Doyle Rd SNWD SE25......17 E3
Drake Av CTHM CR3.......59 E2
Drake Rd CROY/NA CR0....25 F1
  MTCM CR4..............14 A5
Drakewood Rd
  STRHM/NOR SW16........6 D4
Draven CI HAYES BR2.....29 H1
Draxmont WIM/MER SW19...4 A5
Drayton Rd CROY/NA CR0..25 F1
Drew PI CTHM CR3........59 F3
The Driftway BNSTD SM7..41 G5
  MTCM CR4..............14 B2
Driftwood Dr PUR/KEN CR8..55 E2
Drive Rd COUL/CHIP CR5..45 E4
Drive Rd COUL/CHIP CR5..53 G5
The Drive BECK BR3......18 C1
  BELMT SM2.............42 B2
  BNSTD SM7.............51 E2
  COUL/CHIP CR5.........45 E4
  HOR/WEW KT19..........30 D2
  MRDN SM4..............13 G4
  THHTH CR7.............15 H5
  WLGTN SM6.............34 C5
  WWKM BR4..............29 F1
Drovers Rd SAND/SEL CR2..36 B1
Druids Wy HAYES BR2.....19 F5
Drumaline Rdg WPK KT4...20 C3
Drummond Rd CROY/NA CR0..2 C3
Drury Crs CROY/NA CR0...25 E5
Dryden Rd WIM/MER SW19..5 E3
Duchess CI SUT SM1......23 E5
Dudley Dr MRDN SM4......22 A2
Dudley Gv EPSOM KT18....40 A5
Dudley Rd WIM/MER SW19..4 C3
Duke of Edinburgh Rd
  SUT SM1...............23 F4
Dukes HI CTHM CR3.......57 H5
Dukesthorpe Rd SYD SE26..9 H1
Duke St SUT SM1.........23 G5
Dukes Wy WWKM BR4.......29 G6
Dulverton Rd SAND/SEL CR2..37 G5
Dulwich Wood Av NRWD SE19..8 D2
Dulwich Wood Pk NRWD SE19..8 C1
Dunbar Av BECK BR3......18 A3
  STRHM/NOR SW16........16 C1
Duncan Rd
  KWD/TDW/WH KT20.......51 E4
Dundee Rd SNWD SE25.....17 F4
Dundela Gdns WPK KT4....21 F5
Dundonald Rd
  WIM/MER SW19..........4 B4
Dunedin Dr CTHM CR3.....59 G5
Dunfield Rd CAT SE6.....10 D2
Dunheved CI THHTH CR7...15 G5
Dunheved Rd North
  THHTH CR7.............15 G5
Dunheved Rd South
  THHTH CR7.............15 G5
Dunheved Rd West
  THHTH CR7.............15 G5
Dunkeld Rd SNWD SE25....16 B3
Dunkirk St NRWD SE27 *..8 A1
Dunley Dr CROY/NA CR0...39 E2
Dunmail Dr PUR/KEN CR8..46 A5
Dunnymans Rd BNSTD SM7..42 B5
Dunsbury CI BELMT SM2...32 D4
Dunsfold Rd COUL/CHIP CR5..44 D3
Dunsfold Wy CROY/NA CR0..38 D3
Dunstan Rd COUL/CHIP CR5..53 H2
Dunster Av MRDN SM4.....21 H2
Duppas Av CROY/NA CR0...2 B6
Duppas Hill La CROY/NA CR0..2 A6
Duppas Hill Ter CROY/NA CR0..2 B5
Duppas Rd CROY/NA CR0...25 G4
Dura Den CI BECK BR3....10 D4
Durand CI CAR SM5.......23 H5
Durban Rd BECK BR3......18 B1
  NRWD SE27.............8 B3
Durham Av HAYES BR2.....19 H3
Durham HI BMLY BR1......11 H1
Durham Ter PGE/AN SE20 *..9 F4
Durning Rd NRWD SE19....8 B1
Durnsford Rd WIM/MER SW19..4 D1
Dykes Wy HAYES BR2......19 H2

## E

Eagle CI WLGTN SM6......35 E2
Eagle HI NRWD SE19......8 B3
Eardley Rd STRHM/NOR SW16..6 C3
Earlsthorpe Rd SYD SE26..9 H1
Eastwood Av THHTH CR7...15 G4
Easby Crs MRDN SM4......12 D5
East Av WLGTN SM6.......35 F1
Eastbourne Rd TOOT SW17..6 A3
Eastcroft Rd HOR/WEW KT19..30 A2
East Dr CAR SM5.........33 G4
Eastfields Rd MTCM CR4..14 A1
East Gdns TOOT SW17 *...5 H2
Eastgate BNSTD SM7......42 B4
East HI SAND/SEL CR2....36 C5
East India Wy CROY/NA CR0..26 D2
Eastlake CI BELMT SM2...32 D3

Eastney Rd CROY/NA CR0..25 H2
East Parkside WARL CR6..57 G1
East Rd WNWD SE27.......8 A1
East Rd WIM/MER SW19....5 E3
Eastry Av HAYES BR2.....19 H5
East St EW KT17.........40 C2
East Wy CROY/NA CR0.....28 A3
Eastway HOR/WEW KT19....40 A3
Eastwell CI BECK BR3....10 A5
Eastwood St
  STRHM/NOR SW16........6 C3
Eaton Rd BELMT SM2......33 F2
Ebbisham Rd WPK KT4.....21 G3
Ebenezer Wk
  STRHM/NOR SW16........6 C5
Ecclesbourne Rd THHTH CR7..16 A4
Edencourt Rd
  STRHM/NOR SW16........6 B3
Edenfield Gdns WPK KT4..20 D3
Eden Pde BECK BR3.......18 A3
Eden Park Av BECK BR3...27 H1
Eden Rd BECK BR3........18 A5
  CROY/NA CR0...........2 E6
  WNWD SE27.............7 H2
Edenvale Rd MTCM CR4....6 A5
Eden Wy BECK BR3........18 C4
  WARL CR6..............57 E3
Ederline Av
  STRHM/NOR SW16........15 F2
Edgar Rd SAND/SEL CR2...36 B5
Edgecoombe SAND/SEL CR2..37 H4
Edgehill Rd MTCM CR4....6 B5
  PUR/KEN CR8...........35 G5
Edge Point CI
  STRHM/NOR SW16........7 H2
Edgewood Gn CROY/NA CR0..27 H2
Edgeworth CI CTHM CR3...56 A3
Edgington Rd
  STRHM/NOR SW16........6 D3
Edinburgh Rd SUT SM1....23 E4
Edith Rd SNWD SE25......16 B4
  WIM/MER SW19..........4 D1
Edmund Rd MTCM CR4......13 G2
Edridge Rd CROY/NA CR0..2 C5
Edward Av MRDN SM4......13 F4
Edward Rd COUL/CHIP CR5..44 D5
  CROY/NA CR0...........26 C1
  PGE/AN SE20...........9 H4
Edwards CI WPK KT4......21 H5
Edwin PI CROY/NA CR0 *..26 C1
Effingham CI BELMT SM2..32 D3
Effingham Rd CROY/NA CR0..25 F1
Effort St TOOT SW17.....5 G2
Egan CI PUR/KEN CR8.....46 B1
Egerton Rd SNWD SE25....16 C2
Egham CI CHEAM SM3......22 A3
Egham Crs CHEAM SM3.....21 H4
Egleston Rd MRDN SM4....12 D5
Eglise Rd WARL CR6......57 E2
Egmont Rd BELMT SM2.....33 E3
  KWD/TDW/WH KT20.......51 E4
Eighteenth Rd MTCM CR4..15 E3
Eileen Rd SNWD SE25.....16 B4
Eindhoven CI CAR SM5....24 A2
Eland PI CROY/NA CR0 *..2 A4
Eland Rd CROY/NA CR0....2 A4
Elberon Av CROY/NA CR0..14 C5
Elborough Rd SNWD SE25..17 E4
Elder Oak CI PGE/AN SE20..9 F5
Elder Rd WNWD SE27......8 A3
Elderslie CI BECK BR3...18 D5
Elderton Rd SYD SE26....10 A1
Eldertree Wy MTCM CR4...6 B5
Eldon Av CROY/NA CR0....27 G3
Eldon Pk SNWD SE25......17 F3
Eldon Rd CTHM CR3.......59 F1
Eleanora Ter SUT SM1 *..23 G5
Eleanor Av HOR/WEW KT19..30 B5
Elfrida Crs CAT SE6.....10 C1
Elgar Av STRHM/NOR SW16..15 E2
Elgin Crs CTHM CR3......60 A2
Elgin Rd CROY/NA CR0....3 K2
  SUT SM1...............23 G3
  WLGTN SM6.............34 C2
Elizabeth CI SUT SM1....22 B5
Elizabeth Wy NRWD SE19..8 B4
Ellenbridge Wy
  SAND/SEL CR2..........36 C4
Ellery Rd NRWD SE19.....8 B3
Ellesmere Av BECK BR3...18 D1
Ellesmere Dr SAND/SEL CR2..47 F4
Ellington Wy EPSOM KT18..50 B2
Elliott Rd THHTH CR7....15 H3
Ellis CI COUL/CHIP CR5..54 B5
Ellison Rd STRHM/NOR SW16..6 D2
Ellora Rd STRHM/NOR SW16..6 D2
Elm Gdns EPSOM KT18.....50 C4
  MTCM CR4..............14 D5
Elm Gv CTHM CR3.........59 G2
  EPSOM KT18............40 A4
  SUT SM1...............22 D5
  WIM/MER SW19..........4 A4

Elm Grove Pde CAR SM5...24 A4
Elmgrove Rd CROY/NA CR0..27 F2
Elmhurst Av MTCM CR4....6 A4
Elmpark Gdns SAND/SEL CR2..37 G5
Elm Park Rd SNWD SE25...16 C2
Elm Rd BECK BR3.........18 B1
  EW KT17...............30 D2
  PUR/KEN CR8...........45 H3
  THHTH CR7.............16 A3
  WARL CR6..............56 D2
  WLGTN SM6.............24 C2
Elm Rd West CHEAM SM3...22 B1
Elmscott Rd BMLY BR1....11 H2
Elmshorn EW KT17........50 C1
Elmside CROY/NA CR0.....38 D2
Elmslie CI EPSOM KT18...40 B4
Elmstead CI HOR/WEW KT19..30 B3
Elmstead Gdns WPK KT4...21 E4
The Elms WARL CR6.......47 G5
  WLGTN SM6 *...........24 C5
Elm Wy HOR/WEW KT19.....30 B1
  WPK KT4...............21 G5
Elmwood CI EW KT17......31 E5
  WLGTN SM6.............24 B3
Elmwood Dr EW KT17......31 E5
Elmwood Rd CROY/NA CR0..25 H1
  MTCM CR4..............13 H2
Elsrick Av MRDN SM4.....12 C4
Elstan Wy CROY/NA CR0...28 A4
Elstree HI BMLY BR1.....11 G4
Elton Rd PUR/KEN CR8....44 C2
Elvington Gn HAYES BR2..19 H4
Elvino Rd SYD SE26......9 H2
Elwill Wy BECK BR3......19 F1
Ely Rd CROY/NA CR0......16 B4
Elystan CI WLGTN SM6....34 C4
Embassy Ct WLGTN SM6 *..34 B2
Emily Davison Dr
  EPSOM KT18............50 B3
Ena Rd STRHM/NOR SW16...15 E2
Endale CI CAR SM5.......23 H3
Endeavour Wy CROY/NA CR0..24 D1
  WIM/MER SW19..........4 D1
Endsleigh CI SAND/SEL CR2..37 G5
Engadine CI CROY/NA CR0..3 J5
Englefield CI CROY/NA CR0..16 A5
Enmore Av SNWD SE25.....17 E4
Enmore Rd SNWD SE25.....17 E4
Ennerdale CI SUT SM1....22 B5
Ensign CI PUR/KEN CR8...35 G5
Ensign Wy WLGTN SM6.....35 E5
Enterprise CI CROY/NA CR0..25 G3
Eothen CI CTHM CR3......60 A4
Epsom College EW KT17...41 E4
Epsom La North EPSOM KT18..50 B4
Epsom Rd CHEAM SM3 *....22 B1
  CROY/NA CR0...........25 F5
  EW KT17...............40 D1
  MRDN SM4..............12 B5
Eresby Dr BECK BR3......28 C2
Erica Gdns CROY/NA CR0..28 D5
Erin CI BMLY BR1........11 G4
Ernest Av WNWD SE27.....7 H1
Ernest CI BECK BR3......18 C4
Ernest Gv BECK BR3......18 B4
Erridge Rd WIM/MER SW19..12 C1
Erskine CI SUT SM1......23 G4
Erskine Rd SUT SM1......23 F5
Esam Wy STRHM/NOR SW16..7 H2
Esher Av CHEAM SM3......21 H4
Esher Ms MTCM CR4.......14 A2
Eskdale Gdns PUR/KEN CR8..46 B4
Eskmont Rdg NRWD SE19...8 C4
Essendene CI CTHM CR3...59 G3
Essendene Rd CTHM CR3...59 G3
Essenden Rd SAND/SEL CR2..36 C5
Essex CI MRDN SM4.......21 H1
Essex Gv NRWD SE19......8 B3
Estcourt Rd SNWD SE25...17 F5
Estreham Rd
  STRHM/NOR SW16........6 D3
Eswyn Rd TOOT SW17......5 H1
Etherstone Rd
  STRHM/NOR SW16........7 G1
Euston Rd CROY/NA CR0...25 G2
Evelina Rd PGE/AN SE20..9 G4
Eveline Rd MTCM CR4.....5 H5
Evelyn Rd WIM/MER SW19..4 D3
Evelyn Wy WLGTN SM6.....24 D5
Evergreen CI PGE/AN SE20..9 G4
Eversley Rd SNWD SE25...16 B4
Eversley Wy CROY/NA CR0..28 C5
Everton Rd CROY/NA CR0..27 E2
Evesham CI BELMT SM2....32 C5
Evesham Gn MRDN SM4.....12 D5
Evesham Rd MRDN SM4.....12 D5
Ewell By-Pass EW KT17...30 D2
Ewell Court Av HOR/WEW KT19..30 C1
Ewell Downs Rd EW KT17..41 E5
Ewell House Gv EW KT17 *..30 D5
Ewell House Pde EW KT17 *..30 D5
Ewell House Yd EW KT17 *..30 D5
Ewell Park Gdns EW KT17..31 E3
Ewell Park Wy EW KT17...31 E2
Ewell Rd CHEAM SM3......31 G4
Ewhurst Av SAND/SEL CR2..36 D5
Ewhurst CI BELMT SM2....31 G4
Exeter Rd CROY/NA CR0...26 C1
Eylewood Rd WNWD SE27...8 A2

Fairdene Rd COUL/CHIP CR5..53 H3
Fairfax Av EW KT17......31 F4
Fairfield CI HOR/WEW KT19..30 C1
  CROY/NA CR0...........5 C4
Fairfield Pth CROY/NA CR0..3 F4
Fairfield Rd BECK BR3...18 C1
  CROY/NA CR0...........3 F4
Fairfield Wy COUL/CHIP CR5..44 D4
  HOR/WEW KT19..........30 C1
Fairford Av CROY/NA CR0..17 H4
Fairford CI CROY/NA CR0..17 H4
Fairford Ct BELMT SM2 *..32 D5
Fairford Gdns WPK KT4...20 D4
Fairgreen Rd THHTH CR7..15 H4
Fairhaven Av CROY/NA CR0..27 H1
Fairholme Rd CROY/NA CR0..25 G1
  SUT SM1...............32 B2
Fairlands Av SUT SM1....22 C3
  THHTH CR7.............15 F3
Fairlawn Gv BNSTD SM7...43 F5
Fairlawn Pk SYD SE26....10 A2
Fairlawn Rd CAR SM5.....43 E1
  WIM/MER SW19..........4 B4
Fairlight CI WPK KT4....21 G5
Fairlight Rd TOOT SW17..5 F1
Fairmead Rd CROY/NA CR0..25 G1
Fairmile Av STRHM/NOR SW16..6 D2
Fairoak CI PUR/KEN CR8..45 H5
Fairview EW KT17........41 C1
Fairview CI SYD SE26....10 A2
Fairview Rd EW KT17.....40 D1
  STRHM/NOR SW16........7 F5
  SUT SM1...............33 F1
Fairway CAR SM5.........43 E1
Fairway CI CROY/NA CR0..18 A4
  HOR/WEW KT19..........30 A5
Fairway Gdns BECK BR3...19 F5
Fairways PUR/KEN CR8....55 E2
Fairwyn Rd SYD SE26.....10 A1
Falconwood Rd CROY/NA CR0..38 C4
Falcourt CI SUT SM1.....32 D1
Falkland Park Av
  SNWD SE25.............16 C2
Fallsbrook Rd
  STRHM/NOR SW16........6 D3
Fambridge CI SYD SE26...10 B1
Famet Av PUR/KEN CR8....46 A3
Famet CI PUR/KEN CR8....46 A3
Famet Wk PUR/KEN CR8....46 A3
Faraday Rd WIM/MER SW19..4 D3
Farewell PI MTCM CR4....5 F5
Farleigh Court Rd
  CROY/NA CR0...........25 F3
  WARL CR6..............48 B4
Farleigh Dean Crs
  CROY/NA CR0...........48 D1
Farleigh Rd WARL CR6....56 D3
Farley PI SNWD SE25.....17 E5
Farley Rd SAND/SEL CR2..37 F5
Farm Av STRHM/NOR SW16..7 E1
Farm CI BELMT SM2.......33 E5
  COUL/CHIP CR5.........52 D5
  WLGTN SM6.............34 C5
  WWKM BR4..............29 H4
Farmdale Rd CAR SM5.....33 G3
Farm Dr CROY/NA CR0.....28 B3
  PUR/KEN CR8...........44 D2
Farmfield Rd BMLY BR1...11 G2
Farm Flds SAND/SEL CR2..46 D1
Farmhouse Rd
  STRHM/NOR SW16........6 C4
Farmington Av SUT SM1...23 F4
Farm La CROY/NA CR0.....28 B5
  PUR/KEN CR8...........34 C5
Farm Rd BELMT SM2.......33 E5
  MRDN SM4..............12 D4
  WARL CR6..............57 E4
Farmstead Rd CAT SE6....10 D1
Farm Wy WPK KT4.........21 G4
Farnaby Rd BMLY BR1.....11 G5
Farnan Rd STRHM/NOR SW16..7 E2
Farnborough Av
  SAND/SEL CR2..........38 A5
Farnborough Crs HAYES BR2..29 H2
  SAND/SEL CR2..........38 A4
Farningham Crs CTHM CR3..60 A3
Farningham Rd CTHM CR3..60 A3
Farnley Rd SNWD SE25....16 B3
Farquhar Rd NRWD SE19...8 D2
Farquharson Rd
  CROY/NA CR0...........26 A1
Farrier PI SUT SM1......23 G4
Farriers CI EW KT17.....40 C2
Farriers Rd EW KT17.....40 D2
Faversham Rd BECK BR3...18 B1
  MRDN SM4..............12 D5
Fawcett CI STRHM/NOR SW16..7 G1
Fawcett Rd CROY/NA CR0..2 C5
Fayland Av STRHM/NOR SW16..6 C2
Featherbed La
  SAND/SEL CR2..........38 B3
Felbridge CI BELMT SM2..32 D4
  STRHM/NOR SW16........7 G1
Fellmongers Yd CROY/NA CR0..2 C4
Fellowes Rd CAR SM5.....23 G4
Fellows Rd CAR SM5 *....2 D4
Felmingham Rd PGE/AN SE20..17 G3
Felstead Rd HOR/WEW KT19..40 B1
Feltham Rd MTCM CR4.....13 H1
Fendall Rd HOR/WEW KT19..30 A1
Fenmore Rd PUR/KEN CR8..55 F4
Fennel CI CROY/NA CR0...27 H2
Fennells Md EW KT17.....30 C4
Fenwick PI SAND/SEL CR2..35 H5
Ferguson CI BECK BR3....19 E2
Fern CI WARL CR6........57 E5
Ferndale Rd BNSTD SM7...51 F1
  SNWD SE25.............17 F4
Ferndown CI BELMT SM2...33 F2

## F

Fernham Rd THHTH CR7 16 A3
Fernhurst Rd CROY/NA CR0 27 E1
Fernlea Rd MTCM CR4 14 A1
Fernleigh Cl CROY/NA CR0 25 G5
Ferns Cl SAND/SEL CR2 37 F5
Fernthorpe Rd
STRHM/NOR SW16 6 C3
Fern Towers CTHM CR3 60 A5
Fernwood Av
STRHM/NOR SW16 6 D1
Ferrers Av WLGTN SM6 24 D5
Ferrers Rd STRHM/NOR SW16 6 D2
Ferriers Wy EPSOM KT18 50 C4
Ferris Av CROY/NA CR0 28 B4
Fiddicroft Av BNSTD SM7 42 D5
Field Cl SAND/SEL CR2 47 F4
Field End COUL/CHIP CR5 44 D4
Fieldend Rd
STRHM/NOR SW16 6 C5
Fieldhouse Vls BNSTD SM7 * 43 G5
The Fieldings BNSTD SM7 51 F2
Fieldpark Gdns CROY/NA CR0 28 A2
Fieldsend Rd CHEAM SM3 32 A1
Fieldside Rd BMLY BR1 11 F2
Field Wy CROY/NA CR0 38 D3
Figge's Rd MTCM CR4 6 A4
Filey Cl BELMT SM2 33 E3
Finborough Rd TOOT SW17 5 H4
Finch Av WNWD SE27 8 B1
Firdene BRYLDS KT5 20 A2
Firefly Cl WLGTN SM6 * 35 E3
Firle Ct EW KT17 * 40 D2
Fir Rd CHEAM SM3 22 B2
Firsby Av CROY/NA CR0 27 H2
Firs Cl MTCM CR4 14 B1
Firs Rd PUR/KEN CR8 45 H5
First Av HOR/WEW KT19 30 C4
First Quarter HOR/WEW KT19 * 40 C1
Firswood Av HOR/WEW KT19 30 C1
Firtree Av MTCM CR4 14 A1
Fir Tree Cl EW KT17 41 G5
HOR/WEW KT19 20 D5
STRHM/NOR SW16 6 C2
Fir Tree Gdns CROY/NA CR0 28 C5
Fir Tree Gv CAR SM5 33 H3
Fir Tree Rd BNSTD SM7 41 H4
EW KT17 50 B1
Fir Wk CHEAM SM3 31 H2
Fisher Cl CROY/NA CR0 3 K1
Fishponds Rd TOOT SW17 5 G1
Fitzjames Av CROY/NA CR0 27 E3
Fitzroy Gdns NRWD SE19 8 C4
Fiveacre Cl CROY/NA CR0 15 G5
Flag Cl CROY/NA CR0 27 H2
Flanders Crs TOOT SW17 5 H4
Flather Cl STRHM/NOR SW16 6 C3
Flaxley Rd MRDN SM4 12 D5
Fleetwood Cl CROY/NA CR0 3 J4
KWD/TDW/WH KT20 50 D5
Fleming Ct CROY/NA CR0 35 G1
Fleming Md MTCM CR4 5 G4
Flimwell Cl BMLY BR1 11 G2
Flint Cl BNSTD SM7 42 D4
Flora Gdns CROY/NA CR0 49 E1
Florence Av MRDN SM4 13 E4
Florence Rd BECK BR3 17 H1
SAND/SEL CR2 36 B4
WIM/MER SW19 4 D3
Florian Av SUT SM1 23 F5
Florida Rd THHTH CR7 7 H5
Follyfield Rd BNSTD SM7 42 C4
Fontaine Rd
STRHM/NOR SW16 7 F3
Ford Cl THHTH CR7 15 H5
Foresters Cl WLGTN SM6 34 D3
Foresters Dr WLGTN SM6 34 D3
Forestholme Cl SYD SE26 * 9 G2
Forest Rdg BECK BR3 18 C2
Forest Rd CHEAM SM3 22 C2
Forest Side WPK KT4 20 D2
Forge Av COUL/CHIP CR5 54 C5
Forge La CHEAM SM3 32 A3
Forge Ms CROY/NA CR0 38 C1
Forrester Pth SYD SE26 9 G1
Forrest Gdns
STRHM/NOR SW16 15 F2
Forster Rd BECK BR3 18 A2
Forsyte Crs NRWD SE19 8 C5
Fortescue Rd WIM/MER SW19 5 F4
Forval Cl MTCM CR4 13 H4
Foss Av CROY/NA CR0 35 G1
Foss Rd TOOT SW17 5 F1
Foulsham Rd THHTH CR7 16 A2
Founders Gdns NRWD SE19 8 A4
Fountain Dr CAR SM5 33 H4
NRWD SE19 8 D1
WLGTN SM6 44 B1
Fountain Rd THHTH CR7 16 A1
TOOT SW17 5 F2
Four Seasons Crs
CHEAM SM3 22 B3
Fourth Dr COUL/CHIP CR5 53 H1
Foxacre CTHM CR3 59 G2
Foxcombe CROY/NA CR0 38 D2
Foxearth Rd SAND/SEL CR2 37 G5
Foxearth Sp SAND/SEL CR2 37 G4
Foxes Dl HAYES BR2 19 F2
Foxglove Gdns PUR/KEN CR8 45 E1
Foxglove Wy WLGTN SM6 24 A2
Foxgrove Av BECK BR3 10 D4
Foxgrove Rd BECK BR3 10 D4
Fox Hl NRWD SE19 8 D4
Fox Hill Gdns NRWD SE19 8 D4
Foxley Gdns PUR/KEN CR8 45 H3
Foxley Hill Rd PUR/KEN CR8 45 G2
Foxley La PUR/KEN CR8 45 G1
Foxley Rd PUR/KEN CR8 45 H4
THHTH CR7 15 H3
Foxon Cl CTHM CR3 59 G1
Foxon La CTHM CR3 59 F1
Foxon Lane Gdns CTHM CR3 59 G1
Foxton Gv MTCM CR4 13 F1
Framfield Rd MTCM CR4 6 A4
Frampton Cl BELMT SM2 32 C3
Francis Barber Cl
STRHM/NOR SW16 * 7 F1
Franciscan Rd TOOT SW17 6 A1
Francis Cl HOR/WEW KT19 20 B5
Francis Gv WIM/MER SW19 4 B4
Francis Rd CROY/NA CR0 25 H1
CTHM CR3 59 F2
WLGTN SM6 34 C2
Franklin Cl WNWD SE27 7 H1
Franklin Crs MTCM CR4 14 C3
Franklin Rd PGE/AN SE20 9 G4
Franklin Wy CROY/NA CR0 25 E2
Frant Cl PGE/AN SE20 9 G4
Frant Rd THHTH CR7 15 H4
Frederick Cl SUT SM1 22 B5
Frederick Gdns CROY/NA CR0 15 H5
SUT SM1 32 B1
Frederick Rd SUT SM1 32 B1
Freedown La BNSTD SM7 42 D3
Freelands Av SAND/SEL CR2 37 H4
Freeman Rd MRDN SM4 13 F4
Freemasons Pl CROY/NA CR0 26 C2
Freemason's Rd
CROY/NA CR0 26 C2
Freethorpe Cl NRWD SE19 8 C5
Frensham Dr CROY/NA CR0 39 E3
Frensham Rd PUR/KEN CR8 45 H4
Frensham Wy EW KT17 50 C1
Freshfields CROY/NA CR0 28 B1
Freshwater Cl TOOT SW17 6 A3
Freshwater Rd TOOT SW17 6 A3
Freshwood Cl BECK BR3 10 D5
Freshwood Wy WLGTN SM6 34 C4
Friars Wd CROY/NA CR0 38 A4
Friday Rd MTCM CR4 5 H4
Friends' Rd CROY/NA CR0 2 E4
PUR/KEN CR8 45 H2
Frimley Av WLGTN SM6 35 E1
Frimley Cl CROY/NA CR0 39 E3
Frimley Crs CROY/NA CR0 39 E3
Frimley Gdns MTCM CR4 13 G2
Frinton Rd TOOT SW17 6 A3
Frith Rd CROY/NA CR0 2 C3
Frobisher Cl PUR/KEN CR8 55 E2
Frogmore Cl CHEAM SM3 21 H4
Frogmore Gdns CHEAM SM3 22 A5
Fromondes Rd CHEAM SM3 32 A1
Fryern Wd CTHM CR3 59 E4
Fryston Av COUL/CHIP CR5 44 B4
CROY/NA CR0 27 E3
Fulford Rd CTHM CR3 59 F1
HOR/WEW KT19 30 B3
Fullbrooks Av WPK KT4 20 D2
Fuller's Wd CROY/NA CR0 38 C1
Fullerton Rd CAR SM5 33 G4
CROY/NA CR0 26 D1
Furlong Cl WLGTN SM6 24 B2
Furneaux Av WNWD SE27 7 H2
Furness Rd MRDN SM4 12 D5
Furrows Pl CTHM CR3 59 H3
Furtherfield Cl CROY/NA CR0 15 G5
Furzedown Dr TOOT SW17 6 B2
Furzedown Rd BELMT SM2 43 E1
STRHM/NOR SW16 6 B1
Furze Hl PUR/KEN CR8 45 E1
Furze La PUR/KEN CR8 45 E1
Furze Rd THHTH CR7 16 A2
Fyfield Cl HAYES BR2 19 F3

## G

Gable Ct SYD SE26 9 F1
The Gables BNSTD SM7 51 F2
NRWD SE19 * 8 C5
Gables Wy BNSTD SM7 51 F1
Gadesden Rd
HOR/WEW KT19 30 A2
Gainsborough Cl BECK BR3 10 C4
Gainsborough Dr
SAND/SEL CR2 47 E3
Gainsborough Rd
HOR/WEW KT19 30 A5
Gainsborough Ter
BELMT SM2 * 32 B3
Gaist Av CTHM CR3 60 B2
Gale Cl MTCM CR4 13 F2
Gale Crs BNSTD SM7 51 G2
The Gallop BELMT SM2 33 F4
SAND/SEL CR2 37 F3
Galloway Pth CROY/NA CR0 2 E7
Galpin's Rd THHTH CR7 15 E3
Gambole Rd TOOT SW17 5 G1
Gander Green La CHEAM SM3 22 A3
Gap Rd WIM/MER SW19 4 C2
Garbrand Wk EW KT17 30 D4
Garden Av MTCM CR4 6 B4
Garden Cl BNSTD SM7 42 C5
WLGTN SM6 35 E1
Gardeners Rd CROY/NA CR0 2 B1
Garden Rd PGE/AN SE20 9 G5
The Gardens BECK BR3 19 E1
Garden Wk BECK BR3 10 B5
Garendon Gdns MRDN SM4 22 D1
Garendon Rd MRDN SM4 22 D1
Gareth Cl WPK KT4 21 H3
Garfield Rd WIM/MER SW19 5 E3
Garland Wy CTHM CR3 59 F2
Garlichill Rd EPSOM KT18 50 B2
Garnet Rd THHTH CR7 16 A3
Garrard Rd BNSTD SM7 51 G1
Garratt Cl CROY/NA CR0 25 E5
Garratt La TOOT SW17 5 F1
Garratts La BNSTD SM7 51 F1
Garratt Ter TOOT SW17 5 G1
Garrick Crs CROY/NA CR0 3 G3
Garston La PUR/KEN CR8 46 B5
Garth Cl MRDN SM4 21 H1
Garth Rd MRDN SM4 21 H2
Gascoigne Rd CROY/NA CR0 39 E5
Gassiot Rd TOOT SW17 5 H1
Gassiot Wy SUT SM1 23 F4
Gaston Rd MTCM CR4 14 A2
Gatestone Rd NRWD SE19 8 C3
Gatton Cl BELMT SM2 * 32 D4
Gatton Rd TOOT SW17 5 G1
Gauntlet Crs COUL/CHIP CR5 55 F5
Gauntlett Rd SUT SM1 33 F1
Gavina Cl MRDN SM4 13 G4
Gayfere Rd EW KT17 31 E1
Gaynesford Rd CAR SM5 33 H3
Gearing Cl TOOT SW17 6 B1
Gemmell Cl PUR/KEN CR8 45 F4
Geneva Rd THHTH CR7 16 A4
Genoa Rd PGE/AN SE20 9 G5
George Groves Rd
PGE/AN SE20 9 E5
Georges Ter CTHM CR3 59 F2
George St CROY/NA CR0 2 E3
Georgetown Cl NRWD SE19 8 C2
Georgia Rd THHTH CR7 7 H5
Gerald's Gv BNSTD SM7 41 H4
Gerrards Md BNSTD SM7 51 F1
Gibbs Av NRWD SE19 8 B3
Gibbs Cl NRWD SE19 * 8 B2
Gibbs Sq NRWD SE19 * 8 B2
Gibraltar Crs HOR/WEW KT19 30 C5
Gibson Rd SUT SM1 32 D1
Gibson's Hl STRHM/NOR SW16 7 G4
Gidd Hl COUL/CHIP CR5 53 E1
Gilbert Cl WIM/MER SW19 * 4 D5
Gilbert Rd WIM/MER SW19 5 E4
Gilbey Rd TOOT SW17 5 G1
Giles Coppice NRWD SE19 8 D1
Giles Md EPSOM KT18 * 40 C4
Gilham's Av BNSTD SM7 41 H2
Gilhams Cottages
BNSTD SM7 * 42 A2
Gillett Rd THHTH CR7 16 B3
Gilliam Gv PUR/KEN CR8 35 G5
Gillian Park Rd CHEAM SM3 22 B2
Gilpin Cl MTCM CR4 13 G1
Gilsland Rd THHTH CR7 16 B3
Gipsy Hl NRWD SE19 8 C2
Gipsy Rd WNWD SE27 8 B1
Gipsy Road Gdns WNWD SE27 8 A1
Girton Gdns CROY/NA CR0 28 C4
Girton Rd SYD SE26 9 H2
Gisbourne Cl WLGTN SM6 24 D4
Gittens Cl BMLY BR1 11 H1
Glade Gdns CROY/NA CR0 28 A1
Gladeside CROY/NA CR0 17 H5
The Glade BELMT SM2 32 A4
COUL/CHIP CR5 54 C4
CROY/NA CR0 17 H4
EW KT17 31 E2
WWKM BR4 28 D4
Gladstone Ms PGE/AN SE20 9 G4
Gladstone Rd CROY/NA CR0 26 B1
WIM/MER SW19 4 C4
Gladstone Ter WNWD SE27 * 8 A1
Glamorgan Cl MTCM CR4 15 E2
Glanfield Rd BECK BR3 18 B3
Glasford St TOOT SW17 5 H3
Glassmill La HAYES BR2 19 H2
Glastonbury Rd MRDN SM4 12 C5
Glebe Av MTCM CR4 13 G1
Glebe Cl SAND/SEL CR2 46 D2
Glebe Gdns NWMAL KT3 20 C1
Glebe Hyrst SAND/SEL CR2 46 D2
Glebe Pth MTCM CR4 13 H2
Glebe Rd BELMT SM2 32 A4
CAR SM5 33 H2
WARL CR6 56 D2
Glebe Sq MTCM CR4 * 13 H2
The Glebe STRHM/NOR SW16 * 6 D1
WPK KT4 20 D2
Glebe Wy SAND/SEL CR2 46 D2
WWKM BR4 29 F3
Glena Mt SUT SM1 23 E5
Glenbow Rd BMLY BR1 11 G3
Glencairn Rd
STRHM/NOR SW16 7 E4
Glendale Dr WIM/MER SW19 4 B2
Glendale Ms BECK BR3 10 D5
Glendale Ri PUR/KEN CR8 45 H5
Gleneagle Ms
STRHM/NOR SW16 6 D2
Gleneagle Rd
STRHM/NOR SW16 6 D2
Gleneldon Ms
STRHM/NOR SW16 7 E2
Gleneldon Rd
STRHM/NOR SW16 7 E1
Glenfield Rd BNSTD SM7 42 D5
Glen Gdns CROY/NA CR0 25 G4
Glenhurst Ri NRWD SE19 8 A4
Glenister Park Rd
STRHM/NOR SW16 6 D4
Glenn Av PUR/KEN CR8 45 H1
Glen Road End WLGTN SM6 34 B4
Glenside Cl PUR/KEN CR8 46 B5
The Glen BELMT SM2 * 33 E2
CROY/NA CR0 27 H4
HAYES BR2 19 G1
Glenthorne Av CROY/NA CR0 27 G2
Glenthorne Cl CHEAM SM3 22 C2
Glenthorne Gdns
CHEAM SM3 22 C2
Glenwood Rd EW KT17 31 E2
Glenwood Rw NRWD SE19 * 8 D5
Glenwood Wy CROY/NA CR0 17 H5
Glossop Rd SAND/SEL CR2 36 B4
Gloucester Ct MTCM CR4 * 15 E4
Gloucester Gdns SUT SM1 22 D3
Gloucester Rd CROY/NA CR0 26 B1
Glyn Cl EW KT17 31 E4
SNWD SE25 16 C1
Glyn Rd WPK KT4 21 H3
Goat Rd MTCM CR4 24 A1
Godalming Av WLGTN SM6 35 E1
Goddard Rd BECK BR3 17 H3
Godolphin Cl BELMT SM2 42 B1
Godric Crs CROY/NA CR0 39 F5
Godson Rd CROY/NA CR0 25 G4
Godstone Mt PUR/KEN CR8 * 45 H2
Godstone Rd CTHM CR3 60 A4
PUR/KEN CR8 45 H3
SUT SM1 23 E5
Godwin Cl HOR/WEW KT19 30 A2
Goidel Cl WLGTN SM6 24 D5
Goldcliff Cl MRDN SM4 22 C1
Goldcrest Wy CROY/NA CR0 39 F4
PUR/KEN CR8 34 D5
Goldfinch Rd SAND/SEL CR2 38 A5
Goldwell Rd THHTH CR7 15 F3
Golf Cl THHTH CR7 7 G5
Golf Rd PUR/KEN CR8 55 F3
Golf Side BELMT SM2 42 A1
Gomshall Av WLGTN SM6 35 E1
Gomshall Gdns PUR/KEN CR8 46 C5
Gomshall Rd BELMT SM2 31 G5
Gonville Rd THHTH CR7 15 F4
Goodenough Cl
COUL/CHIP CR5 54 C5
Goodenough Rd
WIM/MER SW19 4 B4
Goodenough Wy
COUL/CHIP CR5 54 B5
Goodhart Wy WWKM BR4 19 G5
Goodhew Rd CROY/NA CR0 17 E5
Goodwin Cl MTCM CR4 13 F2
Goodwin Gdns CROY/NA CR0 35 H2
Goodwin Rd CROY/NA CR0 35 H1
Goodwood Cl MRDN SM4 12 C3
Goodwood Pde BECK BR3 * 18 A3
Goossens Cl SUT SM1 33 E1
Gordon Av SAND/SEL CR2 36 A5
Gordon Crs CROY/NA CR0 26 C2
Gordon Rd BECK BR3 18 B2
CAR SM5 33 H2
CTHM CR3 59 F1
Gorringe Park Av MTCM CR4 5 H4
Gorse Cl KWD/TDW/WH KT20 50 B5
Gorse Ri TOOT SW17 6 A2
Gorse Rd CROY/NA CR0 28 C4
Gosfield Rd HOR/WEW KT19 40 B2
Goston Gdns THHTH CR7 15 G2
Goudhurst Rd BMLY BR1 11 H2
Goulding Gdns THHTH CR7 16 A1
Gowland Pl BECK BR3 18 B1
Gowland Cl CROY/NA CR0 27 E1
Gowrie Pl CTHM CR3 59 E2
Gracedale Rd
STRHM/NOR SW16 6 B2
Grace Rd CROY/NA CR0 16 A5
The Gradient SYD SE26 9 E1
Grafton Cl WPK KT4 20 C4
Grafton Park Rd WPK KT4 20 C4
Grafton Rd CROY/NA CR0 25 G2
WPK KT4 20 B4
Graham Av MTCM CR4 6 A5
Graham Cl CROY/NA CR0 28 C3
Graham Rd MTCM CR4 6 A5
PUR/KEN CR8 45 G3
WIM/MER SW19 4 B4
Grampian Cl BELMT SM2 33 E3
Granada St TOOT SW17 5 H2
Granden Rd
STRHM/NOR SW16 * 15 E1
Grandison Rd WPK KT4 21 G3
Grand Stand Rd EPSOM KT18 50 A2
Grange Av SNWD SE25 16 C1
Grangecliffe Gdns
SNWD SE25 16 C1
Grange Ct BELMT SM2 * 32 D3
WLGTN SM6 * 24 B4
Grange Gdns BNSTD SM7 42 D3
SNWD SE25 16 C1
Grange Hl SNWD SE25 16 C1
Grange Meadow
BNSTD SM7 42 D3
Grange Park Rd THHTH CR7 16 B2
Grange Rd BELMT SM2 32 C3
CTHM CR3 59 H5
SAND/SEL CR2 36 A5
SNWD SE25 16 B3
The Grange CROY/NA CR0 28 B3
WPK KT4 20 B5
Grange V BELMT SM2 32 D3
Grangewood La BECK BR3 10 B3
Granton Rd
STRHM/NOR SW16 6 C5
Grant Pl CROY/NA CR0 26 D2
Grant Rd CROY/NA CR0 26 D2
Granville Cl CROY/NA CR0 3 G4
Granville Gdns
STRHM/NOR SW16 7 F5
Granville Rd WIM/MER SW19 4 C4
Grasmere Av WIM/MER SW19 12 C2
Grasmere Rd BMLY BR1 11 H5
PUR/KEN CR8 45 H1
SNWD SE25 17 F5
STRHM/NOR SW16 7 F2
Grassfield Cl COUL/CHIP CR5 53 F4
Grassmount WLGTN SM6 34 C5
Grassway WLGTN SM6 24 C5
Gravel Hl CROY/NA CR0 37 H2
Gravenel Gdns TOOT SW17 * 5 G2
Graveney Gv PGE/AN SE20 9 G4
Graveney Rd TOOT SW17 5 G1
Grayscroft Rd
STRHM/NOR SW16 6 D4
Great Brownings DUL SE21 8 D1
Great Ellshams BNSTD SM7 51 G1
Great Elms EW KT17 * 40 D1
Great Gatton Cl
CROY/NA CR0 28 A1
Great Tattenhams
EPSOM KT18 50 C4
Great Woodcote Dr
PUR/KEN CR8 34 D5
Great Woodcote Pk
PUR/KEN CR8 35
Greaves Pl TOOT SW17 5
Grebe Ct SUT SM1 32
Grecian Crs NRWD SE19 7
Greenacre Pl WLGTN SM6 24
Green Acres CROY/NA CR0 3
Green Chain Wk HAYES BR2 11
SYD SE26 9
Green Cl CAR SM5 23
HAYES BR2 19
Green Court Av
CROY/NA CR0 27
Green Court Gdns
CROY/NA CR0 27
Green Curve BNSTD SM7 42
Greenfield Link
COUL/CHIP CR5 45
Greenford Rd SUT SM1 22
Greenhayes Av BNSTD SM7 42
Greenhayes Gdns
BNSTD SM7 42
Greenhill SUT SM1 23
Greenhill Av CTHM CR3 6
Greenhill La WARL CR6 5
Greenhurst Rd WNWD SE27
Greenland Wy CROY/NA CR0 2
Green La CTHM CR3 5
MRDN SM4 2
PGE/AN SE20
PUR/KEN CR8 4
THHTH CR7
WPK KT4 2
Green Lane Gdns THHTH CR7 1
Green Lanes HOR/WEW KT19 3
Greenlaw Gdns NWMAL KT3 2
Green Leaf Av WLGTN SM6 2
Greenlea Pk WIM/MER SW19 *
Greenmead Cl SNWD SE25 1
Greenock Rd
STRHM/NOR SW16
Greenside Rd CROY/NA CR0 2
The Green CROY/NA CR0 3
CTHM CR3 6
EW KT17 4
KWD/TDW/WH KT20 5
MRDN SM4 1
SUT SM1 2
WLGTN SM6 2
Greenview Av BECK BR3 1
Greenway WLGTN SM6 2
Greenway Gdns
CROY/NA CR0 2
Greenways BECK BR3 1
Greenwood Cl MRDN SM4 1
Greenwood Gdns CTHM CR3 6
Greenwood Rd CROY/NA CR0 2
MTCM CR4 1
Green Wrythe Crs CAR SM5 2
Green Wrythe La CAR SM5 2
Grenaby Av CROY/NA CR0 2
Grenaby Rd CROY/NA CR0 2
Grenadier Pl CTHM CR3 5
Grenfell Rd MTCM CR4
Grennell Cl SUT SM1 2
Grennell Rd SUT SM1 2
Grenville Cl BRYLDS KT5 2
Grenville Rd CROY/NA CR0 3
Gresham Av WARL CR6 5
Gresham Rd BECK BR3 1
SNWD SE25 * 1
Greville Av SAND/SEL CR2 3
Grey Alders BNSTD SM7 4
Greycot Rd BECK BR3 1
Greyfields Cl PUR/KEN CR8 4
Greyhound La
STRHM/NOR SW16
Greyhound Rd SUT SM1 3
Greyhound Ter
STRHM/NOR SW16
Greystone Cl SAND/SEL CR2 4
Greyswood St
STRHM/NOR SW16
Griffiths Rd WIM/MER SW19
Grimwade Av CROY/NA CR0 2
Grindall Cl CROY/NA CR0
Grindley Gdns CROY/NA CR0 * 1
Grisedale Cl PUR/KEN CR8 4
Grisedale Gdns PUR/KEN CR8 4
Groomfield Cl TOOT SW17
Grosvenor Av CAR SM5 3
Grosvenor Gdns WLGTN SM6 3
Grosvenor Hl WIM/MER SW19
Grosvenor Rd SNWD SE25 1
WLGTN SM6 3
WWKM BR4 2
Grove Av EW KT17 4
SUT SM1 3
Groveland Av
STRHM/NOR SW16
Groveland Rd BECK BR3 1
Grovelands Rd PUR/KEN CR8 4
Grove La COUL/CHIP CR5 4
Grove Mill Pl CAR SM5 2
Grove Rd EW KT17 4
MTCM CR4 1
SUT SM1 3
THHTH CR7 1
WIM/MER SW19
Groveside Cl CAR SM5 2
The Grove COUL/CHIP CR5 4
CTHM CR3 5
EW KT17 4
WWKM BR4 2
Grove Wood Hl
COUL/CHIP CR5 4
Guards Av CTHM CR3 5
Guildersfield Rd
STRHM/NOR SW16
Guildford Rd CROY/NA CR0 1
Guildford Wy WLGTN SM6 3
Guinness Ct CROY/NA CR0 *

ell Cl CROY/NA CR0 ... 16 D5
) SE26 ... 9 E2
n Rd TOOT SW17 ... 6 A3
y Crs CROY/NA CR0 ... 25 F2
y Rd CAR SM5 ... 24 A5
t Gdns MTCM CR4 ... 14 A1
d WLGTN SM6 ... 24 D4
or Rd BECK BR3 ... 17 H3
yr Rd HAYES BR2 ... 19 H2
ne Av CROY/NA CR0 ... 27 H1
ne Rd CTHM CR3 ... 59 F3

H

mbe Rd WIM/MER SW19 ... 5 E3
ridge Park Gdns
SM5 ... 23 H3
ridge Rd CAR SM5 ... 24 A3
ngton Crs BECK BR3 ... 10 C3
n Rd SUT SM1 ... 22 D5
igh Cl RYNPK SW20 ... 12 B1
igh Dr BELMT SM2 ... 32 C4
y Rd MTCM CR4 ... 14 D3
y Wood Ri
/KEN CR8 ... 45 H5
w Pl NRWD SE19 ... 9 E4
Cl WIM/MER SW19 ... 5 E3
am Rd TOOT SW17 ... 6 A3
s Wk MRDN SM4 ... 22 D1
wen Rd MRDN SM4 ... 22 D1
Gv SAND/SEL CR2 ... 36 A3
Park Gdns
D/SEL CR2 ... 35 H2
Park Rd
D/SEL CR2 ... 35 H2
Rd SAND/SEL CR2 ... 36 B2
r SYD SE26 ... 9 G2
Valley Rd CTHM CR3 ... 57 F5
ead Rd SUT SM1 ... 22 D4
well Av CROY/NA CR0 ... 25 E5
well Cl MTCM CR4 ... 14 A2
vfield Wy MTCM CR4 ... 13 F2
d WLGTN SM6 ... 34 B4
ad Cl CROY/NA CR0 ... 2 C4
n Rd PUR/KEN CR8 ... 55 G5
ledon Gdns SNWD SE25 ... 16 D2
ledon Rd CTHM CR3 ... 59 F3
leton Cl WPK KT4 ... 21 G3
rook Rd SNWD SE25 ... 17 F2
ro Rd STRHM/NOR SW16 ... 6 D3
ton Av CHEAM SM3 ... 22 A3
ton Cl HOR/WEW KT19 ... 40 A2
/KEN CR8 ... 45 H2
ton Rd THHTH CR7 ... 16 B2
M/MER SW19 ... 4 D4
WD SE27 ... 8 B1
ton Road Ms
M/MER SW19 ... 4 D4
ton Wy WLGTN SM6 ... 34 D4
t Rd NRWD SE19 ... 8 D4
n Gdns NRWD SE19 ... 8 C4
nond Av MTCM CR4 ... 14 B1
nd Cl SAND/SEL CR2 ... 35 H4
den Av BECK BR3 ... 18 A1
den Rd BECK BR3 ... 18 A1
ton Gv EW KT17 ... 40 D1
ton Rd CROY/NA CR0 ... 16 A5
K KT4 ... 21 E3
ey Green Gdns
RL CR6 ... 56 C1
ey Wy SAND/SEL CR2 ... 47 F5
w CROY/NA CR0 ... 18 A5
ck Rd NRWD SE19 ... 8 B3
croft Rd CROY/NA CR0 ... 25 H2
ey Page Rd WLGTN SM6 ... 35 F3
side Cl WPK KT4 ... 21 H2
y Pl BECK BR3 ... 10 C4
ah Cl BECK BR3 ... 18 D2
bal Wy CROY/NA CR0 ... 35 F1
ver Cl CHEAM SM3 ... 22 A5
ver Rd WIM/MER SW19 ... 5 E4
ver St CROY/NA CR0 ... 2 B4
n Cl BECK BR3 * ... 10 D3
edown Rd
D/SEL CR2 ... 47 E1
rough Rd
HM/NOR SW16 ... 7 F1
urfield Rd BNSTD SM7 ... 42 D5
ry Rd CAR SM5 ... 33 G4
urt Av WLGTN SM6 ... 24 B5
urt Fld WLGTN SM6 ... 24 B5
urt Rd THHTH CR7 ... 15 F5
M/MER SW19 ... 4 C4
CTN SM6 ... 24 B5
astle Cl CROY/NA CR0 ... 17 E5
ourts Cl WWKM BR4 ... 28 D5
g Cl CROY/NA CR0 ... 3 K4
ngs La PGE/AN SE20 ... 9 H3
wick Pl
HM/NOR SW16 ... 6 C4
Rd WIM/MER SW19 ... 4 D4
ield Av BELMT SM2 ... 32 A4
ield Rd
HM/NOR SW16 ... 7 F4
Bank CROY/NA CR0 ... 39 F5
tone Dr CTHM CR3 ... 59 H5
tone Hl CTHM CR3 ... 59 H5
tone La CTHM CR3 ... 59 G5
tone Valley Rd
HM CR3 ... 59 H5
wood Gdns
D/SEL CR2 ... 47 F5
wood Rd SAND/SEL CR2 ... 36 C2
M/MER SW19 ... 5 G3
ess Cl EW KT17 ... 50 C1
nd Av CROY/NA CR0 ... 3 K4
nd Cl WIM/MER SW19 ... 12 D2
an Pl PUR/KEN CR8 ... 45 H1
ony Cl WLGTN SM6 ... 35 E4

Harold Rd NRWD SE19 ... 8 B4
SUT SM1 ... 23 F5
Harriet Gdns CROY/NA CR0 ... 27 E3
Harrington Cl CROY/NA CR0 ... 25 E3
Harrington Rd SNWD SE25 ... 17 E3
Harrison's Ri CROY/NA CR0 ... 2 A4
Harrow Gdns WARL CR6 ... 57 F1
Harrow Rd CAR SM5 ... 33 G2
WARL CR6 ... 48 B5
Hartfield Crs WIM/MER SW19 ... 4 B4
Hartfield Gv PGE/AN SE20 ... 9 F5
Hartfield Rd WIM/MER SW19 ... 4 B4
Hartland Rd MRDN SM4 ... 22 C1
Hartland Wy CROY/NA CR0 ... 28 A3
MRDN SM4 ... 22 C1
Hartley Down PUR/KEN CR8 ... 45 F4
Hartley Farm PUR/KEN CR8 ... 45 F5
Hartley Hl PUR/KEN CR8 ... 45 F5
Hartley Old Rd PUR/KEN CR8 ... 45 F4
Hartley Rd CROY/NA CR0 ... 26 A1
Hartley Wy PUR/KEN CR8 ... 45 F5
Hartscroft CROY/NA CR0 ... 38 A4
Hart Sq MRDN SM4 * ... 12 D4
Harvester Rd
HOR/WEW KT19 ... 30 B5
Harwood Av MTCM CR4 ... 13 G2
Haseltine Rd SYD SE26 ... 10 B1
Haslam Av CHEAM SM3 ... 22 A2
Haslemere Av MTCM CR4 ... 13 F1
Haslemere Cl WLGTN SM6 ... 35 E1
Haslemere Rd THHTH CR7 ... 15 H4
Hassocks Rd
STRHM/NOR SW16 ... 6 D5
Hastings Pl CROY/NA CR0 ... 26 D2
Hastings Rd CROY/NA CR0 ... 26 D2
Hatch Gdns
KWD/TDW/WH KT20 ... 50 D5
Hatch La BNSTD SM7 ... 43 H5
Hatch Rd STRHM/NOR SW16 ... 15 E1
Hatfield Cl BELMT SM2 ... 32 C4
MTCM CR4 * ... 13 F3
Hathaway Rd CROY/NA CR0 ... 25 H1
Hatherleigh Cl MRDN SM4 ... 12 C3
Hatton Gdns MTCM CR4 ... 13 H4
Hatton Rd CROY/NA CR0 ... 25 G2
Havelock Rd CROY/NA CR0 ... 3 K2
WIM/MER SW19 ... 5 E2
Havisham Pl NRWD SE19 ... 7 H3
Hawarden Rd CTHM CR3 ... 59 E1
Hawes La WWKM BR4 ... 29 F3
Hawes Rd
KWD/TDW/WH KT20 ... 50 D5
Hawke Rd NRWD SE19 ... 8 B3
Hawker Rd CROY/NA CR0 ... 35 G2
Hawkes Rd MTCM CR4 ... 5 G5
Hawkhirst Rd PUR/KEN CR8 ... 55 F1
Hawkhurst Rd
STRHM/NOR SW16 ... 6 D5
Hawkhurst Wy WWKM BR4 ... 28 D3
Hawkins Wy CAT SE6 ... 10 C2
Hawksbrook La BECK BR3 ... 18 D5
Hawkshead Cl BMLY BR1 ... 11 G4
Hawthorn Av THHTH CR7 ... 7 H5
Hawthorn Cl BNSTD SM7 ... 42 A4
Hawthorn Crs SAND/SEL CR2 ... 47 G1
TOOT SW17 ... 6 A2
Hawthorndene Cl
HAYES BR2 * ... 29 H3
Hawthorn Dr WWKM BR4 ... 29 G5
Hawthorne Av CAR SM5 ... 34 A3
MTCM CR4 ... 13 F1
Hawthorne Pl EW KT17 ... 40 C2
Hawthorn Gv PGE/AN SE20 ... 9 F5
Hawthorn Rd SUT SM1 ... 33 F1
WLGTN SM6 ... 34 B3
The Hawthorns EW KT17 ... 30 D2
Haycroft Cl COUL/CHIP CR5 ... 54 D4
Haydn Av PUR/KEN CR8 ... 45 G5
Haydon Park Rd
WIM/MER SW19 ... 4 C2
Haydon's Rd WIM/MER SW19 ... 4 D2
Hayes Cha WWKM BR4 ... 19 F5
Hayes Crs CHEAM SM3 ... 21 H5
Hayesford Park Dr
HAYES BR2 ... 19 H4
Hayes Hl HAYES BR2 ... 29 G2
Hayes Hill Rd HAYES BR2 ... 29 H2
Hayes La BECK BR3 ... 19 F2
PUR/KEN CR8 ... 54 D1
Hayes Mead Rd HAYES BR2 ... 29 G2
Hayes Wy BECK BR3 ... 19 E3
Haymer Gdns WPK KT4 ... 21 E4
Hayne Rd BECK BR3 ... 18 B1
Haynes La NRWD SE19 ... 8 C3
Haynt Wk RYNPK SW20 ... 12 B2
Haysleigh Gdns PGE/AN SE20 ... 17 E1
Hays Wk BELMT SM2 ... 31 H5
Haywain CTHM CR3 ... 59 E2
Hayward Cl WIM/MER SW19 ... 4 D4
Hazelbank BRYLDS KT5 ... 20 A2
Hazelbury Cl WIM/MER SW19 ... 12 C1
Hazel Cl CROY/NA CR0 ... 27 H1
MTCM CR4 ... 14 D3
Hazeldene Ct PUR/KEN CR8 ... 46 B5
Hazel Gv SYD SE26 ... 9 H1
Hazelhurst BECK BR3 ... 11 F5
Hazelhurst Rd TOOT SW17 ... 5 F1
Hazel Md EW KT17 ... 31 E5
Hazel Wy COUL/CHIP CR5 ... 52 D4
Hazelwood Av MRDN SM4 ... 12 D3
Hazelwood Gv SAND/SEL CR2 ... 47 F4
Hazelwood La
COUL/CHIP CR5 ... 52 D4
Hazledean Rd CROY/NA CR0 ... 3 F3
Hazlemere Gdns WPK KT4 ... 21 E2
Hazon Wy HOR/WEW KT19 ... 40 B2
Headcorn Rd THHTH CR7 ... 15 F3
Headley Av WLGTN SM6 ... 35 F1
Headley Dr CROY/NA CR0 ... 39 E3
EPSOM KT18 ... 50 C4
Headley Gv
KWD/TDW/WH KT20 ... 50 B5

The Headway EW KT17 ... 30 D4
Heath Cl BNSTD SM7 ... 42 D4
SAND/SEL CR2 ... 35 H2
Heathcote Rd EPSOM KT18 ... 40 B4
Heathdene
KWD/TDW/WH KT20 ... 51 E4
Heathdene Rd
STRHM/NOR SW16 ... 7 F4
WLGTN SM6 ... 34 B3
Heath Dr BELMT SM2 ... 33 E4
Heatherdene Cl MTCM CR4 ... 13 F3
Heather Gdns BELMT SM2 ... 32 C2
Heatherset Gdns
STRHM/NOR SW16 ... 7 F4
Heatherside Rd
HOR/WEW KT19 ... 30 B3
Heather Wy SAND/SEL CR2 ... 37 H4
Heathfield Dr MTCM CR4 ... 5 G5
Heathfield Gdns CROY/NA CR0 ... 2 D6
Heathfield Rd BMLY BR1 ... 11 H4
CROY/NA CR0 ... 2 E7
SAND/SEL CR2 ... 36 B1
Heathfield V SAND/SEL CR2 ... 37 H4
Heath Gv PGE/AN SE20 ... 9 G4
Heathhurst Rd
SAND/SEL CR2 ... 36 C4
Heath Rd CTHM CR3 ... 59 F3
THHTH CR7 ... 16 A2
Heathside Pl EPSOM KT18 ... 50 D3
The Heath CTHM CR3 ... 59 E4
Heathview Rd THHTH CR7 ... 15 G3
Heathway CROY/NA CR0 ... 28 B4
CTHM CR3 ... 59 E5
Heaton Rd MTCM CR4 ... 6 A4
Heighton Gdns CROY/NA CR0 ... 35 H1
Heights Cl BNSTD SM7 ... 51 E1
The Heights BECK BR3 * ... 11 E4
Helder St SAND/SEL CR2 ... 36 B2
Helios Rd WLGTN SM6 ... 24 A2
Helme Cl WIM/MER SW19 ... 4 B2
Helmsdale Rd
STRHM/NOR SW16 ... 6 C5
Hemingford Rd CHEAM SM3 ... 21 G5
Hemmingsmead
HOR/WEW KT19 ... 30 A2
Hempshaw Av BNSTD SM7 ... 52 D1
Henbit Cl
KWD/TDW/WH KT20 ... 50 B4
Henderson Rd CROY/NA CR0 ... 16 B5
Heneage Crs CROY/NA CR0 ... 39 E5
Henfield Rd WIM/MER SW19 ... 4 B5
Hengelo Gdns MTCM CR4 ... 13 F3
Hengist Wy HAYES BR2 ... 19 F3
Henley Av CHEAM SM3 ... 22 A4
Henry Doulton Dr TOOT SW17 ... 6 A1
Henry Tate Ms
STRHM/NOR SW16 ... 7 G2
Hensford Gdns SYD SE26 ... 9 F1
Hepburn Gdns HAYES BR2 ... 29 H2
Hepworth Rd
STRHM/NOR SW16 ... 7 E4
Herald Gdns WLGTN SM6 ... 24 B4
Herbert Rd WIM/MER SW19 ... 4 B4
Hereford Cl EPSOM KT18 ... 40 B3
Hereward Av PUR/KEN CR8 ... 35 G5
Hereward Rd TOOT SW17 ... 5 H1
Herlwyn Gdns TOOT SW17 ... 5 H1
Hermes Wy WLGTN SM6 ... 34 D3
Hermitage Gdns NRWD SE19 ... 8 A4
Hermitage La CROY/NA CR0 ... 26 D1
STRHM/NOR SW16 ... 7 F4
Hermitage Rd NRWD SE19 ... 8 B3
PUR/KEN CR8 ... 55 E1
Herondale SAND/SEL CR2 ... 37 H4
Heron Rd CROY/NA CR0 ... 3 H2
Hertford Wy MTCM CR4 ... 15 E3
Hessle Gv EW KT17 ... 40 D1
Hesterman Wy CROY/NA CR0 ... 25 F2
Hewers Wy
KWD/TDW/WH KT20 ... 50 B5
Hewitt Cl CROY/NA CR0 ... 28 C4
Hexham Rd MRDN SM4 ... 22 D2
Heybridge Av
STRHM/NOR SW16 ... 7 F3
Heyford Av RYNPK SW20 ... 12 B2
Heyford Rd MTCM CR4 ... 13 G1
Highbarrow Rd
CROY/NA CR0 ... 26 D2
High Beech SAND/SEL CR2 ... 36 C3
High Beeches BNSTD SM7 ... 41 H4
High Beeches Cl
PUR/KEN CR8 ... 34 D5
High Broom Crs WWKM BR4 ... 28 D1
Highbury Av THHTH CR7 ... 15 G1
Highbury Cl WWKM BR4 ... 28 D3
Highbury Rd WIM/MER SW19 ... 4 A2
Highclere Cl PUR/KEN CR8 ... 46 A5
Highclere St SYD SE26 ... 10 A1
Highdaun Dr
STRHM/NOR SW16 ... 15 F3
Highdown WPK KT4 ... 20 C3
High Down La BELMT SM2 ... 42 D1
High Dr CTHM CR3 ... 61 F2
Higher Dr BNSTD SM7 ... 41 H3
PUR/KEN CR8 ... 45 G3
Higher Gn EW KT17 ... 41 E3
Highfield BNSTD SM7 ... 52 C2
Highfield Dr HAYES BR2 ... 19 G3
HOR/WEW KT19 ... 30 D3
WWKM BR4 ... 28 D4
Highfield Hl NRWD SE19 ... 8 B4
Highfield Rd BRYLDS KT5 ... 20 A1
CTHM CR3 ... 60 A2
PUR/KEN CR8 ... 35 F5
SUT SM1 ... 33 G1
Highgrove Ms CAR SM5 ... 23 G4
High Hill Rd WARL CR6 ... 49 F4
Highland Cottages
WLGTN SM6 * ... 24 B5
Highland Cft BECK BR3 ... 10 D3
Highland Rd BMLY BR1 ... 11 H5
HAYES BR2 ... 19 H1

NRWD SE19 ... 8 C3
PUR/KEN CR8 ... 45 G4
High La CTHM CR3 ... 57 F4
High Level Dr SYD SE26 ... 9 E1
High Limes NRWD SE19 * ... 8 C3
High Md WWKM BR4 ... 29 F3
High Pth WIM/MER SW19 ... 4 D5
High Pines WARL CR6 ... 56 C4
Highridge Cl EPSOM KT18 * ... 40 C5
High Standing CTHM CR3 ... 59 E5
High St BECK BR3 ... 10 C5
BELMT SM2 ... 33 E3
BNSTD SM7 ... 42 C5
CAR SM5 ... 33 H1
CHEAM SM3 ... 32 A2
CROY/NA CR0 ... 2 D4
CTHM CR3 ... 59 G3
HOR/WEW KT19 ... 40 B3
PGE/AN SE20 ... 9 G4
PUR/KEN CR8 ... 45 G1
SUT SM1 ... 32 D2
THHTH CR7 ... 16 A3
WIM/MER SW19 ... 4 A3
WWKM BR4 ... 28 D2
High St Collier's Wd
WIM/MER SW19 ... 5 F4
High Street Ms
WIM/MER SW19 ... 4 A2
High Trees CROY/NA CR0 ... 28 A2
High Trees Cl CTHM CR3 ... 59 H2
High Vw BELMT SM2 ... 42 B1
Highview CTHM CR3 ... 59 G4
High View Av WLGTN SM6 ... 35 F1
High View Cl NRWD SE19 ... 16 D1
High View Rd NRWD SE19 ... 8 B3
The Highway BELMT SM2 ... 33 E4
Highwold COUL/CHIP CR5 ... 53 E3
Highwood Cl PUR/KEN CR8 ... 55 E2
Highwoods CTHM CR3 ... 59 G5
Hilary Av MTCM CR4 ... 14 A2
Hilbert Rd CHEAM SM3 ... 21 H5
Hilborough Cl WIM/MER SW19 ... 5 E4
Hildenborough Gdns
BMLY BR1 ... 11 G3
Hildenlea Pl HAYES BR2 ... 19 G1
Hillars Heath Rd
COUL/CHIP CR5 ... 45 E5
Hillbarn SAND/SEL CR2 ... 46 C1
Hillborough Cl
WIM/MER SW19 * ... 5 E4
Hillbrow Rd BMLY BR1 ... 11 G4
Hillbury Cl WARL CR6 ... 56 B3
Hillbury Gdns WARL CR6 ... 56 C3
Hillbury Rd WARL CR6 ... 56 A2
Hill Cl PUR/KEN CR8 ... 46 A3
Hillcote Av STRHM/NOR SW16 ... 7 G4
Hill Crs WPK KT4 ... 21 G3
Hillcrest Cl BECK BR3 ... 18 B5
EPSOM KT18 ... 40 D5
SYD SE26 ... 9 E1
Hillcrest Rd CTHM CR3 ... 55 H2
PUR/KEN CR8 ... 35 F5
Hillcrest Vw BECK BR3 ... 18 B5
Hillcroft Av PUR/KEN CR8 ... 44 C3
Hillcroome Rd BELMT SM2 ... 33 F2
Hillcross Av MRDN SM4 ... 12 A5
Hilldale Rd SUT SM1 ... 22 B5
Hilldeane Rd PUR/KEN CR8 ... 35 G5
Hilldown Rd HAYES BR2 ... 29 G2
STRHM/NOR SW16 ... 7 E4
Hill Dr STRHM/NOR SW16 ... 15 F2
Hillfield Av MRDN SM4 ... 13 G5
Hillfield Pde MRDN SM4 * ... 13 F5
Hill House Rd
STRHM/NOR SW16 ... 7 F2
Hillhurst Gdns CTHM CR3 ... 55 G5
Hillier Gdns CROY/NA CR0 ... 35 G1
Hillier's La CROY/NA CR0 ... 25 E4
Hillmore Gv SYD SE26 ... 9 H2
Hill Rd CAR SM5 ... 33 G2
MTCM CR4 ... 6 B5
PUR/KEN CR8 ... 45 F2
SUT SM1 ... 32 D1
Hillside BNSTD SM7 ... 42 A5
Hillside Av PUR/KEN CR8 ... 45 H3
Hillside Cl BNSTD SM7 ... 51 E1
MRDN SM4 ... 12 A3
Hillside Cottages
BNSTD SM7 * ... 43 H3
Hillside Gdns WLGTN SM6 ... 34 C3
Hillside Rd BELMT SM2 ... 32 B3
COUL/CHIP CR5 ... 54 A3
CROY/NA CR0 ... 2 A7
CTHM CR3 ... 56 A3
EW KT17 ... 31 G5
HAYES BR2 ... 19 H2
Hillsmead Wy SAND/SEL CR2 ... 47 E4
The Hill CTHM CR3 ... 59 H4
Hill Top CHEAM SM3 ... 22 B1
Hilltop Cottages SYD SE26 * ... 9 F1
Hilltop La CTHM CR3 ... 58 C5
Hilltop Rd CTHM CR3 ... 55 G2
Hilltop Wk CTHM CR3 ... 57 E5
Hillview CTHM CR3 ... 55 H2
Hill View Cl PUR/KEN CR8 ... 45 H1
Hillview Rd SUT SM1 ... 23 E4
Hillworth BECK BR3 * ... 18 D1
Hilton Wy SAND/SEL CR2 ... 47 F5
Himley Rd TOOT SW17 ... 5 G2
Hindhead Wy WLGTN SM6 ... 35 E1
Hinton Rd WLGTN SM6 ... 34 C2
Hitherwood Dr NRWD SE19 ... 8 D1
Hobart Gdns THHTH CR7 ... 16 B2
Hobart Rd WPK KT4 ... 21 F4
Hobbs Rd WNWD SE27 ... 8 A1
Hoffmann Gdns
SAND/SEL CR2 ... 37 E2
Hogarth Crs CROY/NA CR0 ... 26 A1
WIM/MER SW19 ... 5 F5
Hogsmill Wy HOR/WEW KT19 ... 30 A1
Holborn Wy MTCM CR4 ... 13 H1
Holderness Wy WNWD SE27 ... 7 H2

Holland Av BELMT SM2 ... 32 C3
Holland Cl HAYES BR2 ... 29 H3
Holland Rd SNWD SE25 ... 17 E4
The Hollands WPK KT4 ... 20 D2
Holland Wy HAYES BR2 ... 29 H3
Hollies Cl STRHM/NOR SW16 ... 7 G3
Hollingsworth Rd
CROY/NA CR0 ... 37 F2
Hollman Gdns
STRHM/NOR SW16 ... 7 H3
Hollybush Ter NRWD SE19 * ... 8 C3
Holly Cl BECK BR3 ... 19 E3
WLGTN SM6 ... 34 B3
Holly Crs BECK BR3 ... 18 B4
Hollycroft Cl SAND/SEL CR2 ... 36 C1
Holly La BNSTD SM7 ... 52 B3
Holly La East BNSTD SM7 ... 51 H1
Holly La West BNSTD SM7 ... 51 H2
Hollymead CAR SM5 ... 23 H4
Hollymead Rd
COUL/CHIP CR5 ... 53 E3
Hollymoor La
HOR/WEW KT19 ... 30 B5
Holly Tree Rd CTHM CR3 ... 59 G2
Holly Wy MTCM CR4 ... 14 D3
Hollywoods CROY/NA CR0 ... 38 B5
Holman Ct EW KT17 * ... 31 E4
Holman Rd HOR/WEW KT19 ... 30 A1
Holmbury Ct
WIM/MER SW19 ... 5 G4
Holmbury Gv CROY/NA CR0 ... 38 B3
Holmdene Cl BECK BR3 ... 19 E1
Holmes Cl PUR/KEN CR8 ... 45 F3
Holmesdale Cl SNWD SE25 ... 16 D2
Holmesdale Rd
CROY/NA CR0 ... 16 B4
Holmes Rd WIM/MER SW19 ... 5 E4
Holmewood Rd SNWD SE25 ... 16 C2
Holmshaw Cl SYD SE26 ... 10 A1
Holmwood Av
SAND/SEL CR2 ... 46 D3
Holmwood Cl BELMT SM2 ... 31 H4
Holmwood Gdns WLGTN SM6 ... 34 B2
Holmwood Rd BELMT SM2 ... 31 G4
Holne Cha MRDN SM4 ... 12 C5
The Holt MRDN SM4 * ... 12 C3
WLGTN SM6 ... 24 C5
Home Cl CAR SM5 ... 23 H3
Homecroft Rd SYD SE26 ... 9 G2
Home Farm Cl EPSOM KT18 ... 50 D2
Homefield Gdns
KWD/TDW/WH KT20 ... 50 C5
WIM/MER SW19 ... 13 E1
Homefield Ms BECK BR3 * ... 10 C5
Homefield Pk SUT SM1 ... 32 D2
Homefield Rd
COUL/CHIP CR5 ... 54 D5
WARL CR6 ... 56 C5
WIM/MER SW19 ... 4 A3
The Homefield MRDN SM4 * ... 12 C3
Homeland Dr BELMT SM2 ... 32 D4
Homelands Dr NRWD SE19 ... 8 C4
Home Meadow BNSTD SM7 ... 51 G1
Homemead Rd CROY/NA CR0 ... 14 C5
Home Park Rd
WIM/MER SW19 ... 4 B1
Homer Rd CROY/NA CR0 ... 17 H5
Homesdale Rd CTHM CR3 ... 59 F3
Homestead Rd CTHM CR3 ... 59 F3
Homestead Wy
CROY/NA CR0 ... 49 E1
Homewood Gdns
SNWD SE25 * ... 16 C4
Honeysuckle Gdns
CROY/NA CR0 ... 27 H1
Honeywood Wk CAR SM5 ... 23 H5
Honister Hts PUR/KEN CR8 ... 46 B4
Hood Cl CROY/NA CR0 ... 2 B1
Hookfield HOR/WEW KT19 ... 40 A3
Hook Hl SAND/SEL CR2 ... 36 C5
Hook Rd HOR/WEW KT19 ... 30 A5
Hope Cl SUT SM1 ... 33 E1
Hope Pk BMLY BR1 ... 11 H4
Hopton Pde
STRHM/NOR SW16 * ... 7 E2
Hopton Rd
STRHM/NOR SW16 ... 7 E2
Horatius Wy CROY/NA CR0 ... 35 F2
Hornchurch Hl CTHM CR3 ... 55 H2
Horner La MTCM CR4 ... 13 F1
Horsecroft BNSTD SM7 ... 51 F2
Horsecroft Mdw
BNSTD SM7 * ... 51 G1
The Horseshoe BNSTD SM7 ... 42 B5
COUL/CHIP CR5 ... 44 D3
Horsley Cl HOR/WEW KT19 ... 40 B3
Horsley Dr CROY/NA CR0 ... 39 E3
Horton Gdns HOR/WEW KT19 ... 40 A1
Horton Hl HOR/WEW KT19 ... 40 A1
Horton Wy CROY/NA CR0 ... 17 H4
Hotham Road Ms
WIM/MER SW19 ... 5 E4
Houlder Crs CROY/NA CR0 ... 35 H2
Hove Gdns SUT SM1 ... 22 D2
Howard Av EW KT17 ... 31 E5
Howard Rd COUL/CHIP CR5 ... 44 C5
PGE/AN SE20 ... 9 G5
SNWD SE25 ... 17 E4
Howards Crest Cl BECK BR3 ... 19 E1
Howberry Rd THHTH CR7 ... 8 B5
Howden Rd SNWD SE25 ... 16 D1
Howe Dr CTHM CR3 ... 59 F2
Howell Hl BELMT SM2 * ... 31 G5
Howell Hill Cl EW KT17 ... 41 G1
Howell Hill Gv EW KT17 ... 41 G1
How La COUL/CHIP CR5 ... 53 E3
Howley Rd CROY/NA CR0 ... 2 B4
Hoylake Gdns MTCM CR4 ... 14 C2
Hoyle Rd TOOT SW17 ... 5 G2
Hubbard Rd WNWD SE27 ... 8 A1
Hubert Cl WIM/MER SW19 * ... 5 E5
Hughenden Rd WPK KT4 ... 21 E1

Hughes Wk *CROY/NA* CR0 26 A1
Hulverston Cl *BELMT* SM2 32 D5
Hunston Rd *MRDN* SM4 22 D2
Hunter Cl *WLGTN* SM6 35 E3
Hunter Rd *THHTH* CR7 16 B2
Hunters Cl *HOR/WEW* KT19 40 A3
Hunters Meadow
*NRWD* SE19 8 C1
Hunters Wy *CROY/NA* CR0 3 H6
Huntingdon Cl *MTCM* CR4 15 E3
Huntingdon Gdns *WPK* KT4 21 G4
Huntingfield *CROY/NA* CR0 38 B3
Huntly Rd *SNWD* SE25 16 C3
Huntsmans Cl *WARL* CR6 56 C4
Huntsmoor Rd
*HOR/WEW* KT19 30 B1
Hurlstone Rd *SNWD* SE25 16 C4
Hurnford Cl *SAND/SEL* CR2 36 C5
Hurricane Rd *WLGTN* SM6 35 E3
Hurst Cl *HAYES* BR2 29 H2
Hurstcourt Rd *SUT* SM1 22 D2
Hurstdene Av *HAYES* BR2 29 H2
Hurst Rd *CROY/NA* CR0 36 B1
*HOR/WEW* KT19 40 B1
Hurst View Rd *SAND/SEL* CR2 36 C3
Hurst Wy *SAND/SEL* CR2 36 C2
Hutchingson's Rd
*CROY/NA* CR0 49 E1
Hyde Rd *SAND/SEL* CR2 46 C3
Hyde Wk *MRDN* SM4 22 C1
Hylands Ms *EPSOM* KT18 40 A5
Hylands Rd *EPSOM* KT18 40 A5
Hyperion Pl
*HOR/WEW* KT19 30 B4
Hyrstdene *CROY/NA* CR0 2 B7
Hythe Rd *THHTH* CR7 16 B1

## I

Iberian Av *WLGTN* SM6 24 D5
Iden Cl *HAYES* BR2 19 G2
Idlecombe Rd *TOOT* SW17 6 A3
Idmiston Rd *WPK* KT4 20 D1
Idmiston Sq *WPK* KT4 20 D1
Ilex Wy *STRHM/NOR* SW16 7 G2
Ilkley Cl *NRWD* SE19 * 8 B3
Imperial Gdns *MTCM* CR4 14 B2
Imperial Wy *CROY/NA* CR0 35 G2
Inchwood *CROY/NA* CR0 28 D5
Ingatestone Rd *SNWD* SE25 17 F4
Ingham Cl *SAND/SEL* CR2 37 H4
Ingham Rd *SAND/SEL* CR2 37 G4
Ingleboro Dr *PUR/KEN* CR8 46 B3
Ingleby Wy *WLGTN* SM6 34 D4
Inglemere Rd *MTCM* CR4 5 H4
Ingleside Cl *BECK* BR3 10 C4
Ingleton Rd *CAR* SM5 33 G4
Inglewood *CROY/NA* CR0 38 A4
Inglis Rd *CROY/NA* CR0 26 D2
Ingram Rd *THHTH* CR7 8 A5
Innes Cl *RYNPK* SW20 12 A1
Innes Yd *CROY/NA* CR0 2 D5
Inveresk Gdns *WPK* KT4 20 D4
Inverness Rd *WPK* KT4 21 H2
Inwood Av *COUL/CHIP* CR5 54 C5
Inwood Cl *CROY/NA* CR0 28 A3
Iona Cl *MRDN* SM4 22 D1
Ipswich Rd *TOOT* SW17 6 B3
Iris Cl *CROY/NA* CR0 27 H2
Isham Rd
*STRHM/NOR* SW16 15 E1
Island Rd *MTCM* CR4 5 H4
Ivers Wy *CROY/NA* CR0 38 D3
Ivychurch Cl *PGE/AN* SE20 9 F4
Ivydale Rd *CAR* SM5 23 H3
Ivydene Cl *SUT* SM1 23 E5
Ivy Gdns *MTCM* CR4 14 D2
Ivy Rd *TOOT* SW17 5 G2

## J

Jackson Cl *EPSOM* KT18 40 B4
Jackson's Pl *CROY/NA* CR0 3 G1
Jackson's Wy *CROY/NA* CR0 28 C4
Jamaica Rd *THHTH* CR7 15 H5
Jarrow Cl *MRDN* SM4 12 D4
Jarvis Rd *SAND/SEL* CR2 36 B2
Jasmine Gdns *CROY/NA* CR0 28 D4
Jasmine Gv *PGE/AN* SE20 9 F5
Jasper Rd *NRWD* SE19 8 D3
Jean Batten Cl *WLGTN* SM6 35 F3
Jeffs Rd *SUT* SM1 22 B5
Jengar Cl *SUT* SM1 22 D5
Jennett Rd *CROY/NA* CR0 25 G4
Jenson Wy *NRWD* SE19 8 D4
Jeppo's La *MTCM* CR4 13 H3
Jersey Rd *TOOT* SW17 6 B4
Jerviston Gdns
*STRHM/NOR* SW16 7 G3
Jesmond Cl *MTCM* CR4 14 B2
Jesmond Rd *CROY/NA* CR0 26 D1
Jessops Wy *CROY/NA* CR0 14 C5
Jews Wk *SYD* SE26 9 F1
Johns La *MRDN* SM4 13 E4
Johnson Rd *CROY/NA* CR0 26 B1
Johnson's Cl *CAR* SM5 23 H4
John's Ter *CROY/NA* CR0 3 G1
John St *SNWD* SE25 17 E3
Johns Wk *CTHM* CR3 56 A4
Jonson Cl *MTCM* CR4 14 B3
Jordan Cl *SAND/SEL* CR2 46 D1
Joshua Cl *SAND/SEL* CR2 35 H3
Jubilee Rd *CHEAM* SM3 31 H3
Jubilee Wy *WIM/MER* SW19 4 D5
Julien Rd *COUL/CHIP* CR5 44 C5
Junction Rd *SAND/SEL* CR2 36 B2
June Cl *COUL/CHIP* CR5 44 B4
Juniper Gdns *MTCM* CR4 6 C5

## K

Kangley Bridge Rd *SYD* SE26 10 B2
Karen Ct *BMLY* BR1 11 H5
Katharine St *CROY/NA* CR0 2 D4
Katherine Ms *CTHM* CR3 55 H2
Kayemoor Rd *BELMT* SM2 33 G3
Kearton Cl *PUR/KEN* CR8 55 E2
Keats Cl *WIM/MER* SW19 5 F3
Keats Wy *CROY/NA* CR0 17 G5
Keble Cl *WPK* KT4 20 D2
Keble St *TOOT* SW17 5 E1
Keedonwood Rd *BMLY* BR1 11 G1
Keeley Rd *CROY/NA* CR0 2 C3
Keens Cl *STRHM/NOR* SW16 6 D2
Keen's Rd *CROY/NA* CR0 2 D6
Kelling Gdns *CROY/NA* CR0 25 H1
Kellino St *TOOT* SW17 5 H1
Kelsey La *BECK* BR3 18 C2
Kelsey Park Av *BECK* BR3 18 D2
Kelsey Park Rd *BECK* BR3 18 C1
Kelsey Sq *BECK* BR3 18 C1
Kelsey Wy *BECK* BR3 18 C2
Kelso Rd *CAR* SM5 23 E1
Kelvin Gdns *CROY/NA* CR0 25 E1
Kelvington Cl *CROY/NA* CR0 28 A1
Kemble Rd *CROY/NA* CR0 2 A4
Kemerton Rd *BECK* BR3 18 D1
*CROY/NA* CR0 26 D1
Kemp Gdns *CROY/NA* CR0 16 A5
Kempshott Rd
*STRHM/NOR* SW16 7 E4
Kempton Wk *CROY/NA* CR0 18 A5
Kemsing Cl *THHTH* CR7 * 16 A3
Kendale Rd *BMLY* BR1 11 G2
Kendal Gdns *SUT* SM1 23 E3
Kendall Av *BECK* BR3 18 A1
*SAND/SEL* CR2 36 B4
Kendall Av South
*SAND/SEL* CR2 36 B5
Kendall Rd *BECK* BR3 18 A1
Kendor Av *HOR/WEW* KT19 40 A1
Kendra Hall Rd
*SAND/SEL* CR2 35 H3
Kenilworth Av
*WIM/MER* SW19 4 C2
Kenilworth Cl *BNSTD* SM7 51 H1
Kenilworth Rd *EW* KT17 31 E2
*PGE/AN* SE20 9 H5
Kenilworth Ter *BELMT* SM2 32 C3
Kenley Cl *PUR/KEN* CR8 55 F5
Kenley Gdns *THHTH* CR7 15 H3
Kenley La *PUR/KEN* CR8 46 A5
Kenley Rd *WIM/MER* SW19 12 C2
Kenley Wk *CHEAM* SM3 21 H5
Kenlor Rd *TOOT* SW17 5 F2
Kenmare Dr *MTCM* CR4 5 H4
Kenmare Rd *THHTH* CR7 15 G5
Kenmore Rd *PUR/KEN* CR8 45 H4
Kennedy Cl *MTCM* CR4 14 A1
Kennel Wood Crs
*CROY/NA* CR0 49 F2
Kenneth Rd *BNSTD* SM7 43 F5
Kennet Sq *MTCM* CR4 5 G5
Kenny Dr *CAR* SM5 34 A4
Kensington Av *THHTH* CR7 7 G5
Kensington Ter
*SAND/SEL* CR2 36 B3
Kent Cl *MTCM* CR4 15 E3
Kent Gate Wy *CROY/NA* CR0 38 B2
Kent House La *BECK* BR3 10 A3
Kent House Rd *BECK* BR3 9 H4
Kent Rd *WWKM* BR4 28 D2
Kenwood Dr *BECK* BR3 19 E2
Kenwood Rdg
*PUR/KEN* CR8 54 D2
Kerrill Av *COUL/CHIP* CR5 54 C4
Kersey Dr *SAND/SEL* CR2 47 G2
Keston Av *COUL/CHIP* CR5 54 C4
Keston Rd *THHTH* CR7 15 F5
Kestrel Wy *CROY/NA* CR0 39 F4
Keswick Av *WIM/MER* SW19 12 C1
Keswick Cl *SUT* SM1 23 E5
Keswick Rd *WWKM* BR4 29 G3
Kettering St
*STRHM/NOR* SW16 6 B3
Kew Crs *CHEAM* SM3 22 B4
Keynsham Rd *MRDN* SM4 22 D2
Khama Rd *TOOT* SW17 5 G1
Khartoum Rd *TOOT* SW17 5 F1
Kidderminster Pl
*CROY/NA* CR0 25 H2
Kidderminster Rd
*CROY/NA* CR0 25 H2
Kilcorral Cl *EW* KT17 41 E4
Killburns Mill Cl *WLGTN* SM6 24 B4
Killester Gdns *WPK* KT4 21 G5
Kilmartin Av
*STRHM/NOR* SW16 15 G2
Kiln La *EW* KT17 40 C2
Kiln Ms *TOOT* SW17 5 F2
Kimberley Pl *PUR/KEN* CR8 45 G1
Kimberley Rd *BECK* BR3 17 H1
*CROY/NA* CR0 15 H5
Kimble Rd *WIM/MER* SW19 5 F3
Kimpton Park Wy
*CHEAM* SM3 22 B3
Kimpton Rd *CHEAM* SM3 22 B4
King Alfred Av *CAT* SE6 10 C1
Kingcup Cl *CROY/NA* CR0 27 H2
Kingfisher Gdns
*SAND/SEL* CR2 37 H5
Kingfisher Wy *BECK* BR3 17 H4
King Gdns *CROY/NA* CR0 35 H1
King George VI Av
*MTCM* CR4 13 H3
King Henry's Dr
*CROY/NA* CR0 39 E4
Kings Av *BMLY* BR1 11 H3
*CAR* SM5 33 G3
Kingsbridge Rd *MRDN* SM4 21 H1
Kingscote Rd *CROY/NA* CR0 27 F1
Kingscroft Rd *BNSTD* SM7 43 F5
Kingsdale Rd *PGE/AN* SE20 9 H5
Kingsdown Av *SAND/SEL* CR2 35 H5
Kingsdown Rd *CHEAM* SM3 32 A1
*EW* KT17 41 E3
Kings Hall Rd *BECK* BR3 9 H4
Kingshill Av *WPK* KT4 21 E1
Kings Keep *HAYES* BR2 * 19 G2
King's La *SUT* SM1 33 F1
Kingsleigh Pl *MTCM* CR4 13 H2
Kingsleigh Wk *HAYES* BR2 19 H3
Kingsley Av *BNSTD* SM7 42 C5
*SUT* SM1 23 F5
Kingsley Dr *WPK* KT4 20 D3
Kingsley Rd *CROY/NA* CR0 25 G2
*WIM/MER* SW19 4 D2
Kingslyn Crs *NRWD* SE19 16 C1
Kingsmead Av *MTCM* CR4 14 C2
*WPK* KT4 21 F4
Kingsmead Cl
*HOR/WEW* KT19 30 B3
Kings Pde *CAR* SM5 * 23 G4
Kings Rd *BELMT* SM2 32 C5
*MTCM* CR4 14 A2
*SNWD* SE25 17 E2
*WIM/MER* SW19 4 C3
Kings Shade Wk
*HOR/WEW* KT19 * 40 B3
Kingsthorpe Rd *SYD* SE26 9 H1
Kingston Av *CHEAM* SM3 22 A4
Kingston Crs *BECK* BR3 10 B5
Kingston Gdns *CROY/NA* CR0 25 E4
Kingston Rd *HOR/WEW* KT19 30 C1
*RYNPK* SW20 12 A1
*WIM/MER* SW19 4 C4
Kingston Sq *NRWD* SE19 8 B2
Kings Wk *SAND/SEL* CR2 47 F4
Kings Wy *CROY/NA* CR0 35 F1
Kingsway *WWKM* BR4 29 H4
Kingsway Av *SAND/SEL* CR2 37 G4
Kingsway Rd *CHEAM* SM3 32 A3
The Kingsway *EW* KT17 30 D5
Kingswood Av *HAYES* BR2 19 G2
*SAND/SEL* CR2 47 G5
*THHTH* CR7 15 G4
Kingswood Dr *BELMT* SM2 32 D4
*CAR* SM5 23 H2
*DUL* SE21 8 C1
Kingswood La *WARL* CR6 47 G5
Kingswood Rd *HAYES* BR2 19 G2
*PGE/AN* SE20 9 G3
*WIM/MER* SW19 4 B5
Kingswood Wy
*SAND/SEL* CR2 47 H2
*WLGTN* SM6 35 E1
Kingsworth Cl *BECK* BR3 18 A4
Kinloss Rd *CAR* SM5 23 E1
Kinnaird Av *BMLY* BR1 11 H3
Kinnaird Cl *BMLY* BR1 11 H3
Kinross Av *WPK* KT4 21 E3
Kintyre Cl *STRHM/NOR* SW16 15 F1
Kinver Rd *SYD* SE26 9 G1
Kipling Dr *WIM/MER* SW19 5 F3
Kirby Cl *HOR/WEW* KT19 30 D1
Kirkdale *SYD* SE26 9 G1
Kirkdale Cnr *SYD* SE26 * 9 G1
Kirkland Ter *BECK* BR3 10 C3
Kirklees Rd *THHTH* CR7 15 G4
Kirkley Rd *WIM/MER* SW19 4 C5
Kirkly Cl *SAND/SEL* CR2 36 C4
Kirksted Rd *MRDN* SM4 22 D2
Kirkstone Wy *BMLY* BR1 11 G4
Kirtley Rd *SYD* SE26 10 A1
Kitchener Rd *THHTH* CR7 16 B2
Kitley Gdns *NRWD* SE19 8 D5
Kittiwake Cl *SAND/SEL* CR2 38 A5
Knapton Ms *TOOT* SW17 6 A3
Kneller Rd *NWMAL* KT3 20 C1
Knighton Cl *SAND/SEL* CR2 35 H4
Knighton Park Rd *SYD* SE26 9 H2
Knights Hl *WNWD* SE27 7 H2
Knight's Hill Sq *WNWD* SE27 7 H1
Knockholt Cl *BELMT* SM2 32 D5
Knole Cl *CROY/NA* CR0 * 17 G5
Knollmead *BRYLDS* KT5 20 A2
Knolls Cl *WPK* KT4 21 F4
The Knolls *EW* KT17 50 C1
The Knoll *BECK* BR3 10 D5
Knowlton Gn *HAYES* BR2 19 H4
Kohat Rd *WIM/MER* SW19 4 D2
Kooringa *WARL* CR6 56 B4
Kuala Gdns *STRHM/NOR* SW16 7 F5
Kynaston Av *THHTH* CR7 16 A4
Kynaston Ct *CTHM* CR3 59 G5
Kynaston Crs *THHTH* CR7 16 A4
Kynaston Rd *THHTH* CR7 16 A4
Kynersley Cl *CAR* SM5 23 H4

## L

Laburnum Av *SUT* SM1 23 G4
Laburnum Gdns
*CROY/NA* CR0 27 H1
Laburnum Rd *EPSOM* KT18 40 C3
*MTCM* CR4 14 A1
*WIM/MER* SW19 5 E4
Lacey Av *COUL/CHIP* CR5 54 C5
Lacey Dr *COUL/CHIP* CR5 54 C5
Lackford Rd *COUL/CHIP* CR5 52 D3
Lacock Cl *WIM/MER* SW19 5 E3
Lacrosse Wy
*STRHM/NOR* SW16 6 D5
Lacy Gn *COUL/CHIP* CR5 54 C5
Ladas Rd *WNWD* SE27 8 A2
Ladbroke Rd *EPSOM* KT18 40 B4
Ladbrook Rd *SNWD* SE25 16 B3
Ladygrove *CROY/NA* CR0 38 A4
Lady Hay *WPK* KT4 20 D3
Ladymount *WLGTN* SM6 24 D5
Laings Av *MTCM* CR4 13 H1
Lake Gdns *WLGTN* SM6 24 B4
Lakehall Gdns *THHTH* CR7 15 H4
Lakehall Rd *THHTH* CR7 15 H4
Lakehurst Rd
*HOR/WEW* KT19 30 C1
Lake Rd *CROY/NA* CR0 28 B3
*WIM/MER* SW19 4 B2
Lakers Ri *BNSTD* SM7 52 C1
Lakeside *BECK* BR3 18 D2
*HOR/WEW* KT19 30 C2
*WLGTN* SM6 24 B5
Lakeside Cl *SNWD* SE25 17 E1
Lakeview Rd *WNWD* SE27 7 H2
Laleham Ct *SUT* SM1 * 33 E1
Lamberhurst Rd *WNWD* SE27 7 G1
Lambert Rd *BNSTD* SM7 42 C4
Lambert's Pl *CROY/NA* CR0 26 B2
Lambeth Rd *CROY/NA* CR0 25 G2
Lambourn Cl *SAND/SEL* CR2 35 H4
Lambourne Av
*WIM/MER* SW19 4 B1
Lamerock Rd *BMLY* BR1 11 H1
Lammas Av *MTCM* CR4 14 A1
Lancaster Av *MTCM* CR4 15 E4
Lancaster Cl *HAYES* BR2 19 H3
*WPK* KT4 21 F1
Lancaster Gdns
*WIM/MER* SW19 4 A2
Lancaster Rd *SNWD* SE25 16 D1
Lancaster Wy *WPK* KT4 21 G1
Lancastrian Rd *WLGTN* SM6 35 E3
Lancing Rd *CROY/NA* CR0 15 F5
Landgrove Rd
*WIM/MER* SW19 4 C2
Landscape Rd *WARL* CR6 56 B4
Landseer Cl *WIM/MER* SW19 5 E5
Landseer Rd *NWMAL* KT3 20 B1
*SUT* SM1 32 C2
Langcroft Cl *CAR* SM5 23 H4
Langdale Av *MTCM* CR4 13 H2
Langdale Pde *MTCM* CR4 * 13 H1
Langdale Rd *THHTH* CR7 15 G3
Langdon Rd *MRDN* SM4 13 E4
Langdon Wk *MRDN* SM4 13 E4
Langham Dene
*PUR/KEN* CR8 45 H5
Langham Park Pl *HAYES* BR2 19 H3
Langland Gdns *CROY/NA* CR0 28 B3
Langlands Ri *HOR/WEW* KT19 40 A3
Langley Av *WPK* KT4 21 H3
Langley Ct *BECK* BR3 * 18 D3
Langley Oaks Av
*SAND/SEL* CR2 37 F5
Langley Park Rd *BELMT* SM2 33 F3
Langley Pl *WPK* KT4 21 H3
Langley Rd *BECK* BR3 17 H3
*SAND/SEL* CR2 37 H4
*WIM/MER* SW19 4 B5
Langley Wy *WWKM* BR4 29 F2
Langley Wd *BECK* BR3 * 19 G4
Langmead St *WNWD* SE27 7 H1
Langton Av *EW* KT17 40 D1
Langton Wy *CROY/NA* CR0 3 H6
Lankton Cl *BECK* BR3 11 E5
Lansdell Rd *MTCM* CR4 14 A1
Lansdowne Copse *WPK* KT4 * 21 E3
Lansdowne Ct *WPK* KT4 20 D3
Lansdowne Pl *NRWD* SE19 8 D4
Lansdowne Rd *CROY/NA* CR0 2 E2
*HOR/WEW* KT19 30 B3
*PUR/KEN* CR8 45 G2
Lapwing Cl *SAND/SEL* CR2 38 A5
Larbert Rd *STRHM/NOR* SW16 6 C5
Larby Pl *EW* KT17 30 C5
Larch Cl *WARL* CR6 57 E4
Larch Tree Wy *CROY/NA* CR0 28 C4
Larchwood Cl *BNSTD* SM7 51 E1
Larcombe Cl *CROY/NA* CR0 3 J7
Larkbere Rd *SYD* SE26 10 A1
Larkin Cl *COUL/CHIP* CR5 54 B2
Larkspur Wy *HOR/WEW* KT19 30 A1
Lark Wy *CAR* SM5 23 G1
Latham's Wy *CROY/NA* CR0 25 F3
Latimer Cl *WPK* KT4 21 F5
Latimer Rd *CROY/NA* CR0 2 B4
*WIM/MER* SW19 4 D3
Laud St *CROY/NA* CR0 2 C5
Laurel Cl *TOOT* SW17 5 G2
Laurel Crs *CROY/NA* CR0 28 C4
Laurel Gv *PGE/AN* SE20 9 G4
The Laurels *BNSTD* SM7 51 F2
Laurier Rd *CROY/NA* CR0 26 D1
Lavender Av *MTCM* CR4 5 G5
*WPK* KT4 21 G4
Lavender Cl *CAR* SM5 24 A5
*COUL/CHIP* CR5 * 53 G4
*CTHM* CR3 59 E5
Lavender Gv *MTCM* CR4 5 G5
Lavender Rd *CROY/NA* CR0 15 F5
*SUT* SM1 23 F5
*WLGTN* SM6 34 A1
Lavender V *WLGTN* SM6 34 D2
Lavender Wy *CROY/NA* CR0 17 H5
Lavington Rd *CROY/NA* CR0 25 F4
Lawdon Gdns *CROY/NA* CR0 2 B7
Lawford Gdns *PUR/KEN* CR8 55 E1
Lawn Rd *BECK* BR3 10 C4
The Lawns *BELMT* SM2 32 A3
*NRWD* SE19 8 B5
Lawrence Av *NWMAL* KT3 20 C1
Lawrence Rd *SNWD* SE25 16 D3
Lawrie Park Av *SYD* SE26 9 F2
Lawrie Park Crs *SYD* SE26 9 G2
Lawrie Park Gdns *SYD* SE26 9 F2
Lawrie Park Rd *SYD* SE26 9 G3
Laws Cl *SNWD* SE25
Lawson Wk *CAR* SM5
Layard Rd *THHTH* CR7
Layhams Rd *HAYES* BR2
*WWKM* BR4
Layton Crs *CROY/NA* CR0
Lea Cottages *MTCM* CR4 *
Leacroft Cl *PUR/KEN* CR8
Leaf Gv *WNWD* SE27
Leafield Cl *STRHM/NOR* SW16
Leafield Rd *RYNPK* SW20
*SUT* SM1
Leafy Wy *CROY/NA* CR0
Leamington Av *MRDN* SM4
Leander Rd *THHTH* CR7
Lea Rd *BECK* BR3
Leas La *WARL* CR6
Leas Rd *WARL* CR6
Leather Cl *MTCM* CR4
Leaveland Cl *BECK* BR3
Leazes Av *CTHM* CR3
Lebanon Rd *CROY/NA* CR0
Ledbury Rd *CROY/NA* CR0
Ledgers Rd *WARL* CR6
Ledrington Rd *NRWD* SE19
Leechcroft Rd *WLGTN* SM6
Lee Rd *WIM/MER* SW19
The Lees *CROY/NA* CR0
Leeward Gdns
*WIM/MER* SW19
The Leeways *CHEAM* SM3 *
Legion Ct *MRDN* SM4
Leicester Av *MTCM* CR4
Leicester Cl *WPK* KT4
Leicester Rd *CROY/NA* CR0
Leigh Crs *CROY/NA* CR0
Leighton Gdns
*SAND/SEL* CR2
Leighton St *CROY/NA* CR0
Leighton Wy *EPSOM* KT18
Leithcote Gdns
*STRHM/NOR* SW16
Leith Rd *EW* KT17
Leith Towers *BELMT* SM2 *
Lenham Rd *SUT* SM1
*THHTH* CR7
Lennard Av *WWKM* BR4
Lennard Cl *WWKM* BR4
Lennard Rd *CROY/NA* CR0
*PGE/AN* SE20
Lennard Ter *PGE/AN* SE20 *
Lennox Gdns *CROY/NA* CR0
Leof Crs *CAT* SE6
Leominster Rd *MRDN* SM4
Leominster Wk *MRDN* SM4
Leonard Av *MRDN* SM4
Leonard Rd *STRHM/NOR* SW16
Leopold Av *WIM/MER* SW19
Leopold Rd *WIM/MER* SW19
Le Personne Rd *CTHM* CR3
Leslie Gdns *BELMT* SM2
Leslie Grove *CROY/NA* CR0
Leslie Grove Pl *CROY/NA* CR0
Leslie Park Rd *CROY/NA* CR0
Lessingham Av *TOOT* SW17
Lessness Rd *MRDN* SM4
Lestock Cl *SNWD* SE25
Letchworth St *TOOT* SW17
Leveret Cl *CROY/NA* CR0
Leverson St
*STRHM/NOR* SW16
Lewin Rd *STRHM/NOR* SW16
Lewis Rd *MTCM* CR4
*SUT* SM1
Lewiston Cl *WPK* KT4
Lexden Rd *MTCM* CR4
Lexington Ct *PUR/KEN* CR8
Leyburn Gdns *CROY/NA* CR0
Leyfield *WPK* KT4
Leyton Rd *WIM/MER* SW19
Liberty Av *WIM/MER* SW19
Lichfield Wy *SAND/SEL* CR2
Lilac Gdns *CROY/NA* CR0
Lilah Ms *HAYES* BR2
Lilian Rd *STRHM/NOR* SW16
Lilleshall Rd *MRDN* SM4
Limecroft Cl *HOR/WEW* KT19
Lime Gv *WARL* CR6
Limekiln Pl *NRWD* SE19
Lime Meadow Av
*SAND/SEL* CR2
Limes Av *CAR* SM5
*CROY/NA* CR0
*PGE/AN* SE20
Limes Cl *CAR* SM5
Limes Rd *BECK* BR3
*CROY/NA* CR0
Lime Tree Gv *CROY/NA* CR0
Limetree Pl *MTCM* CR4
Lime Tree Wk *WWKM* BR4
Limewood Cl *BECK* BR3
Limpsfield Av *THHTH* CR7
Limpsfield Rd *SAND/SEL* CR2
*WARL* CR6
*WARL* CR6
Lincoln Rd *MTCM* CR4
*SNWD* SE25
*WPK* KT4
Lincoln Ter *BELMT* SM2 *
Linden Av *COUL/CHIP* CR5
*THHTH* CR7
Linden Cl
*KWD/TDW/WH* KT20
Linden Cottages
*WIM/MER* SW19 *
Linden Dr *CTHM* CR3
Linden Gv *PGE/AN* SE20
*WARL* CR6
Linden Leas *WWKM* BR4
Linden Pl *EW* KT17
*MTCM* CR4
The Lindens *CROY/NA* CR0

Linden Wy PUR/KEN CR8 34 C5
Lindfield Rd CROY/NA CR0 16 D5
Lindores Rd CAR SM5 23 E2
Lind Rd SUT SM1 33 E1
Lindsay Cl HOR/WEW KT19 40 A3
Lindsay Rd WPK KT4 21 F3
Lindsey Cl MTCM CR4 15 E3
Lindway WNWD SE27 7 H2
Lingfield Gdns
COUL/CHIP CR5 54 D4
Lingfield Rd WPK KT4 21 G4
Link La WLGTN SM6 34 D2
Link Rd WLGTN SM6 24 A2
Links Av MRDN SM4 12 C3
Links Gdns STRHM/NOR SW16 7 G4
Link's Rd EW KT17 41 E3
TOOT SW17 6 A3
WWKM BR4 29 E2
Links View Rd CROY/NA CR0 28 C4
Links Wy BECK BR3 18 C5
TOOT SW17 5 H3
The Linkway BELMT SM2 33 E4
Linnet Cl SAND/SEL CR2 37 H5
Linton Cl CAR SM5 23 H1
Linton Gld CROY/NA CR0 38 A5
Linton Gv WNWD SE27 7 H2
Linton's La EW KT17 40 C2
Lion Green Rd
COUL/CHIP CR5 44 D5
Lion Rd CROY/NA CR0 16 A4
Lipsham Cl BNSTD SM7 43 F3
Lisle Cl TOOT SW17 6 B1
Lismore WIM/MER SW19 * 4 B2
Lismore Rd SAND/SEL CR2 36 C2
Lissoms Rd COUL/CHIP CR5 53 E3
Lister Cl MTCM CR4 5 G5
Litchfield Av MRDN SM4 22 B1
Litchfield Rd SUT SM1 23 E5
Little Acre BECK BR3 18 C2
Little Bornes DUL SE21 8 C1
Littlebrook Cl CROY/NA CR0 17 H5
Little Ct WWKM BR4 29 G3
Littleheath Rd SAND/SEL CR2 37 F4
Little Orchards EPSOM KT18 40 C4
Little Roke Av PUR/KEN CR8 45 H4
Little Roke Rd PUR/KEN CR8 46 A4
Littlers Cl WIM/MER SW19 5 F5
Littlestone Cl BECK BR3 10 C3
Little Woodcote Est
WLGTN SM6 * 34 B5
Little Woodcote La CAR SM5 44 B2
Liverpool Rd THHTH CR7 16 A2
Livingstone Rd CTHM CR3 59 F2
THHTH CR7 16 B1
Llanthony Rd MRDN SM4 13 F5
Lloyd Av COUL/CHIP CR5 44 A4
STRHM/NOR SW16 7 E5
Lloyd Park Av CROY/NA CR0 3 J7
Lloyd Rd WPK KT4 21 G4
Lloyds Wy BECK BR3 18 A4
Lock's La MTCM CR4 6 A5
Lockwood Cl SYD SE26 9 H1
Lodge Av CROY/NA CR0 25 G4
Lodge Cl EW KT17 31 G5
WLGTN SM6 24 A2
Lodge Gdns BECK BR3 18 B4
Lodge Hl PUR/KEN CR8 45 G5
Lodge La CROY/NA CR0 38 D3
Lodge Pl SUT SM1 32 D1
Lodge Rd CROY/NA CR0 15 H5
SUT SM1 32 D1
WLGTN SM6 34 B1
Lodge Wk WARL CR6 57 G1
Lomas Cl CROY/NA CR0 39 E3
Lombard Rd
WIM/MER SW19 12 D1
Lomond Gdns SAND/SEL CR2 38 A3
London La BMLY BR1 11 H4
London Loop BNSTD SM7 42 C3
COUL/CHIP CR5 58 B1
CROY/NA CR0 27 H4
PUR/KEN CR8 46 C5
SAND/SEL CR2 37 H4
WARL CR6 47 E5
WWKM BR4 29 F5
London Rd BMLY BR1 11 H4
CHEAM SM3 21 H4
CROY/NA CR0 25 H2
CTHM CR3 59 F3
EW KT17 30 D4
MRDN SM4 12 C4
MTCM CR4 13 G3
THHTH CR7 15 G3
THHTH CR7 15 G5
Lonesome Wy MTCM CR4 6 B5
Longacre Pl CAR SM5 * 34 A2
Longcroft Av BNSTD SM7 43 E4
Longdown La North EW KT17 41 E3
Longdown La South
EW KT17 41 E5
Longdown Rd CAT SE6 10 C1
EW KT17 41 E4
Longfellow Rd WPK KT4 21 E2
Longfield BMLY BR1 11 H5
Longfield Av WLGTN SM6 24 A2
Longfield Crs
KWD/TDW/WH KT20 50 C5
Longfield Dr MTCM CR4 5 G5
Longford Ct HOR/WEW KT19 20 A5
Longford Gdns SUT SM1 23 E4
Long Grove Rd
HOR/WEW KT19 40 A1
Longheath Gdns
CROY/NA CR0 17 G4
Long Hl CTHM CR3 61 E1
Longhurst Rd CROY/NA CR0 17 F5
Longlands Av
COUL/CHIP CR5 44 B4
Long La CROY/NA CR0 17 G5
Longley Rd CROY/NA CR0 25 H1
TOOT SW17 5 G3
Longmead Cl CTHM CR3 59 G2
Long Meadow Cl
WWKM BR4 29 E1
Longmead Rd
HOR/WEW KT19 30 C5
TOOT SW17 5 H2
Longmere Gdns
KWD/TDW/WH KT20 50 C4
Longsdon Wy CTHM CR3 60 A4
Longstone Rd TOOT SW17 6 B2
Longthornton Rd
STRHM/NOR SW16 14 C1
Longton Av SYD SE26 9 E1
Longton Gv SYD SE26 9 F1
Long Wk EPSOM KT18 50 D4
Longwood Ct WPK KT4 21 E3
Longwood Rd PUR/KEN CR8 55 F1
Lonsdale Gdns THHTH CR7 15 F3
Lonsdale Rd SNWD SE25 17 F3
Lordsbury Fld WLGTN SM6 34 C5
Lordsgrove Cl
KWD/TDW/WH KT20 50 B5
Lorne Av CROY/NA CR0 27 H1
Lorne Gdns CROY/NA CR0 27 H1
Loubet St TOOT SW17 5 H3
Love La CHEAM SM3 32 A2
MRDN SM4 22 C1
MTCM CR4 13 G2
SNWD SE25 17 F2
Lovelock Cl PUR/KEN CR8 55 E2
Lovett Dr CAR SM5 23 E1
Lower Addiscombe Rd
CROY/NA CR0 3 J1
Lower Barn Rd PUR/KEN CR8 46 B3
Lower Church St
CROY/NA CR0 2 B3
Lower Coombe St
CROY/NA CR0 2 D6
Lower Court Rd
HOR/WEW KT19 40 B1
Lower Dunnymans
BNSTD SM7 42 B4
Lower Green Gdns WPK KT4 21 E2
Lower Gn West MTCM CR4 13 H2
Lower Morden La MRDN SM4 12 A5
Lower Northfield BNSTD SM7 42 B4
Lower Park Rd
COUL/CHIP CR5 52 C3
Lower Pillory Down CAR SM5 44 B2
Lower Rd PUR/KEN CR8 45 H3
SUT SM1 33 F1
Lower Sawleywood
BNSTD SM7 42 B4
Lowry Crs MTCM CR4 13 G1
Loxford Rd CTHM CR3 59 H5
Loxford Wy CTHM CR3 59 H5
Loxley Cl SYD SE26 9 H2
Lucas Rd PGE/AN SE20 9 G3
Lucerne Rd THHTH CR7 15 H4
Lucien Rd TOOT SW17 6 A1
Ludford Cl CROY/NA CR0 2 A6
Lullington Garth BMLY BR1 11 G4
Lullington Rd PGE/AN SE20 9 E4
Lulworth Crs MTCM CR4 13 G1
Lumley Gdns CHEAM SM3 32 A1
Lumley Rd CHEAM SM3 32 A2
Luna Rd THHTH CR7 16 A2
Lunghurst Rd CTHM CR3 61 G1
Lunham Rd NRWD SE19 8 C3
Lupin Cl CROY/NA CR0 27 H2
Lushington Rd CAT SE6 10 D2
Lyall Av DUL SE21 8 C1
Lyconby Gdns CROY/NA CR0 28 A1
Lyle Cl MTCM CR4 24 A1
Lymbourne Cl BELMT SM2 32 C5
Lymer Av NRWD SE19 8 D2
Lyme Regis Rd BNSTD SM7 51 F2
Lymescote Gdns SUT SM1 22 C3
Lymington Cl
STRHM/NOR SW16 14 D1
Lymington Gdns
HOR/WEW KT19 30 D1
Lyncroft Gdns EW KT17 30 D4
Lyndhurst Av
STRHM/NOR SW16 14 D1
Lyndhurst Cl CROY/NA CR0 3 J5
Lyndhurst Ct BELMT SM2 * 32 C3
Lyndhurst Leys HAYES BR2 * 19 F1
Lyndhurst Prior SNWD SE25 * 16 C2
Lyndhurst Rd COUL/CHIP CR5 53 E1
THHTH CR7 15 G3
Lyndhurst Wy BELMT SM2 32 C4
Lyndon Av WLGTN SM6 24 A4
Lyndon Yd TOOT SW17 4 D1
Lynmouth Av MRDN SM4 21 H1
Lynne Cl SAND/SEL CR2 47 G1
Lynscott Wy SAND/SEL CR2 35 H4
Lynsted Ct BECK BR3 18 A1
Lynton Rd CROY/NA CR0 15 G5
Lynwood Av COUL/CHIP CR5 44 B5
EW KT17 40 D4
Lynwood Dr WPK KT4 21 E3
Lynwood Gdns CROY/NA CR0 25 F5
Lynwood Rd EW KT17 40 D4
Lynwood Ter
WIM/MER SW19 * 4 B5
Lyon Rd WIM/MER SW19 5 E5
Lyric Ms SYD SE26 9 G1
Lysander Rd CROY/NA CR0 35 F2
Lytchgate Cl SAND/SEL CR2 36 C3
Lytton Gdns WLGTN SM6 24 D5
Lyveden Rd TOOT SW17 5 G3


## M


Maberley Crs NRWD SE19 9 E4
Maberley Rd BECK BR3 17 H2
BMLY BR1 11 H5
NRWD SE19 8 D5
Macaulay Rd CTHM CR3 59 G2
Macclesfield Rd SNWD SE25 17 G4
Mackenzie Rd BECK BR3 17 H1
Macmillan Wy TOOT SW17 6 B1
Madans Wk EPSOM KT18 40 B4
Madeira Av BMLY BR1 11 G5
Madeira Rd MTCM CR4 13 H3
STRHM/NOR SW16 7 E2
Madeira Wk EPSOM KT18 40 B4
Madeline Rd PGE/AN SE20 9 E4
Magazine Rd CTHM CR3 58 D2
Magdala Rd SAND/SEL CR2 36 B3
Magnolia Wy HOR/WEW KT19 30 A1
Magpie Cl COUL/CHIP CR5 53 G3
Maidenshaw Rd
HOR/WEW KT19 40 B2
The Maisonettes SUT SM1 * 32 B1
Maitland Rd PGE/AN SE20 9 H3
Malcolm Cl PGE/AN SE20 * 9 G4
Malcolm Rd COUL/CHIP CR5 44 D5
PGE/AN SE20 9 G4
SNWD SE25 17 E5
WIM/MER SW19 4 A3
Malden Av SNWD SE25 17 F3
Malden Green Av WPK KT4 20 D2
Malden Rd CHEAM SM3 21 H5
NWMAL KT3 20 D1
Maldon Rd WLGTN SM6 34 B1
Mallard Rd SAND/SEL CR2 37 H5
Mallard Wk BECK BR3 17 H4
Mallard Wy WLGTN SM6 34 C4
Malling Cl CROY/NA CR0 * 17 G5
Malling Gdns MRDN SM4 13 E5
Malling Wy HAYES BR2 29 H1
Mallinson Rd CROY/NA CR0 24 D4
Mallow Cl CROY/NA CR0 27 H2
KWD/TDW/WH KT20 50 B4
Malmains Cl BECK BR3 19 F4
Malmains Wy BECK BR3 19 E3
Malmesbury Rd MRDN SM4 23 E1
Malory Cl BECK BR3 18 A1
The Maltings SNWD SE25 * 16 C2
Malvern Cl MTCM CR4 14 C2
Malvern Rd THHTH CR7 15 G3
Manchester Rd THHTH CR7 16 A2
Mandeville Cl WIM/MER SW19 4 A4
Mann Cl CROY/NA CR0 2 C4
Manor Av CTHM CR3 59 G4
Manor Cl WARL CR6 57 E2
WPK KT4 20 C2
Manor Dr HOR/WEW KT19 30 C2
Manor Dr North NWMAL KT3 20 B1
The Manor Dr WPK KT4 20 D2
Manor Farm Cl WPK KT4 20 C2
Manor Farm Rd
STRHM/NOR SW16 15 G1
Manor Gdns RYNPK SW20 12 B1
SAND/SEL CR2 36 D2
Manor Green Rd
HOR/WEW KT19 40 A2
Manor Gv BECK BR3 18 D1
Manor Hl BNSTD SM7 43 H5
Manor House Ct
EPSOM KT18 * 40 A3
Manor La SUT SM1 33 E1
Manor Park Cl WWKM BR4 28 D2
Manor Park Rd SUT SM1 33 E1
WWKM BR4 28 D2
Manor Pl MTCM CR4 14 C2
SUT SM1 32 D1
Manor Rd BECK BR3 18 C1
BELMT SM2 32 B3
MTCM CR4 14 C2
RYNPK SW20 12 B1
SNWD SE25 17 E3
WLGTN SM6 24 B5
WWKM BR4 28 D3
Manor Rd North WLGTN SM6 24 B5
Manor Wy BECK BR3 18 C2
BNSTD SM7 52 D1
MTCM CR4 14 C2
PUR/KEN CR8 45 E2
SAND/SEL CR2 36 C2
WPK KT4 20 C2
The Manor Wy WLGTN SM6 24 B5
Manor Wood Rd
PUR/KEN CR8 45 E3
Mansard Beeches TOOT SW17 6 A2
Mansell Wy CTHM CR3 59 F2
Mansel Rd WIM/MER SW19 4 A3
Mansfield Rd SAND/SEL CR2 36 B2
Manship Rd MTCM CR4 6 A5
Manston Cl PGE/AN SE20 9 G5
Mantilla Rd TOOT SW17 6 A1
Mantlet Cl STRHM/NOR SW16 6 C4
Maple Cl CTHM CR3 55 H2
MTCM CR4 6 B5
Mapledale Av CROY/NA CR0 27 F4
Maple Ms STRHM/NOR SW16 7 F2
Maple Pl BNSTD SM7 41 H4
Maple Rd CTHM CR3 55 H2
PGE/AN SE20 9 G4
The Maples BNSTD SM7 42 D3
Maplethorpe Rd THHTH CR7 15 G3
Marbles Wy
KWD/TDW/WH KT20 50 D4
Marchmont Rd WLGTN SM6 34 C4
Marcuse Rd CTHM CR3 59 F3
Mardell Rd CROY/NA CR0 17 H4
Marden Crs CROY/NA CR0 15 F5
Marden Rd CROY/NA CR0 15 F5
Maresfield CROY/NA CR0 3 H4
Marfield Cl WPK KT4 21 E2
Marfleet Cl CAR SM5 23 G3
Margaret Wy COUL/CHIP CR5 54 D4
Marham Gdns MRDN SM4 13 E5
Marian Rd STRHM/NOR SW16 6 C5
Mariette Wy WLGTN SM6 35 E4
Marigold Wy CROY/NA CR0 27 H2
Marion Rd THHTH CR7 16 A4
Market Pde EW KT17 * 30 D4
SNWD SE25 * 17 E3
Markfield CROY/NA CR0 48 B1
Markfield Rd CTHM CR3 60 B5
Marks Rd WARL CR6 57 E3
Markville Gdns CTHM CR3 60 B5
Markwell Cl SYD SE26 9 F1
Marlborough Cl
WIM/MER SW19 5 G3
Marlborough Ms BNSTD SM7 42 C5
Marlborough Rd
SAND/SEL CR2 36 A3
SUT SM1 22 C4
WIM/MER SW19 5 G3
Marlings Cl CTHM CR3 55 G2
Marlins Cl SUT SM1 * 33 E1
Marlow Cl PGE/AN SE20 17 F2
Marlow Dr CHEAM SM3 21 H4
Marlowe Sq MTCM CR4 14 C3
Marlowe Wy CROY/NA CR0 25 E3
Marlow Rd PGE/AN SE20 17 F2
Marlpit Av COUL/CHIP CR5 54 A2
Marlpit La COUL/CHIP CR5 53 H1
Maroons Wy CAT SE6 10 C2
Marryat Pl WIM/MER SW19 4 A1
Marshall Cl SAND/SEL CR2 47 E3
Marshalls Cl HOR/WEW KT19 40 A3
Marshall's Rd SUT SM1 22 D5
Marsh Av HOR/WEW KT19 30 C5
MTCM CR4 13 H1
Marston HOR/WEW KT19 40 A1
Marston Dr WARL CR6 57 E3
Marston Wy NRWD SE19 7 H4
Martin Cl SAND/SEL CR2 47 H1
WARL CR6 56 B1
Martin Crs CROY/NA CR0 25 F2
Martin Gv MRDN SM4 12 C2
Martins Cl WWKM BR4 29 F3
Martin's Rd HAYES BR2 19 G1
The Martins SYD SE26 9 F2
Martin Wy MRDN SM4 12 A2
Marwell Cl WWKM BR4 29 H3
Maryhill Cl PUR/KEN CR8 55 E2
Maryland Rd THHTH CR7 7 H5
Mason Rd SUT SM1 32 D1
Mason's Av CROY/NA CR0 2 D5
Masons Ct EW KT17 * 31 E4
Mason's Pl MTCM CR4 5 H5
Massingberd Wy TOOT SW17 6 B1
Masters Cl STRHM/NOR SW16 6 C3
Mathias Cl EPSOM KT18 40 A3
Matilda Cl NRWD SE19 8 B4
Matlock Crs CHEAM SM3 22 A5
Matlock Gdns CHEAM SM3 32 A1
Matlock Pl CHEAM SM3 22 A5
Matlock Rd CTHM CR3 59 G2
Matthew Ct MTCM CR4 14 D4
Matthew's Gdns
CROY/NA CR0 49 F1
Maurice Av CTHM CR3 59 F2
Mavis Av HOR/WEW KT19 30 C1
Mavis Cl HOR/WEW KT19 30 C1
Mawson Cl RYNPK SW20 12 A1
Maxwell Cl CROY/NA CR0 25 E2
Maybourne Cl SYD SE26 9 F3
Maybury Cl
KWD/TDW/WH KT20 51 E4
Maybury St TOOT SW17 5 G2
Maycross Av MRDN SM4 12 B3
Mayday Rd THHTH CR7 15 H5
Mayefield Rd THHTH CR7 15 F3
Mayes Cl WARL CR6 56 D3
Mayfair Av WPK KT4 21 E2
Mayfair Cl BECK BR3 10 D5
Mayfield Cl PGE/AN SE20 9 F5
Mayfield Crs THHTH CR7 15 F3
Mayfield Rd BELMT SM2 33 F2
SAND/SEL CR2 36 B4
WIM/MER SW19 4 B5
Mayford Cl BECK BR3 17 H2
Maynooth Gdns CAR SM5 23 H1
Mayo Rd CROY/NA CR0 16 B4
Mayow Rd SYD SE26 9 H1
May's Hill Rd HAYES BR2 19 H2
Maytree Ct MTCM CR4 14 A2
Maywater Cl SAND/SEL CR2 46 B1
Maywood Cl BECK BR3 * 10 D4
McIntosh Cl WLGTN SM6 35 E3
McRae La MTCM CR4 23 H1
Mead Crs SUT SM1 23 G5
Meadfoot Rd
STRHM/NOR SW16 6 C5
Meadow Av CROY/NA CR0 17 H5
Meadow Cl CAT SE6 10 C2
PUR/KEN CR8 44 D3
Meadow Ct EPSOM KT18 40 A3
Meadow Hl COUL/CHIP CR5 44 C3
Meadow Ri COUL/CHIP CR5 44 D3
Meadow Rd HAYES BR2 11 G5
SUT SM1 23 G5
WIM/MER SW19 5 E4
Meadowside Rd BELMT SM2 32 A4
The Meadows WARL CR6 56 D2
Meadow Stile CROY/NA CR0 2 D5
Meadowview Rd CAT SE6 10 C1
HOR/WEW KT19 30 C4
Meadow View Rd
THHTH CR7 15 H4
Meadow Wk EW KT17 30 D3
WLGTN SM6 24 B4
Meadow Wy
KWD/TDW/WH KT20 51 E2
Mead Pl CROY/NA CR0 2 B1
Mead Rd CTHM CR3 59 H3
Meadside Cl BECK BR3 10 A5
The Meads CHEAM SM3 21 H4
MRDN SM4 * 13 G4
The Mead BECK BR3 19 E1
WLGTN SM6 34 D2
WWKM BR4 29 F2
Meadvale Rd CROY/NA CR0 26 D1
Mead Wy COUL/CHIP CR5 54 A3
CROY/NA CR0 28 A3
HAYES BR2 19 H5
Meadway BECK BR3 11 E5
BRYLDS KT5 20 A2
HOR/WEW KT19 40 A3
WARL CR6 56 C1
Meaford Wy PGE/AN SE20 9 F4
Medland Cl WLGTN SM6 24 A2
Medway Cl CROY/NA CR0 17 G5
Melbourne Cl WLGTN SM6 34 C1
Melbourne Rd
WIM/MER SW19 4 D5
WLGTN SM6 34 B1
Melfield Gdns CAT SE6 10 D1
Melfort Av THHTH CR7 15 H2
Melfort Rd THHTH CR7 15 H2
Meller Cl CROY/NA CR0 25 E4
Mellison Rd TOOT SW17 5 G2
Mellow Cl BNSTD SM7 42 D4
Mellows Rd WLGTN SM6 34 D1
Melrose Av MTCM CR4 6 B4
STRHM/NOR SW16 15 F2
Melrose Rd COUL/CHIP CR5 44 B5
WIM/MER SW19 12 C1
Melrose Vls BECK BR3 * 18 C1
Melsa Rd MRDN SM4 13 E5
Melton Flds HOR/WEW KT19 30 B4
Melton Pl HOR/WEW KT19 30 B4
Melville Av SAND/SEL CR2 36 D1
Melvin Rd PGE/AN SE20 9 G5
Mendip Cl SYD SE26 9 G1
WPK KT4 21 G3
Menlo Gdns NRWD SE19 8 B4
Meopham Rd MTCM CR4 6 C5
Merantum Wy WIM/MER SW19 5 E5
Merchants Cl SNWD SE25 17 E3
Merebank La WLGTN SM6 35 F1
Mere End CROY/NA CR0 27 H1
Merefield Gdns
KWD/TDW/WH KT20 50 D4
Merevale Crs MRDN SM4 13 E5
Merewood Gdns CROY/NA CR0 27 H1
Mereworth Cl HAYES BR2 19 H4
Merland Cl
KWD/TDW/WH KT20 50 C5
Merland Gn
KWD/TDW/WH KT20 50 C5
Merland Ri EPSOM KT18 50 C4
Merlewood Cl CTHM CR3 55 F5
Merlin Cl CROY/NA CR0 3 G6
MTCM CR4 13 G2
WLGTN SM6 35 F2
Merlin Gv BECK BR3 18 B3
Merrilands Rd WPK KT4 21 G2
Merrin Hl SAND/SEL CR2 46 C2
Merrow Rd BELMT SM2 31 H4
Merrow Wy CROY/NA CR0 39 E2
Merrymeet BNSTD SM7 43 H4
Mersham Pl PGE/AN SE20 9 F5
THHTH CR7 16 B1
Mersham Rd THHTH CR7 16 B2
Merton Gdns
KWD/TDW/WH KT20 50 D4
Merton Hall Gdns
RYNPK SW20 4 A5
Merton Hall Rd
WIM/MER SW19 4 B5
Merton High St
WIM/MER SW19 5 E4
Merton Pl WIM/MER SW19 * 5 E5
Merton Rd SNWD SE25 16 D4
WIM/MER SW19 4 D4
Meteor Wy WLGTN SM6 35 E3
The Mews BECK BR3 10 C5
STRHM/NOR SW16 * 7 F5
Michael Rd SNWD SE25 16 C2
Michelham Gdns
KWD/TDW/WH KT20 * 50 C5
Mickleham Gdns CHEAM SM3 32 A2
Mickleham Wy CROY/NA CR0 39 F3
Middle Cl COUL/CHIP CR5 54 C5
EW KT17 40 C2
Middlefields CROY/NA CR0 38 A4
Middle La EW KT17 40 C2
Middle Rd STRHM/NOR SW16 14 C1
Middlesex Rd MTCM CR4 15 E4
Middle St CROY/NA CR0 2 D3
Middleton Rd CAR SM5 23 G1
HOR/WEW KT19 * 30 B5
MRDN SM4 12 D5
Middle Wy STRHM/NOR SW16 14 D1
Midholm Rd CROY/NA CR0 28 A4
Midhurst Av CROY/NA CR0 25 G1
Midway CHEAM SM3 22 B1
Milburn Wk EPSOM KT18 40 C5
Mile Rd WLGTN SM6 24 A2
Miles Rd HOR/WEW KT19 40 B2
MTCM CR4 13 G2
Milestone Cl BELMT SM2 33 F2
Milestone Rd NRWD SE19 8 D3
Milford Gdns CROY/NA CR0 17 G4
Milford Gv SUT SM1 23 E5
Milford Ms STRHM/NOR SW16 7 F1
Millais Crs HOR/WEW KT19 30 C1
Millais Rd NWMAL KT3 20 C1
Millais Wy HOR/WEW KT19 20 A5
Mill Cl CAR SM5 * 24 A3
Miller Cl MTCM CR4 23 H1
Miller Rd CROY/NA CR0 25 F2
WIM/MER SW19 5 F3
Mill Gdns SYD SE26 9 F1
Mill Gn MTCM CR4 * 24 A1
Mill Green Rd MTCM CR4 24 A1
Millhouse Pl WNWD SE27 7 H1
Mill La CAR SM5 24 A5
CROY/NA CR0 25 G4
EW KT17 30 D4
Mill Rd EW KT17 40 D2
WIM/MER SW19 5 E4
Millside CAR SM5 23 H3
Mill View Cl EW KT17 30 D3
Mill View Gdns CROY/NA CR0 27 H4
Milne Pk East CROY/NA CR0 49 F1
Milne Pk West CROY/NA CR0 49 F1
Milner Ap CTHM CR3 60 A1

Milner Cl CTHM CR3 60 A2
Milner Rd CTHM CR3 60 A2
MRDN SM4 13 F4
THHTH CR7 16 A2
WIM/MER SW19 4 D5
Milton Av CROY/NA CR0 26 B1
SUT SM1 23 F4
Milton Cl SUT SM1 23 F4
Milton Gdns EPSOM KT18 40 C4
Milton Rd CROY/NA CR0 26 B1
CTHM CR3 59 F1
MTCM CR4 6 A4
SUT SM1 22 C5
WIM/MER SW19 5 E3
WLGTN SM6 34 C2
Mina Rd WIM/MER SW19 4 C5
Minden Rd CHEAM SM3 22 A3
PGE/AN SE20 9 F5
Minehead Rd
STRHM/NOR SW16 7 F2
Minshull Pl BECK BR3 * 10 C4
Minster Av SUT SM1 22 C3
Minster Dr CROY/NA CR0 3 G6
Mint Rd BNSTD SM7 52 A1
WLGTN SM6 34 B1
Mint Wk CROY/NA CR0 2 D4
WARL CR6 56 D2
Missenden Gdns MRDN SM4 13 E5
Mistletoe Cl CROY/NA CR0 27 H2
Mitcham La
STRHM/NOR SW16 6 C2
Mitcham Pk MTCM CR4 13 H3
Mitcham Rd CROY/NA CR0 25 G1
TOOT SW17 5 H2
Mitchley Av PUR/KEN CR8 46 B3
Mitchley Gv SAND/SEL CR2 47 E3
Mitchley Hl SAND/SEL CR2 46 D3
Mitchley Vw SAND/SEL CR2 47 E3
Mitre Cl BELMT SM2 33 E3
Moffat Rd THHTH CR7 16 A1
TOOT SW17 5 G1
Moir Cl SAND/SEL CR2 37 E4
Mole Ct HOR/WEW KT19 20 A5
Molesey Dr CHEAM SM3 22 A3
Mollison Dr WLGTN SM6 35 E3
Molyneux Dr TOOT SW17 6 B1
Monahan Av PUR/KEN CR8 45 F2
Monarch Cl WWKM BR4 29 H5
Monarch Ms
STRHM/NOR SW16 7 G2
Monarch Pde MTCM CR4 * 13 H1
Money Av CTHM CR3 59 F2
Money Rd CTHM CR3 59 F2
Mongers La EW KT17 30 D5
Monivea Rd BECK BR3 10 B4
Monkleigh Rd MRDN SM4 12 A2
Monksdene Gdns SUT SM1 22 D4
Monks Orchard Rd BECK BR3 28 C2
Monks Rd BNSTD SM7 51 G2
Monks Wy BECK BR3 18 C5
Monmouth Cl MTCM CR4 15 E3
Montacute Rd CROY/NA CR0 39 E4
MRDN SM4 13 F5
Montague Av
SAND/SEL CR2 46 C2
Montague Dr CTHM CR3 59 E2
Montague Rd CROY/NA CR0 25 H2
WIM/MER SW19 4 D4
Montague Ter HAYES BR2 * 19 H3
Montagu Gdns WLGTN SM6 24 C5
Montana Cl SAND/SEL CR2 36 B5
Montana Gdns SUT SM1 33 E1
SYD SE26 10 B2
Montgomery Cl MTCM CR4 * 15 E3
Montgomery Gdns
BELMT SM2 33 F3
Montpelier Rd PUR/KEN CR8 35 H5
SUT SM1 23 E5
Montrave Rd PGE/AN SE20 9 G3
Montrose Gdns MTCM CR4 13 H2
SUT SM1 22 D3
Montrouge Crs EW KT17 50 C1
Montserrat Cl NRWD SE19 8 B2
Moore Cl MTCM CR4 * 14 B1
Mooreland Rd BMLY BR1 11 H4
Moore Rd NRWD SE19 8 A3
Moore Wy BELMT SM2 32 C4
Moormead Dr
HOR/WEW KT19 30 C1
Moorside Rd BMLY BR1 11 G1
Moorsom Wy COUL/CHIP CR5 53 H2
Morden Cl
KWD/TDW/WH KT20 50 D5
Morden Ct MRDN SM4 12 D3
Morden Court Pde
MRDN SM4 * 12 D2
Morden Gdns MTCM CR4 13 F3
Morden Hall Rd MRDN SM4 12 D2
Morden Rd MTCM CR4 13 F3
WIM/MER SW19 12 D1
Morden Wy CHEAM SM3 22 C1
More Cl PUR/KEN CR8 45 F1
Moremead Rd CAT SE6 10 B1
Moreton Rd SAND/SEL CR2 36 B1
WPK KT4 21 E3
Moring Rd TOOT SW17 6 A1
Morland Av CROY/NA CR0 26 C2
Morland Cl MTCM CR4 13 G2
Morland Rd CROY/NA CR0 26 D1
PGE/AN SE20 9 H4
SUT SM1 33 E2
Morley Rd CHEAM SM3 22 B2
SAND/SEL CR2 36 D5
Morningside Rd WPK KT4 21 F3
Morris Cl CROY/NA CR0 18 A5
Morston Cl
KWD/TDW/WH KT20 50 B5
Mortimer Crs WPK KT4 20 B4
Mortimer Rd MTCM CR4 5 H5
Mortlake Cl CROY/NA CR0 25 F4
Mortlake Dr MTCM CR4 5 G5
Morton Cl WLGTN SM6 35 F3
Morton Gdns WLGTN SM6 34 C1
Morton Rd MRDN SM4 13 F4
Mospey Crs EW KT17 40 D5
Moss Gdns SAND/SEL CR2 37 H3
Mosslea Rd CTHM CR3 55 H1
PGE/AN SE20 9 G4
Mossville Gdns MRDN SM4 12 B2
Mostyn Rd WIM/MER SW19 12 B2
Moth Cl WLGTN SM6 35 E3
Mountacre Cl SYD SE26 8 D1
Mount Av CTHM CR3 59 E4
Mountbatten Cl NRWD SE19 8 C2
Mount Cl CAR SM5 34 A4
PUR/KEN CR8 55 E1
Mount Ct WWKM BR4 29 G3
Mount Pk CAR SM5 34 A4
Mount Park Av
SAND/SEL CR2 35 H4
Mount Pleasant EW KT17 30 D5
WNWD SE27 8 A1
Mount Pleasant Rd
CTHM CR3 60 A3
Mount Rd MTCM CR4 13 F1
NRWD SE19 * 8 B3
The Mount COUL/CHIP CR5 44 A5
EW KT17 21 F5
EW KT17 30 D5
WARL CR6 56 A4
Mount Wy CAR SM5 34 A4
Mountwood Cl
SAND/SEL CR2 37 F5
Mowbray Rd NRWD SE19 8 D5
Moys Cl CROY/NA CR0 15 E5
Moyser Rd STRHM/NOR SW16 6 B2
Muchelney Rd MRDN SM4 13 E5
Muggeridge Cl
SAND/SEL CR2 36 B1
Mulberry Cl STRHM/NOR SW16 6 C1
Mulberry Ga BNSTD SM7 51 F1
Mulberry La CROY/NA CR0 3 K1
Mulgrave Rd BELMT SM2 32 B3
CROY/NA CR0 2 E5
Mulholland Cl MTCM CR4 14 B1
Mullards Cl MTCM CR4 23 H2
Munslow Gdns SUT SM1 23 E5
Muschamp Rd CAR SM5 23 G3
Mylis Cl SYD SE26 9 F1
Myrna Cl WIM/MER SW19 5 G4
Myrtle Rd CROY/NA CR0 28 C4
SUT SM1 33 E1

N

Namba Roy Cl
STRHM/NOR SW16 7 F1
Namton Dr THHTH CR7 15 F3
Napier Ct CTHM CR3 59 G2
Napier Rd SAND/SEL CR2 36 B3
SNWD SE25 17 F3
Narrow La WARL CR6 56 C4
Naseby Rd NRWD SE19 8 B3
Nash Cl SUT SM1 23 F4
Natal Rd STRHM/NOR SW16 6 D3
THHTH CR7 16 B2
Neath Gdns MRDN SM4 13 E5
Nello James Gdns
WNWD SE27 8 B1
Nelson Cl CROY/NA CR0 2 B1
Nelson Grove Rd
WIM/MER SW19 4 D5
Nelson Rd CTHM CR3 59 F3
WIM/MER SW19 4 D4
Nesbitt Sq NRWD SE19 * 8 C4
The Netherlands
COUL/CHIP CR5 53 G4
Nethern Court Rd
CTHM CR3 61 G3
Netley Cl CHEAM SM3 31 H1
CROY/NA CR0 39 E3
Netley Gdns MRDN SM4 23 E1
Netley Rd MRDN SM4 23 E1
Nettlecombe Cl BELMT SM2 32 D4
Nettlestead Cl BECK BR3 10 B4
Nettlewood Rd
STRHM/NOR SW16 6 D4
Neville Cl BNSTD SM7 42 D4
Neville Rd CROY/NA CR0 26 B1
Neville Wk CAR SM5 23 G1
Nevil Wk CAR SM5 * 23 G1
Newark Rd SAND/SEL CR2 36 B2
New Barn Cl WLGTN SM6 35 F2
New Barn La CTHM CR3 55 G2
New Barns Av MTCM CR4 14 D3
Newbolt Av CHEAM SM3 31 G1
Newbury Gdns
HOR/WEW KT19 20 D5
New Cl WIM/MER SW19 13 E2
Newcome Gdns
STRHM/NOR SW16 7 E1
Newdigate
STRHM/NOR SW16 * 7 G1
Newent Cl CAR SM5 23 H2
Newgate CROY/NA CR0 26 A2
New Green Pl NRWD SE19 8 C3
Newhaven Rd SNWD SE25 16 B4
Newhouse Cl NWMAL KT3 20 C1
Newhouse Wk MRDN SM4 23 E1
Newlands Pk SYD SE26 9 G3
Newlands Rd
STRHM/NOR SW16 15 E1
The Newlands WLGTN SM6 34 C3
Newlands Woods
CROY/NA CR0 38 B4
Newman Rd CROY/NA CR0 25 F1
Newminster Rd MRDN SM4 23 E1
Newnham Cl THHTH CR7 16 A1
New Rd MTCM CR4 24 A2
Newstead Wk CAR SM5 23 E1
Newton Rd PUR/KEN CR8 44 C2
WIM/MER SW19 4 A4
Nicholas Rd CROY/NA CR0 25 E5
Nicholson Rd CROY/NA CR0 26 D2
Nicola Cl SAND/SEL CR2 36 A2
Nicolls Cl CTHM CR3 59 E2
Niederwald Rd SYD SE26 10 A1
Nightingale Cl CAR SM5 24 A3
Nightingale Ct SUT SM1 33 E1
Nightingale Rd CAR SM5 23 H4
SAND/SEL CR2 47 H1
Nimbus Rd HOR/WEW KT19 30 B5
Nimrod Rd STRHM/NOR SW16 6 B3
Nineacres Wy
COUL/CHIP CR5 54 A1
Ninehams Cl CTHM CR3 55 F5
Ninehams Gdns CTHM CR3 55 F5
Ninehams Rd CTHM CR3 59 F1
Nineteenth Rd MTCM CR4 15 E3
Nonsuch Court Av EW KT17 31 F5
Nonsuch Pl CHEAM SM3 * 31 H3
Nonsuch Wk BELMT SM2 31 H5
Norbury Av STRHM/NOR SW16 7 F5
Norbury Cl STRHM/NOR SW16 7 G5
Norbury Court Rd
STRHM/NOR SW16 15 E1
Norbury Crs
STRHM/NOR SW16 15 G1
Norbury Cross
STRHM/NOR SW16 15 E2
Norbury Hl STRHM/NOR SW16 7 G4
Norbury Ri
STRHM/NOR SW16 15 E2
Norbury Rd THHTH CR7 16 A1
Norfolk Av SAND/SEL CR2 37 E5
Norfolk Rd THHTH CR7 16 A2
WIM/MER SW19 5 G4
Norhyrst Av SNWD SE25 16 D2
Nork Gdns BNSTD SM7 42 A4
Nork Ri BNSTD SM7 50 D1
Nork Wy BNSTD SM7 41 H5
Norman Av EW KT17 40 D2
SAND/SEL CR2 36 A5
Norman Cl EPSOM KT18 50 B4
Norman Colyer Ct
HOR/WEW KT19 * 30 B5
Norman Rd SUT SM1 32 C1
THHTH CR7 15 H4
WIM/MER SW19 5 E4
Normanton Rd
SAND/SEL CR2 36 C2
Normington Cl
STRHM/NOR SW16 7 G2
North Acre BNSTD SM7 51 F1
Northampton Rd
CROY/NA CR0 27 E3
Northanger Rd
STRHM/NOR SW16 7 E3
North Av CAR SM5 34 A3
Northborough Rd
STRHM/NOR SW16 15 E1
Northbrook Rd CROY/NA CR0 16 B4
Northcliffe Cl WPK KT4 20 C4
North Cl MRDN SM4 12 A3
Northcote Rd CROY/NA CR0 16 B5
Northcroft Rd HOR/WEW KT19 30 C3
North Down SAND/SEL CR2 46 C1
Northdown Rd BELMT SM2 32 C5
CTHM CR3 61 G5
North Downs Crs
CROY/NA CR0 38 D5
North Downs Rd
CROY/NA CR0 38 D5
North Dr BECK BR3 18 D3
STRHM/NOR SW16 6 C1
North End CROY/NA CR0 2 C2
Northernhay Wk
MRDN SM4 12 A3
Northey Av BELMT SM2 31 H5
Northfield Crs CHEAM SM3 22 A5
Northfields EW KT17 40 C1
North Gdns WIM/MER SW19 5 F4
North Looe EW KT17 * 41 G3
North Pl MTCM CR4 5 H4
Northpoint Cl SUT SM1 23 E4
North Rd WIM/MER SW19 5 F3
WWKM BR4 28 D2
Northspur Rd SUT SM1 22 C4
North St CAR SM5 23 H5
Northumberland Gdns
MTCM CR4 * 14 D4
North View Crs EPSOM KT18 50 C2
North Wk CROY/NA CR0 38 D2
Northway MRDN SM4 12 A2
WLGTN SM6 24 C5
Northway Rd CROY/NA CR0 16 D5
Northwood Av PUR/KEN CR8 45 G3
Northwood Rd CAR SM5 34 A2
THHTH CR7 16 A1
Norton Gdns
STRHM/NOR SW16 15 E1
Norwich Rd THHTH CR7 16 A2
Norwood High St
WNWD SE27 8 A1
Norwood Park Rd
WNWD SE27 8 A2
Notson Rd SNWD SE25 17 F3
Nottingham Rd
SAND/SEL CR2 2 C7
Nova Ms CHEAM SM3 22 A1
Nova Rd CROY/NA CR0 25 H2
Nubia Wy BMLY BR1 11 G1
Nugent Rd SNWD SE25 16 D2
Nursery Av CROY/NA CR0 27 H3
Nursery Cl CROY/NA CR0 27 H3
EW KT17 30 C5
Nursery Rd MTCM CR4 13 G2
SUT SM1 23 E5
THHTH CR7 16 B3
WIM/MER SW19 12 D1
Nutfield Cl CAR SM5 23 G4
Nutfield Rd COUL/CHIP CR5 53 E1
THHTH CR7 15 H3
Nutwell St TOOT SW17 5 G2

O

Oakapple Cl SAND/SEL CR2 47 F4
Oak Av CROY/NA CR0 28 C3
Oakbank CROY/NA CR0 39 E2
Oakdale Rd HOR/WEW KT19 30 B4
STRHM/NOR SW16 7 E2
Oakdale Wy MTCM CR4 24 A1
Oakdene KWD/TDW/WH KT20 51 E5
Oakdene Dr BRYLDS KT5 20 A2
Oakdene Ms CHEAM SM3 22 B2
Oakfield Gdns BECK BR3 18 D4
CAR SM5 23 G2
Oakfield Rd CROY/NA CR0 26 A2
PGE/AN SE20 9 F5
Oak Gdns CROY/NA CR0 28 C3
Oak Gv WWKM BR4 29 E3
Oak Grove Rd PGE/AN SE20 9 G5
Oakhill Rd BECK BR3 19 E1
STRHM/NOR SW16 7 E5
SUT SM1 22 D4
Oakhurst Ri CAR SM5 33 G5
Oakhurst Rd HOR/WEW KT19 30 A2
Oaklands PUR/KEN CR8 46 A4
Oaklands Av THHTH CR7 15 G3
WWKM BR4 28 D4
Oaklands Gdns PUR/KEN CR8 46 A4
Oaklands Rd BMLY BR1 11 G4
Oaklands Wy WLGTN SM6 34 D3
Oakland Wy HOR/WEW KT19 30 C2
Oak Leaf Cl HOR/WEW KT19 40 A2
Oakleigh Wy MTCM CR4 6 B5
Oakley Av CROY/NA CR0 25 E5
Oakley Ct MTCM CR4 24 A1
Oakley Gdns BNSTD SM7 42 D5
Oakley Rd SNWD SE25 17 F4
WARL CR6 56 A3
Oak Lodge Dr WWKM BR4 28 D1
Oakmead Gn EPSOM KT18 40 A5
Oakmead Pl MTCM CR4 5 G5
Oakmead Rd CROY/NA CR0 14 D5
Oakridge Rd BMLY BR1 11 G1
Oak Rd CTHM CR3 59 G2
Oak Rw MTCM CR4 14 C1
Oaks Av NRWD SE19 8 C2
WPK KT4 21 F5
Oakshade Rd BMLY BR1 11 F1
Oaks La CROY/NA CR0 27 G4
Oaks Pk BNSTD SM7 * 43 H2
Oaks Rd CROY/NA CR0 37 F1
PUR/KEN CR8 45 H4
The Oaks EPSOM KT18 40 C4
MRDN SM4 * 12 A3
Oaks Tr CAR SM5 34 A5
Oaks Wy CAR SM5 33 H3
EPSOM KT18 50 B4
PUR/KEN CR8 46 A4
Oaktree Wk CTHM CR3 59 G2
Oakview Gv CROY/NA CR0 28 A2
Oakview Rd CAT SE6 10 D2
Oak Wy CROY/NA CR0 17 H5
Oakway HAYES BR2 19 F1
Oakwood WLGTN SM6 34 B4
Oakwood Av BECK BR3 19 E1
MTCM CR4 13 F1
PUR/KEN CR8 45 H2
Oakwood Dr NRWD SE19 8 B3
Oakwood Gdns SUT SM1 22 C3
Oakwood Pl CROY/NA CR0 15 G5
Oakwood Ri CTHM CR3 59 G5
Oakwood Rd CROY/NA CR0 15 G5
Oates Cl HAYES BR2 19 F2
Oatlands Rd
KWD/TDW/WH KT20 51 E4
Oban Rd THHTH CR7 16 B3
Ockley Rd CROY/NA CR0 25 F1
STRHM/NOR SW16 7 E1
Octavia Cl MTCM CR4 13 G4
Okeburn Rd TOOT SW17 6 A2
Old Barn Cl BELMT SM2 32 A3
Old Barn La CTHM CR3 55 H1
Old Bromley Rd BMLY BR1 11 F2
Olden La PUR/KEN CR8 45 G2
Old Farleigh Rd
SAND/SEL CR2 37 G5
WARL CR6 48 A3
Oldfield Rd WIM/MER SW19 4 A3
Oldfields Rd SUT SM1 22 C3
Old Fox Cl CTHM CR3 58 D1
Old House Cl EW KT17 30 D5
WIM/MER SW19 4 A2
Old Kingston Rd WPK KT4 20 A4
Old Lodge La PUR/KEN CR8 45 F3
Old London Rd EPSOM KT18 50 A3
Old Malden La WPK KT4 20 C3
Old Oak Av COUL/CHIP CR5 52 C4
Old Palace Rd CROY/NA CR0 2 C4
Old School Cl BECK BR3 17 H1
Old School Pl CROY/NA CR0 25 G5
Old Schools La EW KT17 30 D4
Old School Ter CHEAM SM3 * 31 H3
Oldstead Rd BMLY BR1 11 F1
Old Studio Cl CROY/NA CR0 26 B1
Old Swan Yd CAR SM5 23 H5
Old Town CROY/NA CR0 2 B5
Old Westhall Cl WARL CR6 56 C4
Oliver Av SNWD SE25 16 D3
Oliver Gv SNWD SE25 16 D3
Olive Rd WIM/MER SW19 * 5 E4
Oliver Rd SUT SM1 23 F5
Olley Cl WLGTN SM6 35 E3
Olveston Wk CAR SM5 13 F5
Olyffe Dr BECK BR3 11 E5
Onslow Av BELMT SM2 32 B5
Onslow Gdns SAND/SEL CR2 47 E2
WLGTN SM6 34 C3
Onslow Rd CROY/NA CR0 25 G1
Orchard Av CROY/NA CR0 28 A3
MTCM CR4 24 A2
Orchard Cl BNSTD SM7 42 D4
Orchard Ct WLGTN SM6 * 34 B1
WPK KT4 * 21 E2
Orchard End CTHM CR3 59 G2
Orchard Gdns EPSOM KT18 40 A5
Orchard Gv CROY/NA CR0 28 A1
PGE/AN SE20 9 E4
Orchard Ri CROY/NA CR0 28 A2
Orchard Rd SAND/SEL CR2 47 F4
SUT SM1 32 C1
The Orchard BNSTD SM7 42 C5
EW KT17 30 D3
Orchard Wy CROY/NA CR0 28 A1
SUT SM1 23 F5
Oriel Cl MTCM CR4 14 D3
Orlando Gdns
HOR/WEW KT19 30 B5
Orleans Rd NRWD SE19 8 B3
Ormanton Rd SYD SE26 9 E1
Orme Rd SUT SM1 32 D2
Ormerod Gdns MTCM CR4 14 A1
Ormonde Av HOR/WEW KT19 30 B4
Ormsby BELMT SM2 * 32 D3
Osborne Cl BECK BR3 18 A3
Osborne Gdns THHTH CR7 16 A1
Osborne Rd THHTH CR7 16 A1
Osborne Ter TOOT SW17 * 6 A2
Osier Wy BNSTD SM7 42 A4
MTCM CR4 13 H4
Oslac Rd CAT SE6 10 D2
Osmond Gdns WLGTN SM6 34 C[illegible]
Osney Wk MRDN SM4 13 F5
Osprey Cl SUT SM1 32 B[illegible]
Osprey Gdns SAND/SEL CR2 37 H5
Ospringe Cl PGE/AN SE20 9 G[illegible]
Osterley Gdns THHTH CR7 16 A[illegible]
Osward CROY/NA CR0 38 B5
Otford Cl PGE/AN SE20 9 G5
Otterbourne Rd CROY/NA CR0 2 C[illegible]
Otterburn St TOOT SW17 5 H[illegible]
Otterden St CAT SE6 10 C[illegible]
Outram Rd CROY/NA CR0 3 K[illegible]
Outwood La COUL/CHIP CR5 53 E[illegible]
Oval Rd CROY/NA CR0 3 G[illegible]
The Oval BNSTD SM7 42 C[illegible]
Overbrae BECK BR3 10 C[illegible]
Overbury Av BECK BR3 18 D[illegible]
Overbury Crs CROY/NA CR0 39 E[illegible]
Overdown Rd CAT SE6 10 C[illegible]
Overhill WARL CR6 56 C[illegible]
Overhill Cottages
MTCM CR4 * 14 A[illegible]
Overhill Rd PUR/KEN CR8 35 G[illegible]
Overhill Wy BECK BR3 19 F[illegible]
Overstand Cl BECK BR3 18 C[illegible]
Overstone Gdns
CROY/NA CR0 28 B[illegible]
Overton Rd BELMT SM2 32 C[illegible]
Overton's Yd CROY/NA CR0 2 C[illegible]
Ovett Cl NRWD SE19 8 C[illegible]
Owen Cl CROY/NA CR0 16 B[illegible]
Owen Wk PGE/AN SE20 9 E[illegible]
Owl Cl SAND/SEL CR2 37 H[illegible]
Ownstead Gdns
SAND/SEL CR2 46 D[illegible]
Ownsted Hl CROY/NA CR0 39 E[illegible]
Oxford Av RYNPK SW20 12 A[illegible]
Oxford Cl MTCM CR4 14 C[illegible]
Oxford Rd CAR SM5 33 G[illegible]
NRWD SE19 8 B[illegible]
WLGTN SM6 * 34 C[illegible]
Oxted Cl MTCM CR4 13 F[illegible]
Oxtoby Wy STRHM/NOR SW16 6 D[illegible]

P

Paddock Cl SYD SE26 9 H[illegible]
WPK KT4 20 C[illegible]
Paddock Gdns NRWD SE19 8 C[illegible]
Paddock Wk WARL CR6 56 B[illegible]
Padua Rd PGE/AN SE20 9 C[illegible]
Pageant Wk CROY/NA CR0 3 C[illegible]
Page Crs CROY/NA CR0 35 H[illegible]
Pagehurst Rd CROY/NA CR0 27 E[illegible]
Paget Av SUT SM1 23 F[illegible]
Pain's Cl MTCM CR4 14 B[illegible]
Paisley Rd CAR SM5 23 F[illegible]
Paisley Ter CAR SM5 23 F[illegible]
Palace Gn CROY/NA CR0 38 B[illegible]
Palace Gv NRWD SE19 8 D[illegible]
Palace Rd NRWD SE19 8 D[illegible]
Palace Sq NRWD SE19 8 D[illegible]
Palace Vw CROY/NA CR0 28 B[illegible]
Palestine Gv WIM/MER SW19 5 F[illegible]
Palmer Av CHEAM SM3 21 G[illegible]
Palmer Cl WWKM BR4 29 F[illegible]
Palmersfield Rd BNSTD SM7 42 C[illegible]
Palmers Rd
STRHM/NOR SW16 15 F[illegible]
Palmerston Gv
WIM/MER SW19 4 C[illegible]
Palmerston Rd CAR SM5 23 H[illegible]
CROY/NA CR0 16 B[illegible]
SUT SM1 33 E[illegible]
WIM/MER SW19 4 C[illegible]
Pampisford Rd PUR/KEN CR8 45 G[illegible]
Pams Wy HOR/WEW KT19 30 B[illegible]
Panton Cl CROY/NA CR0 25 H[illegible]
Papermill Cl CAR SM5 24 A[illegible]
The Parade CAR SM5 33 H[illegible]
CROY/NA CR0 * 15 E[illegible]
EPSOM KT18 40 B[illegible]
KWD/TDW/WH KT20 * 51 E[illegible]
PGE/AN SE20 * 9 G[illegible]
SUT SM1 * 22 B[illegible]
SYD SE26 * 9 F[illegible]
WLGTN SM6 * 35 F[illegible]

'rchmore Rd THHTH CR7 ....15 H1
'rchmore Wy THHTH CR7 ....15 H1
'rfour Dr PUR/KEN CR8 ....55 E1
'rish La PGE/AN SE20 ....9 H4
'k Av CAR SM5 ....34 A2
CTHM CR3 ....59 G4
WWKM BR4 ....29 E3
'k Av East EW KT17 ....31 E2
'k Avenue Ms MTCM CR4 ....6 B4
'k Av West EW KT17 ....31 E2
'k Cl CAR SM5 ....33 H2
'k Ct SYD SE26 * ....9 F3
'kdale Crs WPK KT4 ....20 B4
'k End BMLY BR1 ....11 H5
'ker Cl CAR SM5 ....33 H2
'ker Rd CROY/NA CR0 ....2 D6
'kfields CROY/NA CR0 ....28 B2
'kfields Cl CAR SM5 ....24 A5
'kgate Rd WLGTN SM6 ....34 A1
'k Hl CAR SM5 ....33 H2
'k Hill Cl CAR SM5 ....33 H1
'k Hill Ri CROY/NA CR0 ....3 H3
'k Hill Rd CROY/NA CR0 ....3 G3
EW KT17 ....40 D1
HAYES BR2 ....19 G1
WLGTN SM6 ....34 B3
'khurst HOR/WEW KT19 ....30 A5
'khurst Rd SUT SM1 ....23 F5
'klands Rd
STRHM/NOR SW16 ....6 B2
'klands Wy WPK KT4 ....20 C3
'k La CAR SM5 ....24 A5
CHEAM SM3 ....32 A2
CROY/NA CR0 ....2 E5
'kleigh Rd WIM/MER SW19 ....12 D1
'k Ley Rd CTHM CR3 ....60 D1
'k Rd BECK BR3 ....10 B4
BNSTD SM7 ....42 D5
CHEAM SM3 ....32 A2
CTHM CR3 ....59 G3
PUR/KEN CR8 ....46 A5
SNWD SE25 ....16 C3
WARL CR6 ....49 G4
WIM/MER SW19 ....5 F5
WLGTN SM6 ....24 B3
'kside BECK BR3 * ....18 D1
CHEAM SM3 ....32 A2
'kside Cl PGE/AN SE20 ....9 G4
'kside Gdns
COUL/CHIP CR5 ....53 F2
'kside Ms WARL CR6 ....57 G1
'k St CROY/NA CR0 ....2 D3
'k Ter CAR SM5 * ....23 G4
WPK KT4 ....21 E2
Park CAR SM5 ....33 H1
'k Vw CTHM CR3 ....60 A5
EW KT17 * ....40 D3
'k View Dr MTCM CR4 ....13 F1
kview Rd CROY/NA CR0 ....27 E2
'k View Rd CTHM CR3 ....61 F3
'k Vls TOOT SW17 * ....5 G2
'kway CROY/NA CR0 ....38 D5
'kwood BECK BR3 ....10 C4
'k Wood Cl BNSTD SM7 ....41 H5
'k Wood Rd BNSTD SM7 ....41 H5
'kwood Rd WIM/MER SW19 ....4 B2
'k Wood Vw BNSTD SM7 ....50 D1
'r Av EW KT17 ....31 F4
'rs Cl SAND/SEL CR2 ....36 B4
'ry Cl EW KT17 ....31 F3
'ry Rd SNWD SE25 ....16 C2
'sonage Cl WARL CR6 ....57 E1
'sonsfield Cl BNSTD SM7 ....41 H5
'sonsfield Rd BNSTD SM7 ....50 D1
'son's Md CROY/NA CR0 ....2 B1
'thia Cl
KWD/TDW/WH KT20 ....50 B4
'tridge Knoll
PUR/KEN CR8 ....45 H2
'tridge Md BNSTD SM7 ....41 G5
'ton Cl WLGTN SM6 ....24 C4
hfield Rd
STRHM/NOR SW16 ....6 D3
Path WIM/MER SW19 ....4 D5
terdale Cl BMLY BR1 ....11 G3
terson Rd NRWD SE19 ....8 D3
il Gdns CROY/NA CR0 ....3 J3
vement Sq CROY/NA CR0 ....27 E2
Pavement
WIM/MER SW19 * ....4 B3
WNWD SE27 * ....8 A1
vleyne Cl PGE/AN SE20 ....9 G4
vson's Rd THHTH CR7 ....16 A5
xton Pl WNWD SE27 ....8 C1
abody Cl CROY/NA CR0 ....27 G2
ace Cl SNWD SE25 ....16 C3
aches Cl BELMT SM2 ....32 A3
acock Gdns SAND/SEL CR2 ....38 A5
ak Hl SYD SE26 ....9 G1
ak Hill Av SYD SE26 ....9 G1
ak Hill Gdns SYD SE26 ....9 G1
aks Hl PUR/KEN CR8 ....35 E5
aks Hill Ri PUR/KEN CR8 ....35 E5
all Rd CROY/NA CR0 ....15 F5
arce Cl MTCM CR4 ....14 A1
arson Wy MTCM CR4 ....6 A5
artree Av TOOT SW17 ....5 H3
ar Tree Cl MTCM CR4 ....13 H2
artree Cl SAND/SEL CR2 ....47 F4
asus Rd CROY/NA CR0 ....35 G2
ham Rd PGE/AN SE20 ....17 G1
WIM/MER SW19 ....4 C4
ings Cl HAYES BR2 ....19 G2
ton Av BELMT SM2 ....32 D5
nbroke Cl BNSTD SM7 ....51 H2
nbroke Rd MTCM CR4 ....14 A1
SNWD SE25 ....16 C3
nbury Av WPK KT4 ....21 E2
nbury Cl COUL/CHIP CR5 ....44 A4
HAYES BR2 ....29 H1
nbury Rd SNWD SE25 ....17 E3
ndevon Rd CROY/NA CR0 ....25 G1
Pendennis Rd
STRHM/NOR SW16 ....7 E1
Pendle Rd STRHM/NOR SW16 ....6 B3
Penfold Cl CROY/NA CR0 ....25 G4
Penge La PGE/AN SE20 ....9 G4
Penge Rd SNWD SE25 ....17 E2
Penistone Rd
STRHM/NOR SW16 ....7 E4
Pennycroft CROY/NA CR0 ....38 A4
Penrhyn Cl CTHM CR3 ....55 F5
Penrith Cl BECK BR3 ....10 D5
Penrith Rd THHTH CR7 ....16 A1
Penrith St STRHM/NOR SW16 ....6 C3
Penshurst Gn HAYES BR2 ....19 H4
Penshurst Rd THHTH CR7 ....15 H4
Penshurst Wy BELMT SM2 ....32 C3
Pentlands Cl MTCM CR4 ....14 B2
Pentney Rd RYNPK SW20 ....4 A5
Penwortham Rd
SAND/SEL CR2 ....36 B5
STRHM/NOR SW16 ....6 B3
Pepper Cl CTHM CR3 ....59 G5
Peppercorn Cl THHTH CR7 ....16 B1
Peppermint Cl CROY/NA CR0 ....25 E1
Percival Wy HOR/WEW KT19 ....20 A5
Percy Gdns WPK KT4 ....20 B2
Percy Rd MTCM CR4 ....24 A1
PGE/AN SE20 ....9 H5
SNWD SE25 ....16 D4
Peregrine Gdns
CROY/NA CR0 ....28 A3
Perry How WPK KT4 ....20 D2
Persfield Cl EW KT17 ....31 E5
Persfield Ms EW KT17 * ....30 D5
Pershore Gv CAR SM5 ....13 F5
Perth Rd BECK BR3 ....19 E1
Peterborough Rd CAR SM5 ....13 G5
Petersfield Crs
COUL/CHIP CR5 ....45 E5
Petersham Cl SUT SM1 ....32 C1
Petersham Ter
CROY/NA CR0 * ....25 E4
Peterwood Wy CROY/NA CR0 ....25 F3
Petworth Cl COUL/CHIP CR5 ....53 G4
Pevensey Rd TOOT SW17 ....5 F1
Pharaoh Cl MTCM CR4 ....23 H1
Pheasant Cl PUR/KEN CR8 ....45 H3
Philip Gdns CROY/NA CR0 ....28 B3
Philips Cl CAR SM5 ....24 A2
Phipp's Bridge Rd MTCM CR4 ....13 F2
Phoenix Cl WWKM BR4 ....29 G3
Phoenix Rd PGE/AN SE20 ....9 G3
Pickering Gdns CROY/NA CR0 ....16 D5
Pickhurst Gn HAYES BR2 ....29 H1
Pickhurst La WWKM BR4 ....19 H5
Pickhurst Md HAYES BR2 ....29 H1
Pickhurst Pk HAYES BR2 ....19 G5
Pickhurst Ri WWKM BR4 ....29 F2
Picquets Wy BNSTD SM7 ....51 F2
Picton Mt WARL CR6 ....56 A4
Pikes Hl EW KT17 ....40 C3
Pilgrim Cl MRDN SM4 ....22 D1
Pilgrim Hl WNWD SE27 ....8 A1
Pilgrim's Wy SAND/SEL CR2 ....36 D2
Pincott Rd WIM/MER SW19 ....5 E5
Pine Av WWKM BR4 ....28 D2
Pine Cl PGE/AN SE20 ....9 G5
PUR/KEN CR8 ....55 E2
Pine Coombe CROY/NA CR0 ....27 H5
Pine Crs CAR SM5 ....43 F1
Pine Gv WIM/MER SW19 ....4 B2
Pine Pl BNSTD SM7 ....41 H4
Pine Rdg CAR SM5 ....34 A4
The Pines NRWD SE19 * ....7 H3
PUR/KEN CR8 ....45 H3
Pine Wk BELMT SM2 ....33 F5
BNSTD SM7 ....52 D2
CTHM CR3 ....59 G2
Pinewood Cl CROY/NA CR0 ....28 A4
Pinfold Rd
STRHM/NOR SW16 ....7 E1
Pipers Gdns CROY/NA CR0 ....28 A1
Pipewell Rd CAR SM5 ....13 G5
Pippin Cl CROY/NA CR0 ....28 B2
Piquet Rd PGE/AN SE20 ....17 G1
Pirbright Crs CROY/NA CR0 ....39 E2
Pitcairn Rd MTCM CR4 ....5 H4
Pitlake CROY/NA CR0 ....2 B2
Pitt Crs WIM/MER SW19 ....4 D1
Pitt Pl EW KT17 * ....40 C4
Pitt Rd EW KT17 ....40 C4
THHTH CR7 ....16 A4
Pittville Gdns SNWD SE25 ....17 E2
Pit Wood Gn
KWD/TDW/WH KT20 ....50 C5
Pixton Wy CROY/NA CR0 ....38 B3
Placehouse La
COUL/CHIP CR5 ....54 B4
Plantagenet Cl WPK KT4 ....20 B5
Plantation La WARL CR6 ....57 E4
Plawsfield Rd BECK BR3 ....9 H5
Playgreen Wy CAT SE6 ....10 C1
Playground Cl BECK BR3 ....17 H1
Pleasant Gv CROY/NA CR0 ....28 B4
Plesman Wy WLGTN SM6 * ....35 E4
Pleydell Av NRWD SE19 ....8 D4
Pleydell Gdns NRWD SE19 * ....8 D3
Plough La CROY/NA CR0 ....25 E5
PUR/KEN CR8 ....35 F5
WIM/MER SW19 ....4 D2
Plough Lane Cl WLGTN SM6 ....35 E1
Plough Rd HOR/WEW KT19 ....30 B3
Plummer La MTCM CR4 ....13 H1
Plumpton Wy CAR SM5 ....23 G4
Plumtree Cl WLGTN SM6 ....34 D3
Pollard Rd MRDN SM4 ....13 F4
Pollards Crs
STRHM/NOR SW16 ....15 E2
Pollards Hl East
STRHM/NOR SW16 ....15 F2
Pollards Hl North
STRHM/NOR SW16 ....15 F2
Pollards Hl South
STRHM/NOR SW16 ....15 F2
Pollards Hl West
STRHM/NOR SW16 ....15 E2
Pollards Wood Rd
STRHM/NOR SW16 ....15 E1
Polworth Rd
STRHM/NOR SW16 ....7 E2
Pond Cottage La BECK BR3 ....28 C2
Pondfield Rd HAYES BR2 ....29 G2
PUR/KEN CR8 ....54 D1
Pond Hill Gdns CHEAM SM3 * ....32 A2
Pool Cl BECK BR3 ....10 C2
Poole Rd HOR/WEW KT19 ....30 B2
Pope Cl WIM/MER SW19 * ....5 F3
Popes Gv CROY/NA CR0 ....28 B4
Popinjays Rw CHEAM SM3 * ....31 H1
Poplar Av MTCM CR4 ....5 H5
Poplar Crs HOR/WEW KT19 ....30 A2
Poplar Dr BNSTD SM7 ....41 H4
Poplar Farm Cl
HOR/WEW KT19 ....30 A2
Poplar La BECK BR3 ....18 D4
Poplar Rd CHEAM SM3 ....22 B2
WIM/MER SW19 ....12 C1
Poplar Rd South
WIM/MER SW19 ....12 C2
Poplar Wk CROY/NA CR0 ....2 C1
CTHM CR3 ....59 G3
Poppy Cl WLGTN SM6 ....24 A2
Poppy La CROY/NA CR0 ....27 G1
Porchester Md BECK BR3 ....10 D3
Porchfield Cl BELMT SM2 ....32 D5
Porthcawe Rd SYD SE26 ....10 A1
Portland Av NWMAL KT3 ....20 D1
Portland Cl WPK KT4 ....21 F1
Portland Cottages
CROY/NA CR0 * ....24 D1
Portland Pl EW KT17 ....40 C2
SNWD SE25 ....17 E3
Portland Place Flats
EW KT17 * ....40 C2
Portland Rd MTCM CR4 ....13 G1
SNWD SE25 ....17 F3
Portley La CTHM CR3 ....59 G1
Portley Wood Rd CTHM CR3 ....59 H1
Portnalls Cl COUL/CHIP CR5 ....53 F1
Portnalls Ri COUL/CHIP CR5 ....53 G1
Portnalls Rd COUL/CHIP CR5 ....53 F2
Portway EW KT17 ....31 E5
Portway Crs EW KT17 ....31 E5
Postmill Cl CROY/NA CR0 ....27 G4
Potter Cl MTCM CR4 * ....14 B1
Potters Cl CROY/NA CR0 ....28 A2
Potter's La
STRHM/NOR SW16 * ....6 D3
Poulter Pk MRDN SM4 * ....13 G5
Poulton Av SUT SM1 ....23 F4
Pound La HOR/WEW KT19 ....40 B1
Pound Rd BNSTD SM7 ....51 G2
Pound St CAR SM5 ....33 H1
Prentis Rd STRHM/NOR SW16 ....6 D1
Prestbury Crs BNSTD SM7 ....52 D1
Preston Dr HOR/WEW KT19 ....30 C2
Preston La
KWD/TDW/WH KT20 ....50 C5
Preston Rd NRWD SE19 ....7 H3
Prestwood Gdns
CROY/NA CR0 ....26 A1
Pretoria Rd
STRHM/NOR SW16 ....6 B3
Pretty La COUL/CHIP CR5 ....53 G5
Price Rd CROY/NA CR0 ....35 H1
Prickley Wd HAYES BR2 ....29 H2
Priddy's Yd CROY/NA CR0 ....2 D3
Pridham Rd THHTH CR7 ....16 B3
Priestley Rd MTCM CR4 ....14 A1
Primrose Cl CAT SE6 ....11 E2
WLGTN SM6 ....24 B2
Primrose La CROY/NA CR0 ....27 H2
Primrose Wk EW KT17 ....30 D3
Prince Charles Wy
WLGTN SM6 ....24 B4
Prince Georges Rd
WIM/MER SW19 ....5 F5
Prince of Wales' Rd SUT SM1 ....23 F3
Prince Rd SNWD SE25 ....16 C4
Princes Av CAR SM5 ....33 H3
SAND/SEL CR2 ....47 F5
Princes Cl SAND/SEL CR2 ....47 F5
Princes Rd PGE/AN SE20 ....9 H3
WIM/MER SW19 ....4 C3
Princess Rd CROY/NA CR0 ....16 A5
Princes St SUT SM1 ....23 F5
Princes Wy CROY/NA CR0 ....35 F1
WWKM BR4 ....29 H5
Princethorpe Rd SYD SE26 ....9 H1
Pringle Gdns PUR/KEN CR8 ....35 F5
STRHM/NOR SW16 ....6 C1
Prior Av BELMT SM2 ....33 G3
Priory Av CHEAM SM3 ....21 H5
Priory Cl BECK BR3 ....18 A2
WIM/MER SW19 * ....4 D5
Priory Crs CHEAM SM3 ....21 H5
NRWD SE19 ....8 A4
Priory Gdns SNWD SE25 ....16 D3
Priory Rd CHEAM SM3 ....21 H5
CROY/NA CR0 ....25 G1
The Priory CROY/NA CR0 * ....25 G4
Proctor Cl MTCM CR4 ....6 A5
Progress Wy CROY/NA CR0 ....25 F3
Promenade De Verdun
PUR/KEN CR8 ....44 D1
Prospect Cl SYD SE26 ....9 F1
Prospect Pl EW KT17 ....40 C3
Provincial Ter PGE/AN SE20 * ....9 H4
Puffin Cl BECK BR3 ....17 H4
Pump House Cl HAYES BR2 ....19 H1
Purberry Gv EW KT17 ....30 D5
Purberry Shot EW KT17 * ....30 D5
Purcell Cl PUR/KEN CR8 ....46 A4
Purley Bury Av PUR/KEN CR8 ....46 A1
Purley Bury Cl PUR/KEN CR8 ....46 A1
Purley Downs Rd
SAND/SEL CR2 ....46 C1
Purley Hl PUR/KEN CR8 ....45 H2
Purley Knoll PUR/KEN CR8 ....45 F1
Purley Oaks Rd
SAND/SEL CR2 ....36 C5
Purley Pde PUR/KEN CR8 * ....45 G1
Purley Park Rd PUR/KEN CR8 ....45 H1
Purley Ri PUR/KEN CR8 ....45 F2
Purley Rd SAND/SEL CR2 ....36 B3
Purley V PUR/KEN CR8 ....45 H3
Purley Wy CROY/NA CR0 ....35 G4
PUR/KEN CR8 ....45 G1
Pye Cl CTHM CR3 ....59 F3
Pylbrook Rd SUT SM1 ....22 D4
Pylon Wy CROY/NA CR0 ....25 E2
Pytchley Crs NRWD SE19 ....8 A3

## Q

Quadrant Rd THHTH CR7 ....15 H3
The Quadrant BELMT SM2 ....33 E2
RYNPK SW20 ....4 A5
Quail Gdns SAND/SEL CR2 ....38 A5
Quarr Rd CAR SM5 ....13 F5
Quarry Park Rd SUT SM1 ....32 B2
Quarry Ri SUT SM1 ....32 B2
Queen Adelaide Rd
PGE/AN SE20 ....9 G4
Queen Anne's Gdns
MTCM CR4 * ....13 H2
Queen Elizabeth Gdns
MRDN SM4 ....12 C3
Queen Elizabeth's Dr
CROY/NA CR0 ....39 F5
Queen Elizabeth's Gdns
CROY/NA CR0 ....39 F5
Queen Elizabeth's Wk
WLGTN SM6 ....24 D5
Queenhill Rd SAND/SEL CR2 ....37 F5
Queen Mary Rd NRWD SE19 ....7 H3
Queen Mary's Av CAR SM5 ....33 H3
Queens Acre CHEAM SM3 ....31 H3
Queen's Cl WLGTN SM6 ....34 B1
Queens Ct BELMT SM2 * ....42 C1
Queensland Av
WIM/MER SW19 ....4 D5
Queensmead Av EW KT17 ....31 F5
Queen's Mead Rd HAYES BR2 ....19 H1
Queen's Park Rd CTHM CR3 ....59 G3
Queen's Pl MRDN SM4 ....12 C3
Queen's Rd BECK BR3 ....18 A1
BELMT SM2 ....32 C5
CROY/NA CR0 ....15 H5
MRDN SM4 ....12 C3
MTCM CR4 ....13 F2
WIM/MER SW19 ....4 D2
WLGTN SM6 ....34 B1
Queensthorpe Ms SYD SE26 * ....9 H1
Queensthorpe Rd SYD SE26 ....9 H1
Queen St CROY/NA CR0 ....2 C6
Queensway CROY/NA CR0 ....35 F2
Queenswood Av THHTH CR7 ....15 G4
WLGTN SM6 ....24 D5
Quicks Rd WIM/MER SW19 ....4 D4
Quintin Av RYNPK SW20 ....4 A5
Quinton Cl BECK BR3 ....19 E2
WLGTN SM6 ....24 B5

## R

Rackham Ms
STRHM/NOR SW16 ....6 C3
Radcliffe Gdns CAR SM5 ....33 G3
Radcliffe Rd CROY/NA CR0 ....3 K3
Radnor Cl MTCM CR4 ....15 E4
Radnor Wk CROY/NA CR0 ....28 A1
Raglan Ct SAND/SEL CR2 ....35 H1
Railway Ap WLGTN SM6 * ....34 B2
Railway Cottages
BNSTD SM7 * ....42 B4
WIM/MER SW19 * ....4 D1
Raleigh Av WLGTN SM6 ....24 D5
Raleigh Dr BRYLDS KT5 ....20 A2
Raleigh Gdns MTCM CR4 ....13 H2
Raleigh Rd PGE/AN SE20 ....9 H4
Ralph Perring Ct BECK BR3 ....18 C3
Rama Cl STRHM/NOR SW16 ....7 E4
Rama La NRWD SE19 ....8 D4
Rambler Cl STRHM/NOR SW16 ....6 C1
Rame Cl TOOT SW17 ....6 A2
Ramones Ter MTCM CR4 * ....14 C3
Ramsdale Rd TOOT SW17 ....6 A2
Ramsey Pl CTHM CR3 ....59 E2
Ramsey Rd THHTH CR7 ....15 G5
Randlesdown Rd CAT SE6 ....10 C1
Randolph Rd EW KT17 ....40 D4
Ranfurly Rd SUT SM1 ....22 C3
Rangefield Rd BMLY BR1 ....11 G2
Ranmore Av CROY/NA CR0 ....3 K5
Ranmore Rd BELMT SM2 ....31 H4
Rathbone Sq CROY/NA CR0 * ....2 C6
Ravensbourne Av HAYES BR2 ....11 F5
Ravensbury Av MRDN SM4 ....13 E4
Ravensbury Gv MTCM CR4 ....13 F3
Ravensbury La MTCM CR4 ....13 F3
Ravenscar Rd BMLY BR1 ....11 G1
Ravens Cl HAYES BR2 ....19 H1
Ravenscroft Rd BECK BR3 ....17 G1
Ravensdale Gdns NRWD SE19 ....8 B4
Ravensfield Gdns
HOR/WEW KT19 ....30 C1
Ravenshead Cl SAND/SEL CR2 ....47 G1
Ravensmead Rd HAYES BR2 ....11 F4
Ravens Wold PUR/KEN CR8 ....46 A5
Ravenswood Av WWKM BR4 ....29 E2
Ravenswood Crs WWKM BR4 ....29 E2
Ravenswood Rd
CROY/NA CR0 ....2 A5
Rawlings Cl BECK BR3 ....19 E4
Rawlins Cl SAND/SEL CR2 ....38 B3
Rawnsley Av MTCM CR4 ....13 F4
Rayleigh Ri SAND/SEL CR2 ....36 C2
Rayleigh Rd WIM/MER SW19 ....4 B5
Raymead Av THHTH CR7 ....15 G4
Raymond Cl SYD SE26 ....9 G2
Raymond Rd BECK BR3 ....18 A3
WIM/MER SW19 ....4 A3
Rays Rd WWKM BR4 ....29 E1
The Readens BNSTD SM7 ....52 C1
Reading Rd SUT SM1 ....33 E1
Reads Rest La
KWD/TDW/WH KT20 ....51 G5
Recovery St TOOT SW17 ....5 G2
Recreation Rd HAYES BR2 ....19 H1
SYD SE26 ....9 H1
Recreation Wy MTCM CR4 ....15 E2
Rectory Gdns BECK BR3 * ....10 C5
Rectory Gn BECK BR3 ....10 B5
Rectory Gv CROY/NA CR0 ....2 A3
Rectory La BNSTD SM7 ....43 H5
TOOT SW17 ....6 A2
WLGTN SM6 ....24 C5
Rectory Orch WIM/MER SW19 ....4 A1
Rectory Pk SAND/SEL CR2 ....46 C3
Rectory Rd BECK BR3 ....10 C5
SUT SM1 ....22 C4
Redbarn Cl PUR/KEN CR8 ....45 H1
Redclose Av MRDN SM4 ....12 C4
Reddington Cl SAND/SEL CR2 ....36 B4
Reddons Rd BECK BR3 ....10 A4
Reddown Rd COUL/CHIP CR5 ....53 H3
Redford Av COUL/CHIP CR5 ....44 B5
THHTH CR7 ....15 F3
WLGTN SM6 ....34 D3
Redgrave Cl CROY/NA CR0 ....16 D5
Red House Rd CROY/NA CR0 ....14 D5
Redlands COUL/CHIP CR5 ....54 A1
Red Lodge Rd WWKM BR4 ....29 E2
Redroofs Cl BECK BR3 ....10 D5
Redstart Cl CROY/NA CR0 ....39 F5
Redvers Rd WARL CR6 ....56 D3
Redwing Cl SAND/SEL CR2 ....47 H1
Redwing Rd WLGTN SM6 ....35 E3
Redwood Cl PUR/KEN CR8 ....46 A4
Reedham Dr PUR/KEN CR8 ....45 G3
Reedham Park Av
PUR/KEN CR8 ....54 D1
Rees Gdns CROY/NA CR0 ....16 D5
Reeves Cnr CROY/NA CR0 ....2 B3
Regal Ct MTCM CR4 ....13 H2
Regal Crs WLGTN SM6 ....24 B4
Regency Ms BECK BR3 ....11 E5
Regency Wk CROY/NA CR0 ....18 A5
Regent Pde BELMT SM2 * ....33 E2
Regent Pl CROY/NA CR0 ....3 J1
WIM/MER SW19 ....5 E2
Regents Cl CTHM CR3 ....55 H3
SAND/SEL CR2 ....36 C2
Regina Rd SNWD SE25 ....17 E2
Reid Av CTHM CR3 ....59 F1
Reid Cl COUL/CHIP CR5 ....53 F1
Reigate Av SUT SM1 ....22 D2
Reigate Rd EW KT17 ....41 E2
KWD/TDW/WH KT20 ....50 D2
Reigate Wy WLGTN SM6 ....35 E1
Rembrandt Ct
HOR/WEW KT19 ....30 D2
Rendle Cl CROY/NA CR0 ....16 D4
Renmuir St TOOT SW17 ....5 H3
Renown Cl CROY/NA CR0 ....2 B1
Repton Cl CAR SM5 ....33 G1
Repton Ct BECK BR3 ....10 D5
Reservoir Cl THHTH CR7 ....16 B2
Restmor Wy CAR SM5 ....24 A3
The Retreat THHTH CR7 ....16 B3
WPK KT4 ....21 F3
Revell Rd SUT SM1 ....32 B2
Revelstoke Rd
WIM/MER SW19 ....4 A1
Revere Wy HOR/WEW KT19 ....30 C4
Revesby Rd CAR SM5 ....13 G5
Rewley Rd CAR SM5 ....13 F5
Reynard Dr NRWD SE19 ....8 D4
Reynolds Cl CAR SM5 ....23 H2
WIM/MER SW19 ....5 F5
Reynolds Rd NWMAL KT3 ....20 B1
Reynolds Wy CROY/NA CR0 ....3 H6
Rheingold Wy WLGTN SM6 ....35 E4
Rialto Rd MTCM CR4 ....14 A1
Ribblesdale Rd
STRHM/NOR SW16 ....6 B2
Ricards Rd WIM/MER SW19 ....4 B2
Richards Cottages CAR SM5 * ....33 H1
Richards Fld HOR/WEW KT19 ....30 B4
Richland Av COUL/CHIP CR5 ....44 A4
Richlands Av EW KT17 ....31 E1
Richmond Av RYNPK SW20 ....4 A5
Richmond Cl EPSOM KT18 ....40 C4
Richmond Gn CROY/NA CR0 ....25 E4
Richmond Rd
COUL/CHIP CR5 ....44 B5
CROY/NA CR0 ....25 E4
THHTH CR7 ....15 H3
Rickman Hl COUL/CHIP CR5 ....53 F2
Rickman Hill Rd
COUL/CHIP CR5 ....53 F3
The Riddings CTHM CR3 ....59 H5
Riddlesdown Av
PUR/KEN CR8 ....46 A2
Riddlesdown Rd
PUR/KEN CR8 ....46 A3
Ridge Ct CTHM CR3 ....56 A3
Ridge Langley SAND/SEL CR2 ....37 E5
Ridgemount Av
COUL/CHIP CR5 ....53 F2
CROY/NA CR0 ....27 H3

Ridgemount Cl PGE/AN SE20 9 F4
Ridge Pk PUR/KEN CR8 34 D5
Ridge Rd CHEAM SM3 22 B2
MTCM CR4 6 B4
Ridges Yd CROY/NA CR0 2 A4
The Ridge COUL/CHIP CR5 45 E4
PUR/KEN CR8 34 D5
Ridgeway HOR/WEW KT19 40 A2
The Ridgeway CROY/NA CR0 25 F4
The Ridge Wy SAND/SEL CR2 36 C5
Ridgewell Cl SYD SE26 10 B1
Ridgway Pl WIM/MER SW19 4 A3
The Ridgway BELMT SM2 33 F3
Riding Hl SAND/SEL CR2 47 E3
The Ridings EPSOM KT18 40 C5
EW KT17 30 D4
KWD/TDW/WH KT20 51 F5
Ridley Rd WARL CR6 56 C3
WIM/MER SW19 4 D4
Ridsdale Rd PGE/AN SE20 9 F5
Riesco Dr CROY/NA CR0 37 G2
Rigby Cl CROY/NA CR0 25 G4
Riggindale Rd
STRHM/NOR SW16 6 D2
Ringstead Rd SUT SM1 23 F5
Ringwold Cl BECK BR3 10 A4
Ringwood Av CROY/NA CR0 25 E1
Ripley Cl CROY/NA CR0 39 E2
Risborough Dr WPK KT4 21 E1
The Rise EW KT17 30 D5
SAND/SEL CR2 37 G4
Ritchie Rd CROY/NA CR0 17 F5
River Gdns CAR SM5 24 A3
River Grove Pk BECK BR3 10 B5
Riverhead Dr BELMT SM2 32 D5
Riverholme Dr
HOR/WEW KT19 30 B4
Riverpark Gdns HAYES BR2 11 F4
Riverside Cl WLGTN SM6 24 B4
Riverside Dr MTCM CR4 13 E4
Riverside Ms CROY/NA CR0 * 25 E4
Riverside Rd TOOT SW17 4 D1
Riverview Rd
HOR/WEW KT19 30 B1
River Wy HOR/WEW KT19 30 B1
Robertsbridge Rd CAR SM5 23 E1
Roberts Cl CHEAM SM3 31 H3
THHTH CR7 16 B2
Roberts Ct PGE/AN SE20 9 G5
Robert St CROY/NA CR0 2 D4
Robinhood Cl MTCM CR4 14 C3
Robinhood La MTCM CR4 14 C2
Robin Hood La SUT SM1 32 D1
Robinia Cl PGE/AN SE20 9 E5
Robinson Rd TOOT SW17 5 G3
Roche Rd STRHM/NOR SW16 7 E5
Rochester Cl
STRHM/NOR SW16 * 7 E4
Rochester Gdns CROY/NA CR0 3 H4
CTHM CR3 59 G2
Rochester Rd CAR SM5 23 H5
Roche Wk CAR SM5 13 F5
Rochford Wy CROY/NA CR0 15 E5
Rock Cl MTCM CR4 13 F1
Rockhampton Rd
SAND/SEL CR2 36 C2
STRHM/NOR SW16 7 G1
Rock Hl DUL SE21 8 D1
Rockmount Rd NRWD SE19 8 B3
Rockwell Gdns NRWD SE19 8 C1
Roden Gdns CROY/NA CR0 16 C5
Rodney Cl CROY/NA CR0 2 B1
Rodney Pl WIM/MER SW19 5 E5
Rodney Rd MTCM CR4 13 G1
Roe Rd WLGTN SM6 35 E2
Roffes La CTHM CR3 59 F5
Roffey Cl PUR/KEN CR8 54 D1
Rogers Cl COUL/CHIP CR5 54 D3
Rogers La WARL CR6 57 F3
Rogers Rd TOOT SW17 5 F1
Roke Cl PUR/KEN CR8 46 A4
Roke Lodge Rd
PUR/KEN CR8 45 H3
Roke Rd PUR/KEN CR8 45 H4
Roland Wy WPK KT4 20 D3
Rolleston Rd SAND/SEL CR2 36 B3
Rolls Royce Cl WLGTN SM6 35 E3
Romanhurst Av HAYES BR2 19 G3
Romanhurst Gdns
HAYES BR2 19 G3
Roman Rd CAR SM5 33 H4
Roman Ri NRWD SE19 8 B3
Roman Wy CROY/NA CR0 2 B4
Romany Gdns CHEAM SM3 22 C1
Rommany Rd WNWD SE27 8 B1
Ronald Cl BECK BR3 18 B4
The Rookery
STRHM/NOR SW16 * 7 F3
Rook La CTHM CR3 58 C4
Rookley Cl BELMT SM2 32 D5
Rookstone Rd TOOT SW17 5 H2
Rookwood Av WLGTN SM6 24 D5
Roper Wy MTCM CR4 14 A1
Rosamund Cl SAND/SEL CR2 3 F7
Rose Av MRDN SM4 13 E4
MTCM CR4 5 H5
Rosebank EPSOM KT18 40 A4
PGE/AN SE20 9 F4
Rosebery Av EW KT17 40 C4
THHTH CR7 16 A1
Rosebery Gdns SUT SM1 22 D5
Rosebery Pde EW KT17 * 30 D3
Rosebery Rd SUT SM1 32 B2
Rosebriars CTHM CR3 55 G5
Rose Bushes EW KT17 50 C1
Rosecourt Rd CROY/NA CR0 15 F5
Rosedale Pl CROY/NA CR0 27 H1
Rosedale Rd EW KT17 31 E1
Rosedene Av CROY/NA CR0 25 E1
MRDN SM4 12 C4
Rose End WPK KT4 21 H2
Rosefield Cl CAR SM5 33 G1
Rose Hl SUT SM1 22 D3
Rosehill Av SUT SM1 23 E2
Rosehill Court Pde
MRDN SM4 * 23 E1
Rosehill Farm Meadow
BNSTD SM7 42 D5
Rosehill Gdns SUT SM1 22 D3
Rose Hill Pk West SUT SM1 23 E3
Rosemary Cl CROY/NA CR0 25 E1
Rosemead Av MTCM CR4 14 C2
Roseneath Ct CTHM CR3 * 60 A5
Roseneath Pl
STRHM/NOR SW16 7 G1
The Rosery CROY/NA CR0 17 H5
Rose Wk WWKM BR4 29 F3
Rosewell Cl PGE/AN SE20 9 F4
Rosewood Gv SUT SM1 23 E3
Rosewood Ter PGE/AN SE20 * 9 G4
Roslyn Cl MTCM CR4 13 F1
Rossdale SUT SM1 33 G1
Rossetti Gdns
COUL/CHIP CR5 54 B2
Rossignol Gdns CAR SM5 24 A3
Rosslyn Cl WWKM BR4 29 H4
Ross Pde WLGTN SM6 34 B2
Ross Rd SNWD SE25 16 C2
WLGTN SM6 34 C2
Rosswood Gdns WLGTN SM6 34 B2
Rostella Rd TOOT SW17 5 F1
Rostrevor Rd WIM/MER SW19 4 C2
Rotherfield Rd CAR SM5 24 A5
Rotherhill Av
STRHM/NOR SW16 6 D3
Rothermere Rd
CROY/NA CR0 35 F1
Rotherwood Cl RYNPK SW20 4 A5
Rothesay Av RYNPK SW20 12 A1
Rothesay Rd SNWD SE25 16 B3
Rothschild St WNWD SE27 7 H1
Rougemont Av MRDN SM4 12 C5
Round Gv CROY/NA CR0 27 H1
Roundwood Vw BNSTD SM7 41 H5
Roundwood Wy BNSTD SM7 41 H5
Rouse Gdns DUL SE21 8 C1
Rowan Cl STRHM/NOR SW16 6 C5
Rowan Crs STRHM/NOR SW16 6 C5
Rowan Gdns CROY/NA CR0 3 K4
Rowan Md
KWD/TDW/WH KT20 50 B4
Rowan Rd
STRHM/NOR SW16 14 C1
Rowan Ter PGE/AN SE20 * 9 E5
WIM/MER SW19 * 4 A4
Rowden Rd BECK BR3 10 A5
HOR/WEW KT19 20 A5
Rowdown Crs CROY/NA CR0 39 F4
Rowland Wy WIM/MER SW19 4 D5
Rowley Ct CTHM CR3 59 E2
Roxburgh Rd WNWD SE27 7 H2
Roxton Gdns CROY/NA CR0 38 C1
Royal Av WPK KT4 20 C3
Royal Cl WPK KT4 20 C3
Royal Dr EPSOM KT18 50 B3
Royston Av SUT SM1 23 F4
WLGTN SM6 24 D5
Royston Rd PGE/AN SE20 9 H5
Ruden Wy EW KT17 41 F5
Ruffetts Cl SAND/SEL CR2 37 F3
The Ruffetts SAND/SEL CR2 37 F3
Ruffetts Wy
KWD/TDW/WH KT20 51 E3
Rugby La BELMT SM2 31 H4
Ruislip St TOOT SW17 5 H1
Runes Cl MTCM CR4 13 F3
Runnymede WIM/MER SW19 5 F5
Runnymede Crs
STRHM/NOR SW16 6 D5
Rural Wy STRHM/NOR SW16 6 B4
Rushden Cl NRWD SE19 8 B4
Rushmead Cl CROY/NA CR0 3 J6
Rushmere Ct WPK KT4 21 E3
Rushmon Pl CHEAM SM3 * 32 A2
Rusholme Gv NRWD SE19 8 C2
Rushy Meadow La CAR SM5 23 G4
Ruskin Dr WPK KT4 21 F3
Ruskin Rd CAR SM5 34 A1
CROY/NA CR0 2 B2
Ruskin Wy WIM/MER SW19 13 F1
Russel Cl BECK BR3 18 D2
Russell Green Cl
PUR/KEN CR8 35 G5
Russell Hl PUR/KEN CR8 35 F5
Russell Hill Pl PUR/KEN CR8 45 G1
Russell Hill Rd PUR/KEN CR8 35 G5
Russell Rd MTCM CR4 13 G2
WIM/MER SW19 4 C4
Russell Wy SUT SM1 32 D1
Russet Dr CROY/NA CR0 28 A2
Rusthall Cl CROY/NA CR0 17 G5
Rustic Av STRHM/NOR SW16 6 B4
Rustington Wk CHEAM SM3 22 B1
Rutford Rd STRHM/NOR SW16 7 E2
Rutherford Cl BELMT SM2 33 F2
Rutherwyke Cl EW KT17 31 E2
Rutland Cl HOR/WEW KT19 30 B5
WIM/MER SW19 5 G4
Rutland Dr MRDN SM4 22 C1
Rutland Gdns CROY/NA CR0 3 H7
Rutland Ga HAYES BR2 19 H3
Rutlish Rd WIM/MER SW19 4 C5
Rutter Gdns MTCM CR4 13 F3
Ruxley La HOR/WEW KT19 30 B1
Ruxton Cl COUL/CHIP CR5 44 C5
Rydal Cl PUR/KEN CR8 46 B3
Rydal Dr WWKM BR4 29 G3
Rydal Mt HAYES BR2 * 19 H3
Rydal Rd STRHM/NOR SW16 6 D2
Rydon's La COUL/CHIP CR5 55 E5
Rydon's Wood Cl
COUL/CHIP CR5 55 E5
Ryecroft Rd
STRHM/NOR SW16 7 G3
Ryefield Rd NRWD SE19 8 A3
Ryelands Cl CTHM CR3 59 G1
Rylandes Rd SAND/SEL CR2 37 F5
Rymer Rd CROY/NA CR0 26 C1
Ryves Cottages MTCM CR4 * 14 A1


## S


Sackville Rd BELMT SM2 32 C3
Sadler Cl MTCM CR4 13 H1
Saffron Cl CROY/NA CR0 15 E5
Sainsbury Rd NRWD SE19 8 C2
St Agatha's Gv CAR SM5 23 H2
St Alban's Gv CAR SM5 23 G1
St Albans Rd SUT SM1 22 B5
St Amunds Cl CAT SE6 10 C1
St Andrews Cl
WIM/MER SW19 4 D3
St Andrews Rd CAR SM5 23 G4
COUL/CHIP CR5 53 F1
CROY/NA CR0 2 C6
St Ann's Wy CROY/NA CR0 35 H2
St Arvans Cl CROY/NA CR0 3 H4
St Aubyn's Av WIM/MER SW19 4 B2
St Aubyn's Rd NRWD SE19 8 D3
St Augustine's Av
SAND/SEL CR2 36 A3
St Barnabas Cl BECK BR3 19 E1
St Barnabas Rd MTCM CR4 6 A4
SUT SM1 33 F1
St Bartholomew's Cl SYD SE26 9 G1
St Benet's Gv CAR SM5 23 E1
St Bernards CROY/NA CR0 3 G5
St Bernards Cl WNWD SE27 8 B1
St Christopher's Ms
WLGTN SM6 34 C1
St Clair Dr WPK KT4 21 F5
St Clair's Rd CROY/NA CR0 3 G3
St Cloud Rd WNWD SE27 8 A1
St Cyprian's St TOOT SW17 5 H1
St David's COUL/CHIP CR5 54 B2
St David's Cl WWKM BR4 28 D1
St Denis Rd WNWD SE27 8 B1
St Denys Cl PUR/KEN CR8 35 H5
St Dunstan's Hl SUT SM1 22 A5
St Dunstan's Rd SNWD SE25 16 D3
St Edwards Cl CROY/NA CR0 49 F1
St Elizabeth Dr EPSOM KT18 40 A4
St George's Gdns EW KT17 40 D4
St George's Rd BECK BR3 10 D5
MTCM CR4 14 B2
WIM/MER SW19 4 B3
WLGTN SM6 34 B1
St George's Wk CROY/NA CR0 2 D3
St Gothard Rd WNWD SE27 8 B1
St Helen's Crs
STRHM/NOR SW16 7 F5
St Helen's Rd
STRHM/NOR SW16 15 F1
St Helier Av MRDN SM4 23 E1
St Hugh's Rd PGE/AN SE20 9 F5
St James Av EW KT17 40 D1
SUT SM1 32 C1
St James Cl EPSOM KT18 40 C4
St James Ga CTHM CR3 * 60 A2
St James Rd CAR SM5 23 G4
MTCM CR4 6 A4
PUR/KEN CR8 45 H3
SUT SM1 32 C2
St James's Av BECK BR3 18 A2
St James's Cl TOOT SW17 * 6 A2
St James's Pk CROY/NA CR0 26 A1
St James's Rd CROY/NA CR0 26 A1
St Johns Av EW KT17 40 D2
St Johns Cottages
PGE/AN SE20 * 9 G4
St John's Hl COUL/CHIP CR5 54 C2
St John's Rd CAR SM5 23 G4
CROY/NA CR0 2 B4
PGE/AN SE20 9 G4
SUT SM1 22 C3
WIM/MER SW19 4 A4
St Julian's Cl
STRHM/NOR SW16 * 7 G1
St Julian's Farm Rd
WNWD SE27 7 G1
St Katharines Rd CTHM CR3 60 A5
St Kitts Ter NRWD SE19 8 C2
St Lawrence Wy CTHM CR3 59 F3
St Leonard's Rd CROY/NA CR0 2 A5
EPSOM KT18 50 C4
St Leonard's Wk
STRHM/NOR SW16 7 F4
St Louis Rd WNWD SE27 8 B1
St Luke's Cl SNWD SE25 17 F5
St Luke's Rd CTHM CR3 55 H3
St Margaret's Av CHEAM SM3 22 A4
St Margarets Dr EPSOM KT18 40 B4
St Mark's Pl WIM/MER SW19 * 4 B3
St Marks Rd EPSOM KT18 50 C3
MTCM CR4 13 H1
SNWD SE25 17 E3
St Martin's Av EPSOM KT18 40 C4
St Martin's Cl EW KT17 * 40 D3
St Martin's La BECK BR3 18 D4
St Mary Av WLGTN SM6 24 A4
St Mary's Av HAYES BR2 19 G2
St Mary's Cl EW KT17 30 D3
St Mary's Mt CTHM CR3 59 H4
St Mary's Rd SAND/SEL CR2 36 B5
SNWD SE25 16 C2
WIM/MER SW19 4 A2
WPK KT4 20 C3
St Michaels Cl WPK KT4 20 D3
St Michael's Rd CROY/NA CR0 2 D1
CTHM CR3 59 F2
WLGTN SM6 34 C2
St Nicholas Glebe TOOT SW17 6 A3
St Nicholas Rd SUT SM1 32 D1
St Nicholas Wy SUT SM1 22 D5
St Normans Wy EW KT17 31 E5
St Olave's Wk
STRHM/NOR SW16 14 C1
St Oswald's Rd
STRHM/NOR SW16 7 H5
St Paul's Cl CAR SM5 23 G2
St Paul's Rd THHTH CR7 16 A2
St Peter's Rd CROY/NA CR0 2 E7
St Peter's St SAND/SEL CR2 36 B1
St Philip's Av WPK KT4 21 F3
St Saviour's Rd CROY/NA CR0 16 A5
Saints Cl WNWD SE27 7 H1
St Stephen's Crs THHTH CR7 15 G2
St Theresa Cl EPSOM KT18 40 A4
St Vincent Cl WNWD SE27 7 H2
St Winifreds PUR/KEN CR8 46 A5
Salcombe Dr MRDN SM4 21 H2
Salcot Crs CROY/NA CR0 39 E5
Salcott Rd CROY/NA CR0 25 E4
Salem Pl CROY/NA CR0 2 B5
Salisbury Av SUT SM1 32 B2
Salisbury Cl WPK KT4 20 D4
Salisbury Gdns
WIM/MER SW19 * 4 A4
Salisbury Rd BNSTD SM7 42 D5
CAR SM5 33 H2
SNWD SE25 17 E5
WIM/MER SW19 4 A4
WPK KT4 20 B5
Salmons La CTHM CR3 55 H5
Salmons La West CTHM CR3 55 G5
Saltash Cl SUT SM1 22 B5
Salterford Rd TOOT SW17 6 A3
Salter's Hl NRWD SE19 8 B2
Salvador TOOT SW17 5 G2
Samos Rd PGE/AN SE20 17 F1
Sandbourne Av
WIM/MER SW19 12 D2
Sandersfield Gdns
BNSTD SM7 42 D5
Sanders Pde
STRHM/NOR SW16 * 7 E3
Sanderstead Court Av
SAND/SEL CR2 47 E3
Sanderstead Hl
SAND/SEL CR2 46 C1
Sanderstead Rd
SAND/SEL CR2 36 B3
Sandfield Gdns THHTH CR7 15 H2
Sandfield Pl THHTH CR7 16 A2
Sandfield Rd THHTH CR7 15 H2
Sandhills WLGTN SM6 24 D5
Sandhurst Cl SAND/SEL CR2 36 C4
Sandhurst Wy SAND/SEL CR2 36 C3
Sandiford Rd CHEAM SM3 22 B3
Sandiland Crs HAYES BR2 29 H3
Sandilands CROY/NA CR0 27 E4
Sandmartin Wy WLGTN SM6 24 A2
Sandown Ct BELMT SM2 * 32 D3
Sandown Dr CAR SM5 34 A4
Sandown Rd COUL/CHIP CR5 53 E1
SNWD SE25 17 F4
Sandpiper Rd SAND/SEL CR2 47 H1
SUT SM1 32 B1
Sandpit Rd BMLY BR1 11 G2
Sandpits Rd CROY/NA CR0 27 H5
Sandringham Av RYNPK SW20 4 A5
Sandringham Rd
CROY/NA CR0 16 A4
WPK KT4 21 E4
Sandrock Pl CROY/NA CR0 27 H5
Sandy Cft EW KT17 31 G5
Sandy Hill Rd WLGTN SM6 34 C4
Sandy La BELMT SM2 32 A4
MTCM CR4 6 A5
Sandy La North WLGTN SM6 34 D1
Sandy La South WLGTN SM6 34 C4
Sandy Wy CROY/NA CR0 28 B4
Sangley Rd SNWD SE25 16 C3
Saracen Cl CROY/NA CR0 16 B5
Savile Gdns CROY/NA CR0 3 K3
Saville Rw HAYES BR2 29 H2
Sawtry Cl CAR SM5 23 G1
Saxonbury Cl MTCM CR4 13 F2
Saxon Rd SNWD SE25 16 B4
Scarborough Cl BELMT SM2 42 B1
Scarbrook Rd CROY/NA CR0 2 C5
Scawen Cl CAR SM5 24 A5
Scotsdale Cl CHEAM SM3 32 A3
Scotshall La WARL CR6 49 E5
Scott Cl HOR/WEW KT19 30 A1
STRHM/NOR SW16 7 F5
Scotts Av HAYES BR2 19 F1
Scotts Farm Rd
HOR/WEW KT19 30 A2
Scott's La HAYES BR2 19 F2
Seabrook Dr WWKM BR4 29 G3
Seaforth Gdns
HOR/WEW KT19 20 D5
Searchwood Rd WARL CR6 56 B3
Seaton Rd MTCM CR4 13 H1
Seddon Rd MRDN SM4 13 F4
Sedgehill Rd CAT SE6 10 C2
Sedgewood Cl HAYES BR2 29 H1
Seeley Dr DUL SE21 8 C1
Seely Rd TOOT SW17 6 A3
Sefton Rd CROY/NA CR0 27 E2
HOR/WEW KT19 30 B5
Selborne Rd CROY/NA CR0 3 H5
Selby Gn CAR SM5 23 G1
Selby Rd CAR SM5 23 G1
PGE/AN SE20 17 E1
Selcroft Rd PUR/KEN CR8 45 H2
Selhurst New Rd SNWD SE25 16 C5
Selhurst Pl SNWD SE25 16 C5
Selhurst Rd SNWD SE25 16 C4
Selkirk Rd TOOT SW17 5 G1
Sellincourt Rd TOOT SW17 5 G2
Sellindge Cl BECK BR3 10 B4
Selsdon Av SAND/SEL CR2 36 B2
Selsdon Crs SAND/SEL CR2 37 G5
Selsdon Park Rd
SAND/SEL CR2 37
Selsdon Rd SAND/SEL CR2 36
Selwood Rd CHEAM SM3 22
CROY/NA CR0 27
Semley Pl STRHM/NOR SW16 15
Semley Rd STRHM/NOR SW16 15
Seneca Rd THHTH CR7 16
Senga Rd WLGTN SM6 24
Senhouse Rd CHEAM SM3 21
Sergeants Pl CTHM CR3 59
Seven Acres CAR SM5 23
Sevenoaks Cl BELMT SM2 32
Seward Rd BECK BR3 17
Seymour Av CTHM CR3 59
EW KT17 31
MRDN SM4 21
Seymour Ms EW KT17 31
Seymour Pl SNWD SE25 17
Seymour Rd CAR SM5 34
MTCM CR4 24
Seymour Ter PGE/AN SE20 9
Seymour Vls PGE/AN SE20 9
Shadbolt Cl WPK KT4 20
Shaftesbury Rd BECK BR3 18
CAR SM5 23
Shafteswood Ct TOOT SW17 * 5
Shaldon Dr MRDN SM4 12
Shamrock Rd CROY/NA CR0 15
Shannon Wy BECK BR3 10
Shap Crs CAR SM5 23
Sharland Cl THHTH CR7 15
Sharon Cl HOR/WEW KT19 40
Shaw Cl EW KT17 40
SAND/SEL CR2 46
Shaw Crs SAND/SEL CR2 46
Shawford Rd
HOR/WEW KT19 30
Shawley Crs EPSOM KT18 50
Shawley Wy EPSOM KT18 50
Shaw Wy WLGTN SM6 35
Shaxton Crs CROY/NA CR0 39
Shearing Dr CAR SM5 23
Shearwater Rd SUT SM1 32
Sheenewood SYD SE26 9
Sheen Wy WLGTN SM6 35
Sheephouse Wy NWMAL KT3 20
Sheldon Cl PGE/AN SE20 9
Sheldon St CROY/NA CR0 2
Sheldrick Cl MTCM CR4 13
Shelford Ri NRWD SE19 8
Shelley Cl BNSTD SM7 41
COUL/CHIP CR5 54
Shelley Wy WIM/MER SW19 5
Shelton Av WARL CR6 56
Shelton Cl WARL CR6 56
Shelton Rd WIM/MER SW19 4
Shenfield Cl COUL/CHIP CR5 53
Shepherds Wy SAND/SEL CR2 37
Shepley Cl CAR SM5 24
Sheraton Dr HOR/WEW KT19 40
Sherborne Cl EPSOM KT18 50
Sherborne Crs CAR SM5 23
Sherborne Rd CHEAM SM3 22
Sherbrooke Wy WPK KT4 21
Shere Av BELMT SM2 31
Sheridan Rd WIM/MER SW19 4
Sheridan Wk CAR SM5 33
Sheridan Wy BECK BR3 10
Sheringham Rd PGE/AN SE20 17
Sherwood Av
STRHM/NOR SW16 6
Sherwood Park Rd
MTCM CR4 14
SUT SM1 32
Sherwood Rd
COUL/CHIP CR5 53
CROY/NA CR0 27
WIM/MER SW19 4
Sherwood Wy WWKM BR4 29
Shinners Cl SNWD SE25 17
Shire Ct EW KT17 30
Shirley Av BELMT SM2 32
COUL/CHIP CR5 54
CROY/NA CR0 27
SUT SM1 23
Shirley Church Rd
CROY/NA CR0 27
Shirley Crs BECK BR3 18
Shirley Hills Rd CROY/NA CR0 27
Shirley Oaks Rd
CROY/NA CR0 27
Shirley Park Rd
CROY/NA CR0 27
Shirley Rd CROY/NA CR0 27
WLGTN SM6 34
Shirley Rw SNWD SE25 * 17
Shirley Wy CROY/NA CR0 28
Shops SYD SE26 * 9
Shord Hl PUR/KEN CR8 55
Shoreham Cl CROY/NA CR0 17
Shortcroft Rd EW KT17 30
Shortlands Gdns HAYES BR2 19
Shortlands Gv HAYES BR2 19
Shortlands Rd HAYES BR2 19
Shorts Rd CAR SM5 23
Shotfield WLGTN SM6 34
Shott Cl SUT SM1 33
Shrewsbury Rd BECK BR3 18
CAR SM5 23
Shrewton Rd TOOT SW17 * 5
Shroffold Rd BMLY BR1 11
Shropshire Cl MTCM CR4 15
Shrubbery Rd
STRHM/NOR SW16 7
Shrubland Gv WPK KT4 21
Shrubland Rd BNSTD SM7 51
Shrublands Av CROY/NA CR0 28
Sibthorp Rd MTCM CR4 * 13
Sibton Rd CAR SM5 23
Siddons Rd CROY/NA CR0 25
Sidney Rd BECK BR3 18

'NWD SE25 17 E4
ury Av MTCM CR4 5 G5
erdale SYD SE26 9 H1
erdale Cl SUT SM1 22 B5
rgate HOR/WEW KT19 30 A1
r La PUR/KEN CR8 44 D2
'WKM BR4 29 F3
erleigh Rd THHTH CR7 15 F3
rmere Rw SNWD SE25 * 17 E1
rwood Cl BECK BR3 10 C4
ROY/NA CR0 38 B4
ns Cl CAR SM5 23 G3
one Dr PUR/KEN CR8 55 E1
air Dr BELMT SM2 32 D4
'eton Cl CROY/NA CR0 26 A1
OOT SW17 5 H4
yril Black Wy
IM/MER SW19 4 C4
r Rd MTCM CR4 6 A3
ghurst Cl BMLY BR1 11 G2
ghurst Rd
ROY/NA CR0 27 E1
Hill La WARL CR6 49 H5
e Wy MTCM CR4 6 A5
s New Rd CTHM CR3 56 D5
s Oak Rd CTHM CR3 61 G3
ARL CR6 57 G5
ne Wk CROY/NA CR0 18 B5
lwood Rd TOOT SW17 5 F1
ham Bottom La
JR/KEN CR8 44 D2
ham Downs Rd
JR/KEN CR8 45 E4
vdown Cl PGE/AN SE20 9 G5
ns Court Rd BNSTD SM7 52 C2
erfield Cl
VD/TDW/WH KT20 51 E4
erset Cl HOR/WEW KT19 30 C5
erset Gdns
RHM/NOR SW16 15 F2
erset Rd WIM/MER SW19 4 A1
erton Cl PUR/KEN CR8 54 C1
erville Rd PGE/AN SE20 9 H4
hurst Cl CROY/NA CR0 15 F5
ing Rd SNWD SE25 17 E5
r Dr CTHM CR3 59 F3
l Bank CROY/NA CR0 38 A5
nto Rd SUT SM1 22 D4
hampton Gdns
TCM CR4 15 E4
n Av CAR SM5 34 A3
outh Border
IR/KEN CR8 44 D1
nbridge Pl CROY/NA CR0 2 C6
nbridge Rd CROY/NA CR0 2 C6
brook Rd
RHM/NOR SW16 7 E5
acote Rd SAND/SEL CR2 36 D5
WD SE25 17 F4
croft Av WWKM BR4 29 E3
croft Rd
RHM/NOR SW16 6 B3
Croxted Rd DUL SE21 8 B1
down Rd CAR SM5 34 A4
HM CR3 61 F2
Dr BELMT SM2 32 A5
STD SM7 43 G3
UL/CHIP CR5 44 D5
Eden Park Rd
CK BR3 18 D4
End CROY/NA CR0 2 D7
ND/SEL CR2 36 A1
end La CAT SE6 10 C1
end Rd BECK BR3 10 C5
ern Av SNWD SE25 16 D2
ey Rd WIM/MER SW19 4 C4
ey St PGE/AN SE20 9 H4
fields Rd CTHM CR3 61 H5
Gdns WIM/MER SW19 5 F4
Hill Rd HAYES BR2 19 G3
holme Cl NRWD SE19 8 C5
lands Cl
UL/CHIP CR5 54 B2
Lodge Av MTCM CR4 15 E3
Md HOR/WEW KT19 30 D3
Norwood Hl
WD SE25 16 D2
Oak Rd
HM/NOR SW16 7 F1
Pde WLGTN SM6 * 34 C2
Park Hill Rd
ID/SEL CR2 36 C1
Park Rd
M/MER SW19 4 D3
Ri CAR SM5 33 G4
Rd WIM/MER SW19 5 F3
St EPSOM KT18 40 B3
V NRWD SE19 8 C3
view Cl TOOT SW17 6 A2
View Ct NRWD SE19 * 8 A4
view Gdns WLGTN SM6 34 C3
view Rd BMLY BR1 11 F1
HM CR3 61 H5
RL CR6 56 B5
views SAND/SEL CR2 37 H4
ville Cl HOR/WEW KT19 30 B4
Wk WWKM BR4 29 G4
water Cl BECK BR3 10 D4
Wy CAR SM5 33 F5
Y/NA CR0 28 A4
way WLGTN SM6 24 C5
well Rd CROY/NA CR0 15 G5
wood Av
IL/CHIP CR5 44 C5
wood Cl WPK KT4 21 H2
wood Dr BRYLDS KT5 20 A1
eign Cl PUR/KEN CR8 35 F5
NRWD SE19 8 B5
ng Rd TOOT SW17 6 B2
w Farm Rd EW KT17 31 F1
n Cl WLGTN SM6 35 E3
ers Ct CROY/NA CR0 * 26 B2
Speke Rd THHTH CR7 16 B1
Speldhurst Cl HAYES BR2 19 H4
Spencer Hl WIM/MER SW19 4 A3
Spencer Hill Rd
WIM/MER SW19 4 A4
Spencer Pl CROY/NA CR0 26 B1
Spencer Rd BMLY BR1 11 H4
CTHM CR3 59 F1
MTCM CR4 23 H1
SAND/SEL CR2 36 C1
Spices Yd CROY/NA CR0 2 D6
Spindlewood Gdns
CROY/NA CR0 3 F6
Spinney Cl BECK BR3 18 D3
WPK KT4 20 D4
Spinney Gdns NRWD SE19 8 D2
The Spinney CHEAM SM3 21 G5
EPSOM KT18 50 B4
PUR/KEN CR8 45 H1
Spire Pl WARL CR6 56 D3
Spitfire Rd WLGTN SM6 35 F3
Spooner Wk WLGTN SM6 34 D1
Spout Hl CROY/NA CR0 38 C1
Springbourne Ct BECK BR3 11 E5
Springclose La CHEAM SM3 32 A2
Springfield Av RYNPK SW20 12 B2
Springfield Gdns WWKM BR4 28 D3
Springfield Ri SYD SE26 9 F1
Springfield Rd EW KT17 31 G5
SYD SE26 9 F3
THHTH CR7 8 A5
WIM/MER SW19 4 B2
WLGTN SM6 34 B1
Spring Gdns WLGTN SM6 34 C1
Spring Gv MTCM CR4 6 A5
Spring Hl SYD SE26 9 G1
Springhurst Cl CROY/NA CR0 28 B5
Spring La SNWD SE25 17 F5
Spring Park Av CROY/NA CR0 27 H3
Springpark Dr BECK BR3 19 E2
Spring Park Rd CROY/NA CR0 27 H3
Spring St EW KT17 30 D4
Springwell Rd
STRHM/NOR SW16 7 G1
Sprucedale Gdns
CROY/NA CR0 27 H5
WLGTN SM6 35 E4
Spurgeon Av NRWD SE19 8 B5
Spurgeon Rd NRWD SE19 8 B4
The Square CAR SM5 34 A1
The Squerryes CTHM CR3 59 G1
Squires Ct WIM/MER SW19 4 C1
Squirrels Gn WPK KT4 20 D3
Squirrel's Wy EPSOM KT18 40 B5
Stable Ms WNWD SE27 8 A2
Staddon Cl BECK BR3 18 A3
Staddon Ct BECK BR3 18 A3
Stafford Cl CHEAM SM3 32 A2
CTHM CR3 59 H3
Stafford Cross CROY/NA CR0 35 F1
Stafford Gdns CROY/NA CR0 35 F1
Stafford Rd CROY/NA CR0 25 G5
CTHM CR3 59 H3
WLGTN SM6 34 C2
Stagbury Av COUL/CHIP CR5 52 C3
Stagbury Cl COUL/CHIP CR5 52 C4
Stagbury House
COUL/CHIP CR5 52 C4
Stag Leys Cl BNSTD SM7 43 G5
Stainbank Rd MTCM CR4 14 B2
Staines Av CHEAM SM3 21 H3
Staiths Wy
KWD/TDW/WH KT20 50 B5
Stambourne Wy NRWD SE19 8 C4
WWKM BR4 29 F4
Stambourne Woodland Wk
NRWD SE19 8 C4
Stamford Dr HAYES BR2 19 H3
Stane Cl WIM/MER SW19 4 D4
Stane Wy EW KT17 31 E5
Stanford Rd
STRHM/NOR SW16 15 E1
The Stanfords EW KT17 40 D2
Stanford Wy
STRHM/NOR SW16 14 D1
Stanger Rd SNWD SE25 17 E3
Stanhope Gv BECK BR3 18 B4
Stanhope Rd CAR SM5 34 A3
CROY/NA CR0 3 G5
Stanley Av BECK BR3 19 E2
Stanley Cl COUL/CHIP CR5 54 B2
Stanley Gdns MTCM CR4 * 6 A3
SAND/SEL CR2 47 E2
WLGTN SM6 34 C2
Stanley Gv CROY/NA CR0 15 G5
Stanley Park Rd CAR SM5 33 H3
WLGTN SM6 34 B3
Stanley Rd BELMT SM2 32 D2
CAR SM5 33 H4
CROY/NA CR0 25 G1
MRDN SM4 12 C3
MTCM CR4 6 A4
WIM/MER SW19 4 C4
Stanley Sq CAR SM5 33 H4
Stanley St CTHM CR3 59 E2
Stanmore Gdns SUT SM1 23 E4
Stanmore Ter BECK BR3 18 C1
Stannet Wy WLGTN SM6 24 C5
Stanstead Cl HAYES BR2 19 H4
Stanstead Rd CTHM CR3 59 G4
Stanthorpe Cl
STRHM/NOR SW16 * 7 E2
Stanthorpe Rd
STRHM/NOR SW16 7 E2
Stanton Cl WPK KT4 21 H2
Stanton Rd CROY/NA CR0 26 A1
Stanton Wy SYD SE26 10 B1
Staplehurst Rd CAR SM5 33 G3
Stapleton Gdns
CROY/NA CR0 35 G1
Starling Rd CROY/NA CR0 18 A5
Starrock La COUL/CHIP CR5 53 E5
Starrock Rd COUL/CHIP CR5 53 F4
Station Ap BECK BR3 10 A5
BELMT SM2 32 A3
COUL/CHIP CR5 52 D3
CROY/NA CR0 3 F3
CTHM CR3 56 A2
EW KT17 31 F5
HOR/WEW KT19 40 B3
PUR/KEN CR8 * 45 G1
SAND/SEL CR2 36 B4
STRHM/NOR SW16 6 D2
SYD SE26 10 B2
Station Av CTHM CR3 60 A4
HOR/WEW KT19 30 C4
Station Est BECK BR3 17 H3
Station Garage Ms
STRHM/NOR SW16 * 6 D3
Station Pde BECK BR3 * 17 H3
BELMT SM2 * 33 E2
Station Rd BELMT SM2 32 D5
BELMT SM2 42 D1
CAR SM5 23 H5
CROY/NA CR0 2 D1
CTHM CR3 55 H3
HAYES BR2 19 G1
PGE/AN SE20 9 G3
PUR/KEN CR8 46 A4
SNWD SE25 16 D3
WIM/MER SW19 5 E5
WWKM BR4 29 E3
Station Wy CHEAM SM3 32 A2
Station Yd PUR/KEN CR8 * 45 H2
Stavordale Rd CAR SM5 23 E1
Stayton Rd SUT SM1 22 C4
Steep Hl CROY/NA CR0 3 G6
Steeple Cl WIM/MER SW19 4 A2
Steers Md MTCM CR4 5 H5
Stella Rd TOOT SW17 5 H3
Stembridge Rd PGE/AN SE20 17 F1
Stepney Wy MTCM CR4 6 A5
Sterry Dr HOR/WEW KT19 20 C5
Steve Biko La CAT SE6 10 C1
Stevens Cl BECK BR3 10 C3
EW KT17 40 C2
Stevens Pl PUR/KEN CR8 45 H3
Steyning Cl PUR/KEN CR8 54 D1
Stirling Av WLGTN SM6 35 E3
Stirling Cl BNSTD SM7 51 F2
STRHM/NOR SW16 6 C5
Stirling Dr CTHM CR3 59 E1
Stirling Wy CROY/NA CR0 25 E1
Stites Hill Rd COUL/CHIP CR5 54 D5
Stoats Nest Rd
COUL/CHIP CR5 45 E5
Stoats West Village
COUL/CHIP CR5 45 E5
Stockbury Rd CROY/NA CR0 17 G5
Stockhams Cl SAND/SEL CR2 36 B5
Stockport Rd
STRHM/NOR SW16 6 D5
Stodart Rd PGE/AN SE20 9 G5
Stokes Rd CROY/NA CR0 17 H5
Stonecot Cl CHEAM SM3 22 A2
Stonecot Hl CHEAM SM3 22 A2
Stonecroft Wy CROY/NA CR0 25 E1
Stone House Gdns CTHM CR3 59 G5
Stoneleigh Av WPK KT4 21 E4
Stoneleigh Broadway
EW KT17 31 E1
Stoneleigh Crs
HOR/WEW KT19 31 E1
Stoneleigh Park Av
CROY/NA CR0 17 H5
Stoneleigh Park Rd
HOR/WEW KT19 30 D2
Stoneleigh Rd CAR SM5 23 G1
Stone Park Av BECK BR3 18 D3
Stone Pl WPK KT4 21 E3
Stone's Rd EW KT17 40 C1
Stoneyfield Rd
COUL/CHIP CR5 54 B2
Stoney La NRWD SE19 8 D3
Storrington Rd CROY/NA CR0 26 D2
Stoughton Av CHEAM SM3 31 H1
Stowell Av CROY/NA CR0 39 F5
Stratford Rd THHTH CR7 15 G3
Strathbrook Rd
STRHM/NOR SW16 7 F1
Strathdale STRHM/NOR SW16 7 F2
Strathearn Rd SUT SM1 32 C1
WIM/MER SW19 4 C2
Strathmore Cl CTHM CR3 59 G1
Strathmore Rd CROY/NA CR0 26 A1
Strathyre Av
STRHM/NOR SW16 15 G2
Stratton Av WLGTN SM6 34 D4
Stratton Cl WIM/MER SW19 12 B1
Stratton Rd WIM/MER SW19 12 C1
Strawberry La CAR SM5 23 H4
Straw Cl CTHM CR3 59 E3
Streatham Common
STRHM/NOR SW16 * 6 D4
Streatham Common North
STRHM/NOR SW16 7 F2
Streatham Common South
STRHM/NOR SW16 7 E3
Streatham Gn
STRHM/NOR SW16 * 7 E1
Streatham High Rd
STRHM/NOR SW16 7 E2
Streatham Rd MTCM CR4 6 B4
Streatham V
STRHM/NOR SW16 6 C4
Streeters La WLGTN SM6 24 D4
Stretton Rd CROY/NA CR0 26 C1
Strond Green Gdns
CROY/NA CR0 27 G1
Strond Green Wy
CROY/NA CR0 27 G1
Stroudes Cl WPK KT4 20 D1
Stroud Green Wy
CROY/NA CR0 27 F1
Stroud Rd SNWD SE25 17 E5
Stuart Crs CROY/NA CR0 28 B4
Stuart Pl MTCM CR4 5 H5
Stuart Rd THHTH CR7 16 A3
WARL CR6 56 B5
Stubbs Wy WIM/MER SW19 5 F5
Studland Rd SYD SE26 9 H2
Stumps Hill La BECK BR3 10 C3
Styles Wy BECK BR3 19 E3
Succomb's Hl CTHM CR3 56 B5
Succombs Pl WARL CR6 56 B5
Sudbury Gdns CROY/NA CR0 3 H6
Suffield Cl SAND/SEL CR2 47 H2
Suffield Rd PGE/AN SE20 17 G1
Suffolk Rd SNWD SE25 16 D3
WPK KT4 20 D3
Sultan St BECK BR3 17 H1
Summerene Cl
STRHM/NOR SW16 6 C4
Summerhill Wy MTCM CR4 6 A5
Summers Cl BELMT SM2 32 C3
Summerswood Cl
PUR/KEN CR8 55 F1
Summerville Gdns SUT SM1 32 B2
Summit Wy NRWD SE19 8 C4
Sumner Gdns CROY/NA CR0 25 H2
Sumner Rd CROY/NA CR0 25 H2
Sumner Rd South
CROY/NA CR0 25 G2
Sunbury Rd CHEAM SM3 21 H4
Sundale Av SAND/SEL CR2 37 G5
Sundial Av SNWD SE25 16 D1
Sundown Av SAND/SEL CR2 46 D1
Sundridge Pl CROY/NA CR0 27 E2
Sundridge Rd CROY/NA CR0 26 D2
Sunken Rd CROY/NA CR0 37 G1
Sunkist Wy WLGTN SM6 35 E4
Sunlight Cl
WIM/MER SW19 * 5 E3
Sunningdale Rd SUT SM1 22 B4
Sunny Bank SNWD SE25 17 E3
WARL CR6 57 E2
Sunnycroft Rd SNWD SE25 17 E3
Sunnydene Rd PUR/KEN CR8 45 H3
Sunnydene St SYD SE26 10 A1
Sunnyhill Rd
STRHM/NOR SW16 7 E1
Sunnyhurst Cl SUT SM1 22 C4
Sunnymead Av MTCM CR4 14 D2
Sunnymede Av CAR SM5 43 F1
HOR/WEW KT19 30 C4
Sunny Nook Gdns
SAND/SEL CR2 36 B2
Sunny Ri CTHM CR3 59 F4
Sunnyside Pl WIM/MER SW19 4 A3
Sunset Gdns SNWD SE25 16 C1
Sunshine Wy MTCM CR4 13 H1
Surrey Gv SUT SM1 23 F4
Surrey Ms WNWD SE27 8 C1
Surrey Rd WWKM BR4 28 D2
Surrey St CROY/NA CR0 2 C3
Surridge Gdns NRWD SE19 8 B3
Sussex Rd CAR SM5 33 H2
MTCM CR4 * 15 E4
SAND/SEL CR2 36 B2
WWKM BR4 28 D2
Sussex Ter PGE/AN SE20 * 9 G4
Sutherland Dr
WIM/MER SW19 5 F5
Sutherland Gdns WPK KT4 21 F2
Sutherland Rd CROY/NA CR0 25 G1
Sutton Cl BECK BR3 10 D5
Sutton Common Rd
CHEAM SM3 22 C2
Sutton Ct BELMT SM2 33 E3
Sutton Court Rd SUT SM1 33 E2
Sutton Gdns CROY/NA CR0 16 D4
Sutton Gv SUT SM1 33 F1
Sutton La BNSTD SM7 42 D2
Sutton Park Rd SUT SM1 32 D2
Swain Cl STRHM/NOR SW16 6 B3
Swain Rd THHTH CR7 16 A4
Swains Rd MTCM CR4 5 H4
Swallands Rd CAT SE6 10 D1
Swallowdale SAND/SEL CR2 37 H4
Swallow Gdns
STRHM/NOR SW16 6 D2
Swan Cl CROY/NA CR0 * 26 C1
Swiftsden Wy BMLY BR1 11 G3
Swinburne Crs CROY/NA CR0 17 G5
Sycamore Cl CAR SM5 23 H5
SAND/SEL CR2 36 C1
Sycamore Gdns MTCM CR4 13 F1
Sycamore Gv PGE/AN SE20 9 E5
Sycamore Ri BNSTD SM7 41 H4
Sydenham Av SYD SE26 9 F2
Sydenham Rd CROY/NA CR0 2 E1
SYD SE26 9 H2
Sydenham Station Ap
SYD SE26 9 G1
Sydney Av PUR/KEN CR8 45 F2
Sydney Rd SUT SM1 22 C5
Sylvan Cl SAND/SEL CR2 37 F5
Sylvan Hl NRWD SE19 8 D5
Sylvan Rd NRWD SE19 8 D5
Sylvan Wy WWKM BR4 29 G5
Sylverdale Rd CROY/NA CR0 2 A4
PUR/KEN CR8 45 H3

## T

Tabarin Wy EW KT17 50 C1
Tabor Gdns CHEAM SM3 32 B2
Tabor Gv WIM/MER SW19 4 A4
Taffy's How MTCM CR4 13 G2
Tait Rd CROY/NA CR0 26 C1
Talbot Rd CAR SM5 34 A1
THHTH CR7 16 B3
Talisman Sq SYD SE26 9 E1
Talisman Wy EW KT17 50 C1
Tall Elms Cl HAYES BR2 19 H4
Tall Trees STRHM/NOR SW16 15 F2
Tamesis Gdns WPK KT4 20 C3
Tamworth La MTCM CR4 14 B2
Tamworth Pk MTCM CR4 14 B3
Tamworth Pl CROY/NA CR0 2 C3
Tamworth Rd CROY/NA CR0 2 C3
Tandridge Gdns
SAND/SEL CR2 46 D3
Tandridge Rd WARL CR6 56 D4
Tanfield Rd CROY/NA CR0 2 C6
Tangier Wy
KWD/TDW/WH KT20 51 E2
Tangier Wd
KWD/TDW/WH KT20 51 E3
Tanglewood Cl CROY/NA CR0 27 G4
Tankerton Ter
CROY/NA CR0 * 25 F1
Tankerville Rd
STRHM/NOR SW16 6 D4
Tannery Cl CROY/NA CR0 17 H4
Tannsfeld Rd SYD SE26 9 H2
Tapestry Cl BELMT SM2 32 D3
Taplow Ct MTCM CR4 13 G3
Tarragon Gv SYD SE26 9 H3
Tarrington Cl
STRHM/NOR SW16 * 6 D1
Tate Rd SUT SM1 32 C1
Tattenham Corner Rd
EPSOM KT18 50 A3
Tattenham Crs EPSOM KT18 50 B3
Tattenham Gv EPSOM KT18 50 B4
Tattenham Wy
KWD/TDW/WH KT20 51 E2
Taunton Av CTHM CR3 59 H3
Taunton Cl CHEAM SM3 22 C2
Taunton La COUL/CHIP CR5 54 C4
Tavern Cl CAR SM5 23 G1
Tavistock Crs MTCM CR4 15 E3
Tavistock Gv CROY/NA CR0 26 B1
Tavistock Rd CAR SM5 23 F2
CROY/NA CR0 26 B2
Tayles Hill Dr EW KT17 30 D5
Taylor Rd MTCM CR4 5 G4
WLGTN SM6 34 B1
Taylor's La SYD SE26 9 F1
Teal Cl SAND/SEL CR2 47 H1
Tealing Dr HOR/WEW KT19 20 B5
Teal Pl SUT SM1 32 B1
Teasel Cl CROY/NA CR0 27 H2
Tedder Rd SAND/SEL CR2 37 H3
Teddington Cl
HOR/WEW KT19 30 B5
Teesdale Gdns SNWD SE25 16 C1
Teevan Cl CROY/NA CR0 27 E1
Teevan Rd CROY/NA CR0 27 E1
Telegraph Tr CAR SM5 34 A5
WLGTN SM6 44 A1
Telford Cl NRWD SE19 8 D3
Temple Av CROY/NA CR0 28 B4
Templecombe Wy
MRDN SM4 12 A4
Templeman Cl PUR/KEN CR8 54 C1
Temple Rd CROY/NA CR0 2 E7
HOR/WEW KT19 40 B2
Templeton Cl NRWD SE19 8 B5
Temple Wy SUT SM1 23 F4
Tennison Cl COUL/CHIP CR5 54 D5
Tennison Rd SNWD SE25 16 D3
Tennyson Rd PGE/AN SE20 9 H4
WIM/MER SW19 5 E3
Tenterden Gdns
CROY/NA CR0 27 E1
Tenterden Rd CROY/NA CR0 27 F1
Tewkesbury Rd CAR SM5 23 F2
Thakeham Cl SYD SE26 9 F2
Thames Down Link
HOR/WEW KT19 20 A5
Thanescroft Gdns
CROY/NA CR0 3 H5
Thanet Pl CROY/NA CR0 2 D6
Tharp Rd WLGTN SM6 34 D1
Thayers Farm Rd BECK BR3 10 A5
Theobald Rd CROY/NA CR0 2 A2
Therapia La CROY/NA CR0 24 D1
Theresa's Wk SAND/SEL CR2 36 B4
Thesiger Rd PGE/AN SE20 9 H4
Thicket Crs SUT SM1 23 E5
Thicket Gv PGE/AN SE20 9 E4
Thicket Rd PGE/AN SE20 9 F4
SUT SM1 23 E5
Thicket Ter PGE/AN SE20 * 9 E4
Thirlmere Ri BMLY BR1 11 H3
Thirlmere Rd
STRHM/NOR SW16 6 D1
Thirsk Rd MTCM CR4 6 A4
SNWD SE25 16 B3
Thistlewood Crs
CROY/NA CR0 49 F2
Thomas Av CTHM CR3 59 E1
Thomas Dean Rd SYD SE26 * 10 B1
Thomas Wall Cl SUT SM1 32 D1
Thompson Cl CHEAM SM3 22 C2
Thomson Crs CROY/NA CR0 25 G2
Thorburn Wy
WIM/MER SW19 * 5 F5
Thorn Ct BELMT SM2 * 32 D3
Thorncroft Cl COUL/CHIP CR5 54 C4
Thorncroft Rd SUT SM1 22 D5
Thorndon Gdns
HOR/WEW KT19 20 C5
Thorneloe Gdns
CROY/NA CR0 35 H1
Thorne's Cl BECK BR3 19 E2
Thornhill Rd CROY/NA CR0 26 A1
Thornlaw Rd WNWD SE27 7 G1
Thornsett Pl PGE/AN SE20 17 F1
Thornsett Rd PGE/AN SE20 17 F1
Thornsett Ter PGE/AN SE20 * 17 F1
Thornton Av CROY/NA CR0 15 F5
Thornton Crs COUL/CHIP CR5 54 C4

Thornton Dene BECK BR3 18 C1
Thornton Hl WIM/MER SW19 4 A4
Thornton Rd CAR SM5 23 G1
THHTH CR7 15 G4
Thornton Rw THHTH CR7 15 G4
Thornville Gv MTCM CR4 13 F1
Thorold Cl SAND/SEL CR2 37 H5
Thorpe Cl CROY/NA CR0 49 F1
SYD SE26 * 9 H1
Thorpe Ct TOOT SW17 5 G1
Thorsden Wy NRWD SE19 * 8 C2
Thrale Rd STRHM/NOR SW16 6 C2
Throwley Rd SUT SM1 32 D1
Throwley Wy SUT SM1 22 D5
Thrupp Cl MTCM CR4 14 B1
Thurbarn Rd CAT SE6 10 D2
Thurlby Rd WNWD SE27 7 G1
Thurleston Av MRDN SM4 12 A4
Thurnham Wy
KWD/TDW/WH KT20 50 D5
Thursley Crs CROY/NA CR0 39 F3
Thurso St TOOT SW17 5 F1
Tichmarsh HOR/WEW KT19 30 A5
Tidenham Gdns CROY/NA CR0 3 H4
Tideswell Rd CROY/NA CR0 28 C4
Tiepigs La WWKM BR4 29 G3
Tilehurst Rd CHEAM SM3 32 A1
Tilford Av CROY/NA CR0 39 E3
Tilia Cl SUT SM1 32 B1
Tillingdown Hl CTHM CR3 60 B2
Tillingdown La CTHM CR3 60 B5
Timbercroft HOR/WEW KT19 20 C5
Timber Hill Rd CTHM CR3 60 A4
Timberling Gdns
SAND/SEL CR2 36 B5
Timberslip Dr WLGTN SM6 34 D4
The Timbers CHEAM SM3 * 32 A2
Times Sq SUT SM1 * 32 D1
Tindale Cl SAND/SEL CR2 46 B1
Tinsley Cl SNWD SE25 17 F2
Tintagel Cl EW KT17 40 D4
Tintern Cl WIM/MER SW19 5 E4
Tintern Rd CAR SM5 23 F2
Tipton Dr CROY/NA CR0 3 H6
Tirlemont Rd SAND/SEL CR2 36 A3
Tirrell Rd CROY/NA CR0 16 A5
Tisbury Rd STRHM/NOR SW16 15 E1
Titchfield Rd CAR SM5 23 F2
Titchfield Wk CAR SM5 23 F1
Tithepit Shaw La WARL CR6 56 B2
Tiverton Cl CROY/NA CR0 26 D1
Tivoli Rd WNWD SE27 8 A2
Tollers La COUL/CHIP CR5 54 B4
Tollhouse La WLGTN SM6 34 C4
Tolworth Ri North
BRYLDS KT5 20 A1
Tolworth Ri North
(Kingston By-Pass)
BRYLDS KT5 20 A2
Tolworth Ri South
BRYLDS KT5 20 A2
Tomlin Cl HOR/WEW KT19 40 B1
Tonbridge Cl BNSTD SM7 43 H4
Tonfield Rd CHEAM SM3 22 B2
Tonge Cl BECK BR3 18 C4
Tonstall Rd HOR/WEW KT19 30 B5
MTCM CR4 14 A1
Tooting Bec Gdns
STRHM/NOR SW16 6 D1
Tooting Gv TOOT SW17 5 G2
Tooting High St TOOT SW17 5 G3
Tooting Market TOOT SW17 * 5 H1
Tootswood Rd HAYES BR2 19 G4
Top Pk BECK BR3 19 G4
Tormead Cl SUT SM1 32 C2
Torridge Rd THHTH CR7 15 H4
Torrington Sq
CROY/NA CR0 * 26 B1
Torrington Wy MRDN SM4 22 C1
Torr Rd PGE/AN SE20 9 H4
Torwood La CTHM CR3 55 H5
Totterdown St TOOT SW17 5 H1
Totton Rd THHTH CR7 15 G2
Tovil Cl PGE/AN SE20 17 E1
Tower Cl PGE/AN SE20 9 F4
Tower Pl WARL CR6 48 C5
The Towers PUR/KEN CR8 46 A5
Tower Vw CROY/NA CR0 28 A2
Townend CTHM CR3 59 G2
Town End Cl CTHM CR3 59 G2
Towpath Wy CROY/NA CR0 16 D5
Toynbee Rd RYNPK SW20 4 A5
The Tracery BNSTD SM7 42 D5
Trafalgar Av WPK KT4 21 H2
Trafalgar Rd WIM/MER SW19 4 D4
Trafalgar Wy CROY/NA CR0 25 G3
Trafford Rd THHTH CR7 15 F4
Tramway Cl PGE/AN SE20 9 G5
Tramway Pth MTCM CR4 13 G3
Treadwell Rd EPSOM KT18 40 D5
Tredown Rd SYD SE26 9 G2
Tredwell Rd WNWD SE27 7 H1
Tree Tops CTHM CR3 56 A3
Tree View Cl NRWD SE19 8 C5
Treloar Gdns NRWD SE19 8 B3
Tremaine Rd PGE/AN SE20 17 F1
Trenham Dr WARL CR6 56 C1
Trenholme Rd PGE/AN SE20 9 F4
Trenholme Ter PGE/AN SE20 9 F4
Trent Wy WPK KT4 21 G4
Tresco Cl BMLY BR1 11 G3
Trevelyan Rd TOOT SW17 5 H3
Trevor Rd WIM/MER SW19 4 A4
Trewsbury Rd SYD SE26 9 H2
Trinity Cl SAND/SEL CR2 36 C4
Trinity Ms PGE/AN SE20 17 F1
Trinity Rd WIM/MER SW19 4 C3
Tristram Rd BMLY BR1 11 H1
Tritton Av CROY/NA CR0 25 E5
Trojan Wy CROY/NA CR0 25 F4
Troy Rd NRWD SE19 8 B3
Truslove Rd WNWD SE27 7 G2
Tudor Av WPK KT4 21 F4
Tudor Cl BNSTD SM7 42 A5
CHEAM SM3 31 H1
COUL/CHIP CR5 54 C3
SAND/SEL CR2 47 F5
WLGTN SM6 34 C3
Tudor Dr MRDN SM4 22 B1
Tudor Gdns WWKM BR4 29 E4
Tudor Pl MTCM CR4 5 G4
NRWD SE19 * 8 D4
Tudor Rd BECK BR3 19 E2
NRWD SE19 8 D4
SNWD SE25 17 F4
Tugela Rd CROY/NA CR0 16 B5
Tulip Cl CROY/NA CR0 27 H2
Tull St CAR SM5 23 H1
Tulse Cl BECK BR3 19 E2
Tulyar Cl KWD/TDW/WH KT20 50 B4
Tumblewood Rd BNSTD SM7 51 E1
Tummons Gdns SNWD SE25 16 C1
Tunstall Rd CROY/NA CR0 3 H1
Tupwood Ct CTHM CR3 60 A5
Tupwood Scrubbs Rd
CTHM CR3 * 56 A5
Turkey Oak Cl NRWD SE19 8 C5
Turle Rd STRHM/NOR SW16 15 E1
Turner Av MTCM CR4 5 H5
Turner Ms BELMT SM2 32 D3
Turner Rd NWMAL KT3 20 B1
Turners Meadow Wy
BECK BR3 10 B5
Turners Wy CROY/NA CR0 25 G3
Turnpike La SUT SM1 33 E1
Turnpike Link CROY/NA CR0 3 H3
Turnstone Cl SAND/SEL CR2 38 A5
Turpin Wy WLGTN SM6 34 B3
Tweeddale Rd CAR SM5 23 F2
Twickenham Cl CROY/NA CR0 25 F4
Twyford Rd CAR SM5 23 F2
Tybenham Rd
WIM/MER SW19 12 C2
Tydcombe Rd WARL CR6 56 C4
Tylecroft Rd
STRHM/NOR SW16 15 E1
Tylney Av NRWD SE19 8 D2
Tynemouth Rd MTCM CR4 6 A4

U

Uckfield Gv MTCM CR4 6 A5
Uffington Rd WNWD SE27 7 G1
Ullathorne Rd
STRHM/NOR SW16 6 C1
Ullswater Cl BMLY BR1 11 G3
Ullswater Crs COUL/CHIP CR5 54 A1
Ulstan Cl CTHM CR3 61 G3
Underwood CROY/NA CR0 39 E2
Underwood Ct CTHM CR3 59 H4
Underwood Rd CTHM CR3 59 G5
Undine St TOOT SW17 5 H2
Union Rd CROY/NA CR0 26 A1
Unity Cl CROY/NA CR0 38 D4
NRWD SE19 8 A2
University Rd
WIM/MER SW19 5 F3
Upfield CROY/NA CR0 27 F4
Upland Rd BELMT SM2 33 F3
CTHM CR3 61 H1
SAND/SEL CR2 36 B1
Uplands BECK BR3 18 C1
Uplands Rd PUR/KEN CR8 55 E2
Upland Wy EPSOM KT18 50 C3
Upper Beulah Hl NRWD SE19 8 C5
Upper Court Rd CTHM CR3 61 G4
HOR/WEW KT19 40 A1
Upper Dunnymans
BNSTD SM7 42 B4
Upper Elmers End Rd
BECK BR3 18 A4
Upper Gn East MTCM CR4 13 H1
Upper Gn West MTCM CR4 13 H1
Upper Gv SNWD SE25 16 C3
Upper High St EW KT17 40 D3
Upper Mulgrave Rd
BELMT SM2 32 A3
Upper Pillory Down CAR SM5 44 A3
Upper Pines BNSTD SM7 52 D2
Upper Rd WLGTN SM6 34 D1
Upper Sawleywood
BNSTD SM7 42 B4
Upper Selsdon Rd
SAND/SEL CR2 36 D4
Upper Shirley Rd
CROY/NA CR0 27 G4
Upper Tooting Rd TOOT SW17 5 H1
Upper Vernon Rd SUT SM1 33 F1
Upper Woodcote Village
PUR/KEN CR8 44 D3
Upton Dene BELMT SM2 32 D3
Upton Rd THHTH CR7 16 B1
Upwood Rd
STRHM/NOR SW16 7 E5
Uvedale Cl CROY/NA CR0 49 F1
Uvedale Crs CROY/NA CR0 49 F1

V

Valan Leas HAYES BR2 19 G2
Vale Cl COUL/CHIP CR5 45 E4
Valentyne Cl CROY/NA CR0 49 G1
Vale Rd HOR/WEW KT19 20 D5
MTCM CR4 14 D2
SUT SM1 22 D5
Valeswood Rd BMLY BR1 11 H2
The Vale COUL/CHIP CR5 45 E4
CROY/NA CR0 27 H3
Valleyfield Rd
STRHM/NOR SW16 7 F2
Valley Gdns WIM/MER SW19 5 F4
Valley Rd HAYES BR2 19 G1
PUR/KEN CR8 46 B5
STRHM/NOR SW16 7 F1
Valley View Gdns
PUR/KEN CR8 46 C5
Valley Wk CROY/NA CR0 27 G3
Valnay St TOOT SW17 5 H2
Vancouver Cl
HOR/WEW KT19 40 A1
Van Dyck Av NWMAL KT3 20 B1
Vanguard Cl CROY/NA CR0 2 B1
Vanguard Wy CROY/NA CR0 3 K7
WARL CR6 48 B3
WLGTN SM6 35 E3
Vant Rd TOOT SW17 5 H2
Varley Wy MTCM CR4 13 F1
Vauxhall Gdns SAND/SEL CR2 36 A2
Veals Md MTCM CR4 5 G5
Vectis Gdns TOOT SW17 6 B3
Vectis Rd TOOT SW17 6 B3
Vellum Dr CAR SM5 24 A4
Venner Rd SYD SE26 9 G3
Ventnor Rd BELMT SM2 32 D3
Venus Ms MTCM CR4 13 G2
Verdayne Av CROY/NA CR0 27 H2
Verdayne Gdns WARL CR6 56 C1
Vermont Rd NRWD SE19 8 C3
SUT SM1 22 D4
Vernon Cl HOR/WEW KT19 30 A2
Vernon Dr CTHM CR3 59 E2
Vernon Rd SUT SM1 33 E1
Vernon Wk
KWD/TDW/WH KT20 50 D5
Veronica Gdns
STRHM/NOR SW16 6 C5
Versailles Rd PGE/AN SE20 9 E4
Verulam Av PUR/KEN CR8 44 C2
Vicarage Cl WPK KT4 20 C2
Vicarage Ct BECK BR3 * 18 A2
Vicarage Dr BECK BR3 10 C5
Vicarage Gdns MTCM CR4 13 G2
Vicarage Rd CROY/NA CR0 25 G4
SUT SM1 22 C5
Vicars Oak Rd NRWD SE19 8 C3
Vickers Cl WLGTN SM6 35 F3
Victoria Av SAND/SEL CR2 36 A5
WLGTN SM6 24 A4
Victoria Crs NRWD SE19 8 C3
WIM/MER SW19 * 4 B4
Victoria Pl EW KT17 40 C2
Victoria Rd COUL/CHIP CR5 44 D5
SUT SM1 33 F1
WIM/MER SW19 5 G4
Victor Rd PGE/AN SE20 9 H4
Victory Av MRDN SM4 13 E4
Victory Pl NRWD SE19 * 8 C3
Victory Rd WIM/MER SW19 5 E4
Victory Road Ms
WIM/MER SW19 5 E4
Vigilant Cl SYD SE26 9 E1
Village Gdns EW KT17 30 D5
Village Rw BELMT SM2 32 C3
Village Wy BECK BR3 18 C3
SAND/SEL CR2 47 E3
Villiers Gv BELMT SM2 31 H4
Villiers Rd BECK BR3 17 H1
Vincennes Est WNWD SE27 8 B1
Vincent Av CAR SM5 43 F1
Vincent Rd COUL/CHIP CR5 53 G1
CROY/NA CR0 26 C1
Vincents Cl COUL/CHIP CR5 52 D5
Vine Cl SUT SM1 23 E4
Vineyard Hill Rd
WIM/MER SW19 4 C1
Viney Bank CROY/NA CR0 38 B4
Violet Cl CHEAM SM3 22 A2
WLGTN SM6 24 A2
Violet Gdns CROY/NA CR0 35 H1
Violet La CROY/NA CR0 2 B7
SAND/SEL CR2 35 H1
Virginia Rd THHTH CR7 7 H5
Volta Wy CROY/NA CR0 25 F2
Voss Ct STRHM/NOR SW16 7 E3
Vulcan Wy CROY/NA CR0 39 G5
WLGTN SM6 35 E4

W

Waddington Av
COUL/CHIP CR5 54 C4
Waddington Cl
COUL/CHIP CR5 54 D4
Waddington Wy NRWD SE19 8 A5
Waddon Cl CROY/NA CR0 25 G4
Waddon Court Rd
CROY/NA CR0 25 G5
Waddon Marsh Wy
CROY/NA CR0 25 F2
Waddon New Rd
CROY/NA CR0 2 A4
Waddon Park Av
CROY/NA CR0 25 G5
Waddon Rd CROY/NA CR0 25 G4
Waddon Wy CROY/NA CR0 35 G2
Wadhurst Cl PGE/AN SE20 17 F1
Wagtail Gdns SAND/SEL CR2 37 H5
Wagtail Wk BECK BR3 19 E4
Wakefield Gdns NRWD SE19 8 C4
Walburton Rd PUR/KEN CR8 44 C3
Waldegrave Rd NRWD SE19 8 D4
Waldegrove CROY/NA CR0 3 J5
Waldemar Rd WIM/MER SW19 4 C2
Walden Gdns THHTH CR7 15 F3
Waldo Pl MTCM CR4 5 G4
Waldorf Cl SAND/SEL CR2 35 H4
Waldron Gdns HAYES BR2 19 F2
Waldronhyrst SAND/SEL CR2 2 B7
The Waldrons CROY/NA CR0 2 C6
Wales Av CAR SM5 33 H1
Waleton Acres WLGTN SM6 * 34 C2
Walham Ri WIM/MER SW19 4 A3
Walkfield Dr EPSOM KT18 50 B2
Wallace Crs CAR SM5 33 H1
Wallace Flds EW KT17 40 D2
Walled Garden Cl BECK BR3 18 D3
Waller La CTHM CR3 59 H3
Walnut Cl CAR SM5 33 H1
EPSOM KT18 40 D5
Walnut Gv BNSTD SM7 41 H4
Walnut Ms BELMT SM2 33 E3
Walnut Tree Av MTCM CR4 * 13 G2
Walnut Tree Cl BNSTD SM7 42 A2
Walpole Av COUL/CHIP CR5 52 D4
Walpole Rd CROY/NA CR0 2 E2
WIM/MER SW19 5 F3
Walsh Crs CROY/NA CR0 49 G2
Walsingham Gdns
HOR/WEW KT19 20 C5
Walsingham Rd
CROY/NA CR0 39 E5
MTCM CR4 13 H4
Walter's Rd SNWD SE25 16 C3
Waltham Rd CAR SM5 23 F2
CTHM CR3 60 B2
Walton Av CHEAM SM3 22 B4
Walton Gn CROY/NA CR0 38 D4
Walton Wy MTCM CR4 14 C3
Wandle Bank CROY/NA CR0 25 E4
WIM/MER SW19 5 F3
Wandle Ct HOR/WEW KT19 20 A5
Wandle Court Gdns
CROY/NA CR0 25 E4
Wandle Rd CROY/NA CR0 2 C5
MRDN SM4 13 F4
WLGTN SM6 24 B3
Wandle Side CROY/NA CR0 25 F4
WLGTN SM6 24 B4
Wandle Wy MTCM CR4 13 H4
Warbank Cl CROY/NA CR0 39 G5
Warbank Crs CROY/NA CR0 39 G5
Ward Cl SAND/SEL CR2 36 C1
Ward La WARL CR6 56 C1
Warham Rd SAND/SEL CR2 36 A1
Waring St WNWD SE27 8 A1
Warlingham Rd THHTH CR7 15 H3
Warminster Rd SNWD SE25 17 E1
Warminster Sq SNWD SE25 17 E1
Warminster Wy MTCM CR4 6 B5
Warner Av CHEAM SM3 22 A3
Warner Rd BMLY BR1 11 H4
Warnham Court Rd CAR SM5 33 H3
Warren Av BELMT SM2 32 B5
BMLY BR1 11 G4
SAND/SEL CR2 37 H3
Warren Dr South BRYLDS KT5 20 A2
Warren Md BNSTD SM7 41 G5
Warren Pk WARL CR6 56 D3
Warren Park Rd SUT SM1 33 F2
Warren Rd BNSTD SM7 41 H4
CROY/NA CR0 26 C2
PUR/KEN CR8 45 H2
WIM/MER SW19 5 G3
The Warren BELMT SM2 33 F4
WPK KT4 20 B5
Warrington Rd CROY/NA CR0 2 A5
Warwick Gdns THHTH CR7 * 15 G3
Warwick Rd COUL/CHIP CR5 44 C4
PGE/AN SE20 17 F2
SUT SM1 33 E1
THHTH CR7 15 G2
Washington Rd WPK KT4 21 F3
Watcombe Rd SNWD SE25 17 F4
Waterer Gdns
KWD/TDW/WH KT20 51 E3
Waterer Ri WLGTN SM6 34 D2
Waterfall Cottages
WIM/MER SW19 5 F3
Waterfall Rd WIM/MER SW19 5 F3
Waterfall Ter TOOT SW17 5 G3
Waterfield
KWD/TDW/WH KT20 50 B5
Waterfield Dr WARL CR6 56 B4
Waterfield Gdns SNWD SE25 16 C3
Waterfield Gn
KWD/TDW/WH KT20 50 B5
Waterhouse La
PUR/KEN CR8 55 E4
Waterloo Pl CAR SM5 * 23 H4
Waterloo Rd HOR/WEW KT19 40 B3
SUT SM1 33 F1
Waterman Sq PGE/AN SE20 9 G4
Water Md COUL/CHIP CR5 52 D2
Watermead La CAR SM5 13 H5
Watermead Rd CAT SE6 11 E1
Watermens Sq PGE/AN SE20 * 9 G4
Watermill Wy WIM/MER SW19 5 E5
Watersedge HOR/WEW KT19 20 A5
Waterside Av BECK BR3 18 D4
Waterside Wy TOOT SW17 5 E1
Water Tower Hl CROY/NA CR0 3 G6
Watery La RYNPK SW20 12 B1
Wates Wy MTCM CR4 13 H5
Watlings Cl CROY/NA CR0 18 A5
Watlington Gv SYD SE26 10 A2
Watney Cl PUR/KEN CR8 45 F3
Watneys Rd CROY/NA CR0 14 D4
Watson Av CHEAM SM3 22 A3
Watson Cl WIM/MER SW19 5 G3
Wattendon Rd PUR/KEN CR8 54 D1
Wavel Pl SYD SE26 8 D1
Waverley Av PUR/KEN CR8 55 G1
SUT SM1 22 D3
Waverley Rd EW KT17 31 F1
SNWD SE25 17 F3
Waverley Wy CAR SM5 33 G2
Waynflete Av CROY/NA CR0 2 A5
Wayside CROY/NA CR0 * 38 D2
Wealdstone Rd CHEAM SM3 22 B3
Weall Cl PUR/KEN CR8
Weaver Cl CROY/NA CR0
Weaver Wk WNWD SE27
Wedgwood Wy NRWD SE19
Weighton Rd PGE/AN SE20
Weihurst Gdns SUT SM1
Welbeck Cl EW KT17
Welbeck Rd CAR SM5
Welcomes Cottages
CTHM CR3*
Welcomes Rd PUR/KEN CR8
Welford Pl WIM/MER SW19
Welham Rd TOOT SW17
Welhouse Rd CAR SM5
Well Cl STRHM/NOR SW16
Wellesford Cl BNSTD SM7
Wellesley Court Rd
CROY/NACR0 *
Wellesley Gv CROY/NA CR0
Wellesley Rd BELMT SM2
CROY/NA CR0
Well Farm Rd CTHM CR3
Wellfield Gdns CAR SM5
Wellfield Rd
STRHM/NOR SW16
Wellhouse Rd BECK BR3
Wellington Av WPK KT4
Wellington Dr PUR/KEN CR8
Wellington Rd CROY/NA CR0
CTHM CR3
Wells Cl SAND/SEL CR2
Wellwood Cl COUL/CHIP CR5
Wendling Rd SUT SM1
The Wend COUL/CHIP CR5
Wentworth Cl MRDN SM4
Wentworth Rd CROY/NA CR0
Wentworth Wy
SAND/SEL CR2
Werndee Rd SNWD SE25
Wessex Av WIM/MER SW19
Wessex Ct BECK BR3 *
Wessex Ter MTCM CR4 *
West Av WLGTN SM6
Westbourne Av CHEAM SM3
Westbourne Rd
CROY/NA CR0
SYD SE26
Westbrook Rd THHTH CR7
Westbury Cl CTHM CR3 *
Westbury Rd BECK BR3
CROY/NA CR0
PGE/AN SE20
Westcombe Av CROY/NA CR0
Westcote Rd
STRHM/NOR SW16
Westcott Cl CROY/NA CR0
Westcott Wy BELMT SM2
Westcroft Gdns MRDN SM4
Westcroft Rd CAR SM5
West Dr BELMT SM2
CAR SM5
KWD/TDW/WH KT20
STRHM/NOR SW16
Westerham Cl BELMT SM2 *
Westerley Crs SYD SE26 *
Western Rd MTCM CR4
SUT SM1
Westfield Av SAND/SEL CR2
Westfield Cl SUT SM1
Westfield Rd BECK BR3
CROY/NA CR0
MTCM CR4
SUT SM1
West Gdns EW KT17
TOOT SW17
Westgate Rd BECK BR3
SNWD SE25
Westhall Pk WARL CR6
Westhall Rd WARL CR6
West Hl HOR/WEW KT19
SAND/SEL CR2
West Hill Av HOR/WEW KT19
Westland Dr HAYES BR2
Westlands Ct EPSOM KT18
Westleigh Av COUL/CHIP CR5
West Md HOR/WEW KT19
Westmead Rd SUT SM1
Westminster Av THHTH CR7
Westminster Rd SUT SM1
Westmoat Cl BECK BR3
Westmoreland Dr
BELMT SM2
Westmoreland Rd
HAYES BR2
Westmoreland Ter
PGE/AN SE20 *
Westmorland Cl
HOR/WEW KT19
Westmorland Wy MTCM CR4
West Oak BECK BR3
Weston Cl COUL/CHIP CR5
Weston Dr CTHM CR3
Weston Gv BMLY BR1
Weston Rd BMLY BR1
EW KT17
Westover Cl BELMT SM2
Westow Hl NRWD SE19
Westow St NRWD SE19
West Parkside WARL CR6
West St CAR SM5
CROY/NA CR0
EPSOM KT18
EW KT17
SUT SM1
West Street La CAR SM5
West Street Pl CROY/NA CR0
West View Av CTHM CR3
West View Rd WARL CR6
West Wy CAR SM5
CROY/NA CR0
WWKM BR4
Westway CTHM CR3

Way Gdns
OY/NA CR0 ....27 H3
ways HOR/WEW KT19 ....20 D5
well Rd
RHM/NOR SW16 ....7 E3
well Road Ap
RHM/NOR SW16 ....7 E3
wood Av NRWD SE19 ....8 A5
wood HI SYD SE26 ....9 E2
wood PI SYD SE26 * ....9 E2
wood Rd
UL/CHIP CR5 ....53 H3
ern CI SAND/SEL CR2 ....36 C5
ourne PI SAND/SEL CR2 ....36 B5
ridge Rd THHTH CR7 ....15 G3
Ct HOR/WEW KT19 ....20 A5
nouth Ct BELMT SM2 * ....32 D3
fedale Gdns THHTH CR7 ....15 F3
ncliffe Gdns
WD SE25 ....16 C1
ncliffe Rd SNWD SE25 ....16 B1
eley Rd PGE/AN SE20 ....9 H4
thill Rd PGE/AN SE20 ....17 F1
t Knoll PUR/KEN CR8 ....55 E1
tstone CI
M/MER SW19 ....5 F5
lers La EPSOM KT18 ....40 A4
an Wy WLGTN SM6 ....24 D4
brel CI SAND/SEL CR2 ....46 B1
Fell CI STRHM/NOR SW16 ....6 D2
y Gdns SUT SM1 ....23 F3
y Rd SUT SM1 ....23 F3
Bridge Av MTCM CR4 ....13 F3
croft CI BECK BR3 ....19 F3
croft Wy BECK BR3 ....19 E3
field Av PUR/KEN CR8 ....54 C1
foot La BMLY BR1 ....11 F1
gate Wy
D/TDW/WH KT20 ....50 B5
hall PI WLGTN SM6 ....24 B5
hall Rd THHTH CR7 ....15 G4
HI SAND/SEL CR2 ....36 B5
Horse Dr EPSOM KT18 ....40 A5
horse La SNWD SE25 ....16 C3
horse Rd CROY/NA CR0 ....26 A1
Knobs Wy CTHM CR3 ....60 A5
ley Rd NRWD SE19 ....8 B2
Ldg NRWD SE19 ....7 H4
Lodge CI BELMT SM2 ....33 E3
Oak Dr BECK BR3 ....19 E1
oaks BNSTD SM7 ....42 D3
thorn Av
UL/CHIP CR5 ....44 A5
thorn Gdns
OY/NA CR0 ....27 F3
ord Gdns MTCM CR4 ....13 H2
ift Av SAND/SEL CR2 ....36 A1
ift St CROY/NA CR0 ....2 D4
and Rd CAR SM5 ....23 F2
head CI SAND/SEL CR2 ....36 B2
nore Rd BECK BR3 ....18 B2
nores CI EPSOM KT18 * ....40 A5
table CI BECK BR3 ....10 B5
table PI CROY/NA CR0 ....2 D7
tone La BECK BR3 ....18 D4
aker Rd CHEAM SM3 ....22 B4
ebury CI CAR SM5 ....33 H3
vorth Rd SNWD SE25 ....16 C2
ebeam Vw CTHM CR3 ....55 H3
ecliffe Rd North
R/KEN CR8 ....45 H1
ecliffe Rd South
R/KEN CR8 ....45 G2
eleafe HI CTHM CR3 ....55 H3
eleafe Rd CTHM CR3 ....59 H2
rs Oake NRWD SE19 * ....8 D1
icket CROY/NA CR0 ....38 C1
am Av CHEAM SM3 ....31 G1
OY/NA CR0 ....28 A3
am Cha WWKM BR4 ....29 F1
am Ct WWKM BR4 * ....29 F5
am Court Rd
VKM BR4 ....29 E3
am Crs WWKM BR4 ....29 E3
am Rd BECK BR3 ....18 D2
OY/NA CR0 ....27 G3
am Wy BECK BR3 ....19 E3

Wide Wy MTCM CR4 ....14 D2
Wigmore Rd CAR SM5 ....23 F3
Wilbury Av BELMT SM2 ....32 B5
Wilcox Rd SUT SM1 * ....22 D5
Wildwood Ct PUR/KEN CR8 ....46 B5
Wilfred Owen Cl
WIM/MER SW19 ....5 E3
Wilhelmina Av
COUL/CHIP CR5 ....53 G4
Wilkins Cl MTCM CR4 ....5 G5
Wilkinson Gdns SNWD SE25 ....8 C5
Wilks Gdns CROY/NA CR0 ....28 A2
Willett Rd THHTH CR7 ....15 G4
Willey Broom La CTHM CR3 ....58 C5
Willey La CTHM CR3 ....59 F5
William Booth Rd
PGE/AN SE20 ....9 E5
William Rd CTHM CR3 ....59 F2
SUT SM1 ....33 E1
WIM/MER SW19 ....4 A4
Williams La MRDN SM4 ....13 E5
Williams Ter CROY/NA CR0 ....35 G2
William St CAR SM5 ....23 G4
Willis Av BELMT SM2 ....33 G2
Willis Rd CROY/NA CR0 ....26 A1
Willmore End WIM/MER SW19 ....4 D5
Willoughby Av CROY/NA CR0 ....25 F5
The Willow Centre
MTCM CR4 ....13 H4
Willowhayne Gdns WPK KT4 ....21 G5
Willow La MTCM CR4 ....13 H4
Willow Mt CROY/NA CR0 * ....3 H5
Willow Rd WLGTN SM6 ....34 B3
Willows Av MRDN SM4 ....12 D4
The Willows BECK BR3 * ....10 C5
Willow Ter PGE/AN SE20 * ....9 F5
Willowtree Wy THHTH CR7 ....7 G5
Willow Vw WIM/MER SW19 ....5 F5
Willow Wk CHEAM SM3 ....22 B4
Willow Wy HOR/WEW KT19 ....30 B2
Willow Wood Crs SNWD SE25 ....16 C5
Wilmar Gdns WWKM BR4 ....28 D2
Wilmot Cottages
BNSTD SM7 * ....42 D5
Wilmot Rd CAR SM5 * ....33 H1
PUR/KEN CR8 ....45 G2
Wilmot Wy BNSTD SM7 ....42 C5
Wilson Av MTCM CR4 ....5 G4
Wilson Cl SAND/SEL CR2 ....36 B1
Wilton Crs WIM/MER SW19 ....4 B5
Wilton Gv WIM/MER SW19 ....4 B4
Wilton Rd WIM/MER SW19 ....5 G4
Wiltshire Rd THHTH CR7 ....15 G2
Wimbledon Br
WIM/MER SW19 ....4 B3
Wimbledon Hill Rd
WIM/MER SW19 ....4 A3
Wimbledon Rd TOOT SW17 ....5 E1
Wimborne Cl EW KT17 ....40 D3
WPK KT4 ....21 G2
Wimborne Wy BECK BR3 ....17 H3
Wimshurst Cl CROY/NA CR0 ....25 E2
Winchcombe Rd CAR SM5 ....23 F1
Winchelsey Ri SAND/SEL CR2 ....36 D2
Winchester Cl HAYES BR2 ....19 H2
Winchester Ms WPK KT4 ....21 H3
Winchester Pk HAYES BR2 ....19 H2
Winchester Rd HAYES BR2 ....19 H2
Winchfield Rd SYD SE26 ....10 A2
Windall Cl NRWD SE19 ....9 E5
Windborough Rd CAR SM5 ....34 A3
Windermere Av
WIM/MER SW19 ....12 D2
Windermere Rd
COUL/CHIP CR5 ....45 E5
CROY/NA CR0 ....26 D2
STRHM/NOR SW16 ....6 C5
WWKM BR4 ....29 G3
Windfield Cl SYD SE26 ....9 H1
Windham Av CROY/NA CR0 ....39 F5
The Windings SAND/SEL CR2 ....46 D1
Windmill Av EW KT17 ....40 D1
Windmill Cl CTHM CR3 ....59 E1
EW KT17 ....40 D2
Windmill End EW KT17 ....40 D2
Windmill Gv CROY/NA CR0 ....26 A1
Windmill La EW KT17 ....40 D2

Windmill Rd CROY/NA CR0 ....26 A1
MTCM CR4 ....14 C4
Windsor Av CHEAM SM3 ....22 A4
WIM/MER SW19 ....5 E5
Windsor Cl WNWD SE27 ....8 A1
Windsor Gdns CROY/NA CR0 ....25 E4
Windsor Gv WNWD SE27 ....8 A1
Windsor Rd THHTH CR7 ....15 H1
WPK KT4 ....21 E3
Windycroft Cl PUR/KEN CR8 ....44 D3
Wingate Crs CROY/NA CR0 ....15 E5
Wings Cl SUT SM1 ....22 C5
Winifred Rd COUL/CHIP CR5 ....53 E1
WIM/MER SW19 ....4 C5
Winkworth Pl BNSTD SM7 ....42 B4
Winkworth Rd BNSTD SM7 ....42 C4
Winlaton Rd BMLY BR1 ....11 F1
Winterbourne Rd THHTH CR7 ....15 G3
Winton Wy STRHM/NOR SW16 ....7 G2
Wisbeach Rd CROY/NA CR0 ....16 B4
Wisborough Rd
SAND/SEL CR2 ....36 D4
Witham Rd PGE/AN SE20 ....17 G2
Witherby Cl CROY/NA CR0 ....36 C1
Witley Crs CROY/NA CR0 ....39 E2
Wittersham Rd BMLY BR1 ....11 H2
Wiverton Rd SYD SE26 ....9 G3
Woburn Av PUR/KEN CR8 ....45 G1
Woburn Cl WIM/MER SW19 ....5 E3
Woburn Rd CAR SM5 ....23 G2
CROY/NA CR0 ....26 A2
Woldingham Rd WARL CR6 ....56 B5
The Wold CTHM CR3 ....61 G2
Wolfington Rd WNWD SE27 ....7 H1
Wolseley Rd MTCM CR4 ....24 A1
Wolsey Cl WPK KT4 ....21 E5
Wolsey Crs CROY/NA CR0 ....39 E4
MRDN SM4 ....22 B1
Wonersh Wy BELMT SM2 ....31 H4
Wontford Rd PUR/KEN CR8 ....45 G5
Woodbastwick Rd SYD SE26 ....9 H3
Woodbine Gv PGE/AN SE20 ....9 F4
Woodbine La WPK KT4 ....21 F4
Woodbourne Gdns
WLGTN SM6 ....34 B3
Woodbury Cl CROY/NA CR0 ....3 K3
Woodbury Dr BELMT SM2 ....33 F5
Woodbury St TOOT SW17 ....5 G2
Woodcote Av THHTH CR7 ....15 H3
WLGTN SM6 ....34 B4
Woodcote Cl EPSOM KT18 ....40 B4
Woodcote End EPSOM KT18 ....40 B5
Woodcote Gn WLGTN SM6 ....34 C4
Woodcote Green Rd
EPSOM KT18 ....40 B4
Woodcote Grove Rd
COUL/CHIP CR5 ....44 D5
Woodcote House Ct
EPSOM KT18 * ....40 B5
Woodcote La PUR/KEN CR8 ....44 D1
Woodcote Ms WLGTN SM6 ....34 B2
Woodcote Pk
COUL/CHIP CR5 * ....44 B3
Woodcote Park Av
PUR/KEN CR8 ....44 C1
Woodcote Pl
WNWD SE27 * ....7 H2
Woodcote Rd EPSOM KT18 ....40 B5
WLGTN SM6 ....34 B2
Woodcote Valley Rd
PUR/KEN CR8 ....44 D3
Wood Crest BELMT SM2 * ....33 E3
Woodcrest Rd PUR/KEN CR8 ....45 E3
Woodcroft Rd THHTH CR7 ....15 H4
Woodend NRWD SE19 ....8 A3
SUT SM1 ....23 E3
The Wood End WLGTN SM6 ....34 B4
Wooderson Cl SNWD SE25 ....16 C3
Woodfield Av CAR SM5 ....34 A2
Woodfield Cl COUL/CHIP CR5 ....53 G4
NRWD SE19 ....8 A4
Woodfield Hl COUL/CHIP CR5 ....53 F4
The Woodfields
SAND/SEL CR2 ....46 D1
Woodgate Dr
STRHM/NOR SW16 ....6 D4
Woodgavil BNSTD SM7 ....51 F1

Woodhatch Spinney
COUL/CHIP CR5 ....54 A1
Woodhyrst Gdns
PUR/KEN CR8 ....45 H5
Woodland Cl
HOR/WEW KT19 * ....30 C2
NRWD SE19 ....8 C3
Woodland Gdns
SAND/SEL CR2 ....47 G1
Woodland Gv CROY/NA CR0 ....35 G3
Woodland Hl NRWD SE19 ....8 C3
Woodland Rd NRWD SE19 ....8 C2
THHTH CR7 ....15 G3
Woodlands Av WPK KT4 ....20 D3
Woodlands Gdns
EPSOM KT18 ....50 C2
Woodlands Gv
COUL/CHIP CR5 ....53 F2
The Woodlands NRWD SE19 ....8 A4
WLGTN SM6 ....34 B4
Woodland Wy CROY/NA CR0 ....28 A2
MRDN SM4 ....12 B3
MTCM CR4 ....6 A4
PUR/KEN CR8 ....45 G3
WWKM BR4 ....29 E4
Wood La CTHM CR3 ....59 F4
KWD/TDW/WH KT20 ....51 F2
Woodlea Dr HAYES BR2 ....19 G4
Woodley Cl TOOT SW17 ....5 H4
Woodley La SUT SM1 ....23 G4
Wood Lodge La WWKM BR4 ....29 E4
Woodman Rd
COUL/CHIP CR5 ....44 C5
Woodmansterne La
BNSTD SM7 ....42 D5
Woodmansterne Rd
CAR SM5 ....33 G5
COUL/CHIP CR5 ....44 C5
STRHM/NOR SW16 ....6 C4
Woodmansterne St
BNSTD SM7 ....43 G5
Woodmere Av CROY/NA CR0 ....27 H1
Woodmere Cl CROY/NA CR0 ....27 H1
Woodmere Gdns
CROY/NA CR0 ....27 H1
Woodmere Wy BECK BR3 ....19 F4
Woodnook Rd
STRHM/NOR SW16 ....6 B2
Woodpecker Mt
CROY/NA CR0 ....38 A4
Woodplace Cl
COUL/CHIP CR5 ....53 G4
Woodplace La
COUL/CHIP CR5 ....53 G5
Woodside WIM/MER SW19 ....4 B2
Woodside Av SNWD SE25 ....17 F5
Woodside Cl BRYLDS KT5 ....20 A1
CTHM CR3 ....59 G4
Woodside Court Rd
CROY/NA CR0 ....27 E1
Woodside Gn SNWD SE25 ....17 F5
Woodside Pk SNWD SE25 ....17 F5
Woodside Rd PUR/KEN CR8 ....45 E3
SNWD SE25 ....17 F5
SUT SM1 ....23 E4
Woodside Wy CROY/NA CR0 ....17 G5
MTCM CR4 ....6 B5
Woodstock Av CHEAM SM3 ....22 B1
Woodstock Ct
HOR/WEW KT19 ....40 B2
Woodstock Gdns BECK BR3 ....10 D5
Woodstock Ri CHEAM SM3 ....22 B2
Woodstock Rd CAR SM5 ....34 A1
COUL/CHIP CR5 ....53 F1
CROY/NA CR0 ....2 E5
Woodstock Wy MTCM CR4 ....14 C1
Woodstone Av EW KT17 ....31 E1
Wood St MTCM CR4 ....24 A1
Woodsyre SYD SE26 ....8 D1
Woodvale Av SNWD SE25 ....16 D2
Woodview Cl SAND/SEL CR2 ....47 F4
Woodville Rd MRDN SM4 ....12 C3
THHTH CR7 ....16 B2
Worbeck Rd PGE/AN SE20 ....17 F1
Worcester Cl CROY/NA CR0 ....28 B3
MTCM CR4 ....14 A1
Worcester Gdns WPK KT4 ....20 C4

Worcester Park Rd WPK KT4 ....20 A4
Worcester Rd BELMT SM2 ....32 C3
WIM/MER SW19 ....4 B3
Wordsworth Av
PUR/KEN CR8 ....46 B5
Wordsworth Dr CHEAM SM3 ....21 G5
Wordsworth Rd PGE/AN SE20 ....9 H4
WLGTN SM6 ....34 C2
Worple Rd EPSOM KT18 ....40 C4
WIM/MER SW19 ....4 A4
Worple Road Ms
WIM/MER SW19 ....4 B3
Worslade Rd TOOT SW17 ....5 F1
Worsley Bridge Rd SYD SE26 ....10 B2
Worthfield Cl
HOR/WEW KT19 ....30 B3
Worthington Cl MTCM CR4 ....14 B3
Wortley Rd CROY/NA CR0 ....25 G1
Wotton Wy BELMT SM2 ....31 G5
Wrayfield Rd CHEAM SM3 ....21 H4
Wray Rd BELMT SM2 ....32 B4
Wren Cl SAND/SEL CR2 ....37 H5
Wrenthorpe Rd BMLY BR1 ....11 G1
Wrights Rd SNWD SE25 ....16 C2
Wright's Rw WLGTN SM6 ....24 B5
Wrythe Gn CAR SM5 ....23 H4
Wrythe Green Rd CAR SM5 ....23 H4
Wrythe La CAR SM5 ....23 F2
Wyche Gv SAND/SEL CR2 ....36 A4
Wychwood Av THHTH CR7 ....15 H2
Wycliffe Rd WIM/MER SW19 ....4 D3
Wydenhurst Rd
CROY/NA CR0 ....27 E1
Wyeth's Ms EW KT17 ....40 D3
Wyeth's Rd EW KT17 ....40 D3
Wyncote Wy SAND/SEL CR2 ....37 H4
Wyndham Cl BELMT SM2 ....32 C3
Wyndhurst Cl SAND/SEL CR2 ....35 H3
Wynton Gdns SNWD SE25 ....16 D4
Wyvern Rd PUR/KEN CR8 ....35 G5

Y

Yarborough Rd
WIM/MER SW19 ....5 F5
Yarbridge Cl BELMT SM2 * ....32 D5
Yenston Cl MRDN SM4 ....12 C5
Yeomanry Cl EW KT17 ....40 D2
Yewbank Cl PUR/KEN CR8 ....46 B5
Yewdale Cl BMLY BR1 ....11 G3
Yewlands Cl BNSTD SM7 ....42 D5
Yew Tree Bottom Rd
EW KT17 ....50 B2
Yew Tree Cl COUL/CHIP CR5 ....52 D4
WPK KT4 ....20 C2
Yew Tree Dr CTHM CR3 ....59 H5
Yew Tree Gdns EPSOM KT18 ....40 A5
Yew Tree Rd BECK BR3 ....18 B2
Yew Tree Wk PUR/KEN CR8 ....36 A5
York Cl MRDN SM4 ....12 D3
Yorke Ga CTHM CR3 ....59 F2
York Rd BELMT SM2 ....32 C2
CROY/NA CR0 ....25 G1
SAND/SEL CR2 ....37 H5
WIM/MER SW19 ....4 D3
Yorkshire Rd MTCM CR4 ....15 E4
York St MTCM CR4 ....24 A1

Z

Zermatt Rd THHTH CR7 ....16 A4
Zig Zag Rd PUR/KEN CR8 ....55 E1
Zion Pl THHTH CR7 ....16 B3
Zion Rd THHTH CR7 ....16 B3


## ndex - featured places


Industrial Estate
CM CR4 ....13 H4
Mills
M/MER SW19 ....5 E5
Primary School
DN SM4 ....22 C1
Trading Estate
SE26 ....10 A2
sbury Primary School
DN SM4 ....12 C4
our School
D/TDW/WH KT20 ....51 F3
en (Anglo School)
WD SE19 ....8 C5
gton Business Centre
OY/NA CR0 ....39 G5
gton Court Golf Club
OY/NA CR0 ....38 B4
gton Golf Club
OY/NA CR0 ....28 B5
gton High School
OY/NA CR0 ....49 G2
gton Palace
f Club
OY/NA CR0 ....38 A2

Addiscombe CC
CROY/NA CR0 ....27 E4
Aerodrome Hotel
CROY/NA CR0 ....35 G2
Albany Clinic
WIM/MER SW19 ....4 D4
Alexandra Infant School
PGE/AN SE20 ....9 H4
Alexandra Junior School
SYD SE26 ....9 H3
All Saints Benhilton CE
Primary School SUT SM1 ....22 D4
All Saints CE Junior School
NRWD SE19 ....8 C5
All Saints CE Primary School
CAR SM5 ....34 A1
WIM/MER SW19 ....5 E4
Anerley School
NRWD SE19 ....9 E5
Applegarth Primary School
CROY/NA CR0 ....38 D2
Aragon Primary School
MRDN SM4 ....22 A1
The Archbishop Lanfranc
School CROY/NA CR0 ....15 E5

Archbishop Tenisons CE School
CROY/NA CR0 ....3 J5
Art School
BECK BR3 ....18 A4
Ashburton Community School
CROY/NA CR0 ....27 F1
Ashburton Primary School
CROY/NA CR0 ....17 F5
Ashgrove Trading Estate
BMLY BR1 ....11 F3
Ashley Centre Shopping
Precinct
EPSOM KT18 ....40 B3
Atwood Primary School
SAND/SEL CR2 ....47 E4
Audley Primary School
CTHM CR3 ....59 G1
Auriol Junior School
HOR/WEW KT19 ....20 D5
The Avenue Primary School
BELMT SM2 ....32 C5
Back Care Clinic
WPK KT4 ....21 E2
Balgowan Primary School
BECK BR3 ....18 A1

Bandon Hill Cemetery
WLGTN SM6 ....34 D1
Bandon Hill Primary School
WLGTN SM6 ....34 D2
Banstead Athletic FC
KWD/TDW/WH KT20 ....50 C5
Banstead Clinic
BNSTD SM7 ....42 C5
Banstead County Junior School
BNSTD SM7 ....51 F1
Banstead Downs Golf Club
BELMT SM2 ....42 C1
Banstead Infant School
BNSTD SM7 ....42 B5
Banstead Sports Centre
KWD/TDW/WH KT20 ....50 C5
Banstead Village Clinic
BNSTD SM7 ....42 D5
Barrow Hedges Primary
School
CAR SM5 ....33 G3
Beacon School
BNSTD SM7 ....51 E2
Beaumont Primary School
PUR/KEN CR8 ....45 F4

Beckenham Business Centre
BECK BR3 ....10 A3
Beckenham Crematorium
BECK BR3 ....17 G2
Beckenham CC
BECK BR3 ....10 D4
Beckenham Hospital
BECK BR3 ....18 B1
Beckenham Leisure Centre
BECK BR3 ....10 A5
Beckenham Place Park
Golf Course
BECK BR3 ....10 D3
Beckenham RFC
BECK BR3 ....18 A3
Beckenham Town FC
BECK BR3 ....18 C4
Beckmead School
BECK BR3 ....28 C2
Beddington Infant School
WLGTN SM6 ....24 C4
Beddington Medical Centre
CROY/NA CR0 ....25 E5
Beddington Park Primary
School CROY/NA CR0 ....24 D4

Beddington Trading Estate *CROY/NA* CR0 25 E2
Bedington Infant School *WLGTN* SM6 24 C5
Beech House School *SAND/SEL* CR2 36 D5
Beecholme Primary School *MTCM* CR4 6 B5
Benedict Primary School *MTCM* CR4 13 F2
Bensham Manor School *THHTH* CR7 16 A4
Benson Primary School *CROY/NA* CR0 28 A4
Best Western Bromley Court Hotel *BMLY* BR1 11 G3
Bethlem Royal Hospital *BECK* BR3 28 C1
Beulah Infant School *THHTH* CR7 16 A1
Beverley Trading Estate *MRDN* SM4 21 H1
Bishop Challoner School *HAYES* BR2 19 F1
Bishop Gilpin Primary School *WIM/MER* SW19 4 B2
Bishop Thomas Grant School *STRHM/NOR* SW16 7 F2
Blenheim Business Centre *MTCM* CR4 5 H5
Blenheim High School *HOR/WEW* KT19 30 B5
Blenheim Shopping Centre *PGE/AN* SE20 9 G4
Bond First School *MTCM* CR4 13 H1
Bond Primary School *MTCM* CR4 13 H1
Bonus Pastor Roman Catholic School *BMLY* BR1 11 F1
Boundary Business Park *MTCM* CR4 13 F1
Bourne Hall Health Centre *EW* KT17 30 D4
Bourne Hall Museum *EW* KT17 30 D4
The Bridge Leisure Centre *SYD* SE26 10 B2
Brigstock Medical Centre *THHTH* CR7 15 H4
Brit School for Performing Arts *CROY/NA* CR0 16 B5
Broadmead J&I School *CROY/NA* CR0 16 B5
Broadwater Primary School *TOOT* SW17 5 F1
Bromley Cemetery *BMLY* BR1 11 H4
Bromley Road Infant School *BECK* BR3 10 D5
Brookfield Primary School *CHEAM* SM3 22 A2
Brookmead Industrial Estate *CROY/NA* CR0 14 C5
Broomsleigh Business Park *SYD* SE26 10 B2
Burghwood Clinic *BNSTD* SM7 51 F1
Burnhill Business Centre *BECK* BR3 18 C1
Byron Primary School *COUL/CHIP* CR5 54 A2
Camden Junior School *CAR* SM5 23 H5
The Canons Leisure Centre *MTCM* CR4 13 H3
Capital Business Centre *MTCM* CR4 13 H4
*SAND/SEL* CR2 36 B2
Caplan Estate *MTCM* CR4 6 C5
Carew Manor School *WLGTN* SM6 24 D4
Carshalton AFC *SUT* SM1 23 G4
Carshalton College of Further Education *CAR* SM5 23 H4
Carshalton High School for Boys *CAR* SM5 23 F3
Carshalton High School for Girls *CAR* SM5 23 G4
Carshalton War Memorial Hospital *CAR* SM5 33 H1
Castle Hill Primary School *CROY/NA* CR0 39 E2
The Caterham Dene Hospital *CTHM* CR3 59 H3
Catford Wanderers Sports Club *CAT* SE6 11 E1
Cator Park School for Girls *BECK* BR3 10 A4
Centrale Shopping Centre *CROY/NA* CR0 2 C2
Central Medical Centre *MRDN* SM4 13 E3
Centre Court Shopping Centre *WIM/MER* SW19 4 B3
Chaffinch Business Park *BECK* BR3 17 H2
Chalk Lane Hotel *EPSOM* KT18 40 B5
Chandos Business Centre *WLGTN* SM6 34 C2
Cheam Common J&I School *WPK* KT4 21 F3
Cheam Fields Primary School *CHEAM* SM3 32 A1
Cheam High School *CHEAM* SM3 22 A5
Cheam Leisure Centre *CHEAM* SM3 21 H5
Cheam Park Farm Junior School *CHEAM* SM3 22 A4
Cheam Sports Club *CHEAM* SM3 32 A3
Chelsea Fields Industrial Estate *WIM/MER* SW19 5 F5
Chipstead Golf Club *COUL/CHIP* CR5 52 D3
Chipstead Valley Primary School *COUL/CHIP* CR5 53 E1
Christ Church Primary School *PUR/KEN* CR8 35 H5
Christian Meeting Hall *BECK* BR3 10 C5
Churchfields Primary School *BECK* BR3 17 H2
Clare House Primary School *BECK* BR3 19 E1
Clifton Hill School *CTHM* CR3 59 F4
College Fields Business Centre *WIM/MER* SW19 5 G5
Collingwood Preparatory School *WLGTN* SM6 34 B1
Coloma Convent Girls School *CROY/NA* CR0 27 H4
Colonnades Leisure Park *CROY/NA* CR0 35 G2
Colours Sports Club *SUT* SM1 33 E1
Coney Hill School *HAYES* BR2 29 H3
Connaught Business Centre *CROY/NA* CR0 35 F2
*MTCM* CR4 13 H4
Coulsdon CE Primary School *COUL/CHIP* CR5 54 B3
The Coulsdon Eye Clinic *COUL/CHIP* CR5 44 C5
Coulsdon High School *COUL/CHIP* CR5 54 D5
Coulsdon Manor Golf Club *COUL/CHIP* CR5 54 B1
Coulsdon Sixth Form College *COUL/CHIP* CR5 54 C4
Courtwood Primary School *CROY/NA* CR0 38 B5
Cranmer Primary School *MTCM* CR4 13 H3
Cricket Green School *MTCM* CR4 13 G2
Croham Hurst Golf Club *SAND/SEL* CR2 36 D2
Crown Lane Primary School *WNWD* SE27 8 A1
Croydon Airport Industrial Estate *CROY/NA* CR0 35 G3
Croydon Bowling Club *SAND/SEL* CR2 36 A1
Croydon Cemetery *CROY/NA* CR0 15 F4
Croydon Clocktower Cinema *CROY/NA* CR0 2 D4
Croydon College *CROY/NA* CR0 2 E3
Croydon Crematorium *THHTH* CR7 15 E4
Croydon Fairfield Halls Cinema *CROY/NA* CR0 2 E4
Croydon FC *SNWD* SE25 17 G4
Croydon High Junior School *SAND/SEL* CR2 47 F1
Croydon Road Industrial Estate *BECK* BR3 17 G3
Croydon Sports Arena *SNWD* SE25 17 G4
Crystal Palace FC (Selhurst Park) *SNWD* SE25 16 C3
Crystal Palace Museum *NRWD* SE19 8 D3
Cuaco Sports Ground *BECK* BR3 10 C3
Cuddington Cemetery *WPK* KT4 21 F3
Cuddington CP School *WPK* KT4 20 D4
Cuddington Croft Primary School *BELMT* SM2 31 H4
Cuddington Golf Club *BNSTD* SM7 42 A3
Culvers House Primary School *MTCM* CR4 24 A2
Cumnor House School *SAND/SEL* CR2 35 H4
Cypress Infant School *SNWD* SE25 16 C1
Cypress Junior School *SNWD* SE25 16 C1
Cyprus College of Art *WNWD* SE27 7 H1
Danetree School *HOR/WEW* KT19 30 A3
David Livingstone Primary School *THHTH* CR7 8 A5
Davidson Primary School *CROY/NA* CR0 26 D1
De Stafford College *CTHM* CR3 59 H1
Devonshire Primary School *BELMT* SM2 33 E3
Dorchester Primary School *WPK* KT4 21 G2
Downderry Primary School *BMLY* BR1 11 G1
Downham Health Centre *BMLY* BR1 11 G1
Downsend School Epsom Lodge *EW* KT17 40 D3
Downsview Primary School *NRWD* SE19 8 A4
Dundonald Primary School *WIM/MER* SW19 4 B4
Duppas Junior School *CROY/NA* CR0 35 H1
Eagle Trading Estate *MTCM* CR4 13 H5
Eardley Primary School *STRHM/NOR* SW16 6 C3
East Surrey Museum *CTHM* CR3 59 H4
Ebbisham County Infants School *EPSOM* KT18 40 A4
Ebbisham Sports Club *HOR/WEW* KT19 40 A2
Ecclesbourne Primary School *THHTH* CR7 16 A4
Eclipse Estate *HOR/WEW* KT19 40 A3
Edenham High School *CROY/NA* CR0 28 A1
Edenvale Child Health Clinic *MTCM* CR4 6 A4
Edes Business Park *WLGTN* SM6 24 A3
Elfrida Primary School *CAT* SE6 10 D1
Elmhurst School *SAND/SEL* CR2 36 B1
Elmhurst School for Boys *SAND/SEL* CR2 3 F7
Elmwood Junior School *CROY/NA* CR0 25 H1
Ensham Secondary School *TOOT* SW17 5 H2
Epsom Bowls *EPSOM* KT18 40 C4
Epsom Business Park *EW* KT17 40 C1
Epsom College *EW* KT17 41 E4
Epsom County & Magistrates Court *EPSOM* KT18 40 B3
Epsom & Ewell High School *HOR/WEW* KT19 30 A2
Epsom General Hospital *EPSOM* KT18 40 A5
Epsom Golf Club *EW* KT17 41 E5
Epsom Health Clinic *EPSOM* KT18 40 C3
Epsom Primary School *HOR/WEW* KT19 40 B1
Epsom Sports Club *EPSOM* KT18 40 B5
Essendene Lodge School *CTHM* CR3 59 H2
Eversley Medical Centre *CROY/NA* CR0 15 G5
Ewell Athletics Track *HOR/WEW* KT19 30 B2
Ewell Castle Junior School *EW* KT17 30 D4
Ewell Castle School *EW* KT17 31 E4
Ewell Grove Infant School *EW* KT17 30 D4
Fairchildes Primary School *CROY/NA* CR0 49 G2
Fairview Medical Centre *STRHM/NOR* SW16 7 E5
Farleigh Court Golf Club *WARL* CR6 48 C2
Farleigh Primary School *WARL* CR6 56 D2
Farleigh Rovers FC *WARL* CR6 57 F1
Felnex Trading Estate *WLGTN* SM6 24 A3
First Quarter Business Park *HOR/WEW* KT19 40 B1
Follys End Christian High School *SNWD* SE25 16 C5
The Foot Clinic *WIM/MER* SW19 4 A3
The Foot Health Centre *COUL/CHIP* CR5 44 D5
Forestdale Primary School *CROY/NA* CR0 38 A4
Foresters Primary School *WLGTN* SM6 34 D2
Franciscan Primary School *TOOT* SW17 6 A1
Franklin Industrial Estate *PGE/AN* SE20 9 G5
Furzedown Primary School *TOOT* SW17 6 B3
Gardener Industrial Estate *SYD* SE26 10 A2
Garden Primary School *MTCM* CR4 14 D2
Garfield Primary School *WIM/MER* SW19 5 E3
Garth Primary School *MRDN* SM4 13 F4
The Garth Road Industrial Centre *MRDN* SM4 21 G1
Gateway Business Centre *SYD* SE26 10 A3
Gatton School *TOOT* SW17 5 G1
Gilbert Scott Primary School *SAND/SEL* CR2 38 A3
Glebe School *WWKM* BR4 29 F2
Glenthorne High School *CHEAM* SM3 22 C2
Glyn Technology School *EW* KT17 40 D1
Gonville Primary School *THHTH* CR7 15 F4
Good Shepherd RC Primary School *BMLY* BR1 11 H1
*CROY/NA* CR0 38 D3
Gorringe Park Primary School *MTCM* CR4 6 A5
Grace Business Centre *MTCM* CR4 13 H5
Grand Avenue Primary School *BRYLDS* KT5 20 A1
Granton Primary School *STRHM/NOR* SW16 6 C4
Graveney School *TOOT* SW17 6 B3
Greenacre School for Girls *BNSTD* SM7 43 E3
Green Lane Primary School *WPK* KT4 21 F1
Green Lane Sports Ground *THHTH* CR7 15 H1
Greenshaw High School *SUT* SM1 23 E3
Greenvale Primary School *SAND/SEL* CR2 47 H1
Green Wrythe Primary School *CAR* SM5 13 F5
Gresham Primary School *SAND/SEL* CR2 46 D2
Hackbridge Primary School *WLGTN* SM6 24 A2
Haling Manor High School *SAND/SEL* CR2 35 H3
Hamilton Road Industrial Estate *WNWD* SE27 8 B1
Hampton Road Industrial Park *CROY/NA* CR0 16 A5
Hamsey Green Infant School *WARL* CR6 56 B1
Hamsey Green Junior School *WARL* CR6 56 B1
Harris City Technology College *NRWD* SE19 8 D5
Haseltine Primary School *SYD* SE26 10 B1
Haslemere Primary School *MTCM* CR4 13 F1
Hatfield Primary School *MRDN* SM4 12 A5
Hawes Down Clinic *WWKM* BR4 29 F3
Hawes Down primary School *WWKM* BR4 29 F2
Hawkins Clinic *EW* KT17 41 G5
The Hayes Primary School *PUR/KEN* CR8 54 D1
Heavers Farm Primary School *SNWD* SE25 16 D4
Henderson Hospital *BELMT* SM2 32 C4
Highfield Infant School *HAYES* BR2 19 H3
Highfield Junior School *HAYES* BR2 19 G3
Highview Primary School *WLGTN* SM6 35 E1
Hillbrook Primary School *TOOT* SW17 5 H1
Hillcroft Primary School *CTHM* CR3 59 G3
Hillcross Primary School *MRDN* SM4 12 B3
HM Prison *BELMT* SM2 43 E2
Holy Trinity CE Junior School *WLGTN* SM6 24 C5
Holy Trinity Primary School *WIM/MER* SW19 4 C3
Homefield Preparatory School *SUT* SM1 32 C1
Horton Hospital *HOR/WEW* KT19 40 A1
Horton Park Golf & Country Club *HOR/WEW* KT19 30 A3
Howard Primary School *SAND/SEL* CR2 2 C7
HSBC Sports Club *BECK* BR3 10 A3
IKEA Store Croydon *CROY/NA* CR0 25 F2
Immanuel CE Primary School *STRHM/NOR* SW16 7 E3
Innkeeper's Lodge *BECK* BR3 18 C5
*CHEAM* SM3 22 C2
*SAND/SEL* CR2 36 A4
James Dixon Primary School *PGE/AN* SE20 9 E5
John Ruskin College *SAND/SEL* CR2 38 A3
Joseph Hood Primary School *RYNPK* SW20 12 A1
Julians Primary School *STRHM/NOR* SW16 7 G1
Jurys Inn *CROY/NA* CR0 2 D2
Kangley Business Centre *SYD* SE26 10 B2
Kelsey Park School *BECK* BR3 18 C2
Kenley Primary School *PUR/KEN* CR8 55 G1
Kenley Sports Club *PUR/KEN* CR8 46 A4
Kensington Avenue Primary School *THHTH* CR7 7 G5
Keston Primary School *COUL/CHIP* CR5 54 C4
Kiln Park Business Centre *EW* KT17 40 C1
Kimpton Industrial Estate *CHEAM* SM3 22 B3
Kingsley Primary School *CROY/NA* CR0 25 F2
Kings School of English *BECK* BR3
Kingswood Primary School *WNWD* SE27
Knollmead Primary School *BRYLDS* KT5
Laine Theatre Arts *EW* KT17
Laker Industrial Estate *BECK* BR3
Laleham Lea Preparatory School *PUR/KEN* CR8
Lambeth Cemetery *TOOT* SW17
Lambeth Crematorium *TOOT* SW17
Lamont Business Centre *CROY/NA* CR0
Langley Park Girls School & Sports Centre *BECK* BR3
Langley Park Golf Club *BECK* BR3
Langley Park School for Boys *BECK* BR3
Lewin Mead Community Mental Health Centre *STRHM/NOR* SW16
Lewis Clinic *CAR* SM5
Liberty Middle School *MTCM* CR4
Linden Bridge School *WPK* KT4
The Link Day Primary School *CROY/NA* CR0
The Link Secondary School *CROY/NA* CR0
Links Primary School *TOOT* SW17
Lodge School *PUR/KEN* CR8
Lombard Business Park *CROY/NA* CR0
*WIM/MER* SW19
London Ladies & Girls FC *CAT* SE6
London Lane Clinic *BMLY* BR1
London Living Theatre *SYD* SE26
London Road Medical Centre *CROY/NA* CR0
Lonesome Primary School *MTCM* CR4
The Longcroft Clinic *BNSTD* SM7
Longmead Business Centre *HOR/WEW* KT19
Longmead Industrial Estate *HOR/WEW* KT19
Lower Sydenham Industrial Estate *SYD* SE26
Lynton Preparatory School *EW* KT17
Malcolm Primary School *PGE/AN* SE20
Malden Manor Primary School *NWMAL* KT3
Malden Parochial Primary School *WPK* KT4
Malden Road Baths *CHEAM* SM3
Malmesbury Primary School *MRDN* SM4
Manor Drive Health Centre *WPK* KT4
Manor Park Primary School *SUT* SM1
Maple House School *THHTH* CR7
Marden Lodge Primary School *CTHM* CR3
Margaret Roper Catholic Primary School *PUR/KEN* CR8
Mariner Business Centre *CROY/NA* CR0
Marion Vian Primary School *BECK* BR3
Mayday University Hospital *THHTH* CR7
The Mead Infant School *WPK* KT4
Melrose Special School *MTCM* CR4
Merland Rise Primary School *EPSOM* KT18
Merton Abbey Primary School *WIM/MER* SW19
Merton Adult College *RYNPK* SW20
Merton College *MRDN* SM4
Merton Industrial Park *WIM/MER* SW19
Merton Park Primary School *WIM/MER* SW19
Metro Business Centre *SYD* SE26
Metropolitan Police Hayes Sports Club *HAYES* BR2
Mill Green Business Park *MTCM* CR4
Mill Lane Trading Estate *CROY/NA* CR0
Mitcham CC *MTCM* CR4
Mitcham Golf Club *MTCM* CR4
Mitcham Industrial Estate *MTCM* CR4

Index - featured places 79

am Vale High School
CM CR4 ... 14 B1
on Drive Health Centre
TN SM6 ... 35 E3
s Hill Sports Centre
D/SEL CR2 ... 37 H3
s Orchard Primary
ool CROY/NA CR0 ... 17 H4
en First School
DN SM4 ... 12 C4
en Hall Medical Centre
/MER SW19 ... 12 D2
en Hall Park (NT)
DN SM4 ... 13 E3
n Park Pool
DN SM4 ... 12 B4
en Road Clinic
/MER SW19 ... 12 D2
amp Primary School
SM5 ... 23 G3
College of
ther Education
KM BR4 ... 29 H4
al Sports Centre
VD SE19 ... 9 E3
al Therapy Clinic
T SW17 ... 6 B2
est Sports Club
K BR3 ... 10 B3
Hospital
PK SW20 ... 12 B1
Trading Estate
/MER SW19 ... 4 D5
ddington Pools &
ess Centre
Y/NA CR0 ... 39 E5
Woodlands School
LY BR1 ... 11 G1
ch High School for Girls
AM SM3 ... 31 H3
ch House Hotel
KT17 ... 31 G1
ch Industrial Estate
/WEW KT19 ... 40 C1
ch Primary School
KT17 ... 31 F1
ry Complementary
rapy Clinic
HM/NOR SW16 ... 7 F5
ry Health Centre
HM/NOR SW16 ... 15 F1
ry Manor Primary School
HM/NOR SW16 ... 7 E5
ry Manor Secondary
s School
HM/NOR SW16 ... 7 G5
ry Trading Estate
HM/NOR SW16 ... 15 F1
Croydon Medical Centre
TH CR7 ... 15 H5
Downs Golf Club
M CR3 ... 61 G5
East Surrey
ege of Technology
KT17 ... 41 E1
od Heights Shopping
tre NRWD SE19 ... 8 C3
od School
VD SE19 ... 8 A2
ld Road Industrial Estate
/AN SE20 ... 9 F4
dge JMI School
KM BR4 ... 28 D1
ports Centre
SM5 ... 43 H1
od Independent School
/KEN CR8 ... 45 H3
ational Health Centre
Y/NA CR0 ... 2 E5
Cinema
K BR3 ... 18 C1
KT17 ... 40 C3
/MER SW19 ... 4 C4
ckenhamian RFC
KM BR4 ... 29 F4
d Cottage Hospital
KT17 ... 40 D3
ds Trading Estate
SM1 ... 22 C4
lace School
Y/NA CR0 ... 2 B4
lsonians Sports Club
KM BR4 ... 29 G2
d Business Centre
K BR3 ... 10 B2
d Hill College
TN SM6 ... 34 B2
d Way Primary School
Y/NA CR0 ... 28 A1
pathic Clinic
/WEW KT19 ... 30 B1
dy & St Phillip Neri RC
mary School
SE26 ... 10 A1
rimary School
Y/NA CR0 ... 3 G1
on Grange School
MT SM2 ... 32 D4
rston Business Centre
SM1 ... 33 E1
more Medical Centre
TH CR7 ... 16 A2
Church CE
mary School
Y/NA CR0 ... 2 A5
ill Junior School
Y/NA CR0 ... 3 G5
atrick Doody Clinic &
lth Centre
/MER SW19 ... 4 C4
Primary School
VD SE19 ... 8 D3

Payne Clinic
EW KT17 ... 41 E3
Peall Road Industrial Estate
CROY/NA CR0 ... 15 F5
Pelham Primary School
WIM/MER SW19 ... 4 C4
Penwortham Primary School
STRHM/NOR SW16 ... 6 B3
Phoenix College
MRDN SM4 ... 12 D4
Pickhurst Infant School
WWKM BR4 ... 19 G5
Pickhurst Junior School
WWKM BR4 ... 19 H5
Pilton Estate
CROY/NA CR0 ... 2 B2
Pinnacles Cricket & Squash
Club SUT SM1 ... 32 C2
Pioneers Industrial Park
CROY/NA CR0 ... 25 E2
Pitwood Park Industrial Estate
KWD/TDW/WH KT20 ... 50 D5
Playhouse Cinema
EPSOM KT18 ... 40 B4
Playhouse Theatre
EPSOM KT18 ... 40 A3
Polka Theatre for Children
WIM/MER SW19 ... 4 D3
Poplar Primary School
WIM/MER SW19 ... 12 C2
Portland Medical Centre
SNWD SE25 ... 17 F4
Premier Travel Inn
CROY/NA CR0 ... 35 G2
CROY/NA CR0 ... 37 E1
EPSOM KT18 ... 40 A4
HOR/WEW KT19 ... 30 C1
KWD/TDW/WH KT20 ... 51 E4
WIM/MER SW19 ... 5 E5
Priory CE Primary School
WIM/MER SW19 ... 4 D2
Priory Retail Park
WIM/MER SW19 ... 5 F4
Priory School
BNSTD SM7 ... 42 C5
Priory Special School
SNWD SE25 ... 16 D3
Progress Business Park
CROY/NA CR0 ... 25 F3
Purley Community Health
Clinic PUR/KEN CR8 ... 45 G1
Purley & District War
Memorial Hospital
PUR/KEN CR8 ... 45 G1
Purley Downs Golf Club
SAND/SEL CR2 ... 46 B1
Purley John Fisher RFC
COUL/CHIP CR5 ... 54 C5
Purley Oaks Primary School
SAND/SEL CR2 ... 36 B3
Purley Secretarial & Language
College PUR/KEN CR8 ... 45 G1
Purley Sports Club
PUR/KEN CR8 ... 34 D5
Queen Elizabeth Hospital
BNSTD SM7 ... 52 A3
Queen Mary's Hospital for
Children SUT SM1 ... 23 E2
Queen's Road Cemetery
CROY/NA CR0 ... 16 A5
Rainbow Leisure Centre
EW KT17 ... 40 C2
Rangefield Primary School
BMLY BR1 ... 11 G2
Red Gates School
CROY/NA CR0 ... 35 G1
Reedham Park School
PUR/KEN CR8 ... 45 G4
Regina Coeli RC Primary
School SAND/SEL CR2 ... 35 H3
The Retail Business Centre
EW KT17 ... 30 D5
Ricards Lodge High School
WIM/MER SW19 ... 4 B1
Riddlesdown High School
PUR/KEN CR8 ... 46 C4
Ridgeway Primary School
SAND/SEL CR2 ... 36 C4
Riverside Business Park
WIM/MER SW19 ... 5 E5
Riverside Wandle Trading
Estate MTCM CR4 ... 23 H1
Riverview CE Primary School
HOR/WEW KT19 ... 20 A5
Roan Industrial Estate
MTCM CR4 ... 5 G5
Robin Hood Infant School
SUT SM1 ... 32 C1
Robin Hood Junior School
SUT SM1 ... 32 D1
Robin Hood Lane Health
Centre SUT SM1 ... 32 C1
Rockmount Primary School
NRWD SE19 ... 8 A3
Roke Primary School
PUR/KEN CR8 ... 46 A4
Roman Industrial Estate
CROY/NA CR0 ... 26 C1
Rosebery School
EPSOM KT18 ... 40 A4
Roundshaw J&I School
WLGTN SM6 ... 35 E3
Royal Marsden Hospital
BELMT SM2 ... 33 E5
Royal Russell School
CROY/NA CR0 ... 37 F2
Royston Primary School
PGE/AN SE20 ... 9 H5
Rutlish School
RYNPK SW20 ... 12 B1
Ryelands Primary School
SNWD SE25 ... 17 F4

Safari Cinema
CROY/NA CR0 ... 25 H2
St Andrews CE School
CROY/NA CR0 ... 2 B5
St Annes Catholic Primary
School BNSTD SM7 ... 51 G1
St Anne's Special School
MRDN SM4 ... 12 C4
St Anthonys Hospital
WPK KT4 ... 21 H2
St Anthonys RC Primary
School PGE/AN SE20 ... 9 F5
St Augustines RC Primary
School CAT SE6 ... 10 D2
St Bartholomews CE Primary
School SYD SE26 ... 9 G1
St Boniface RC Primary School
TOOT SW17 ... 5 H2
St Cecilias RC Primary School
WPK KT4 ... 21 H3
St Chads RC Primary School
SNWD SE25 ... 16 C4
St Christophers School
BECK BR3 ... 19 E1
EPSOM KT18 ... 40 C4
St Clements Primary School
EW KT17 ... 30 D4
St Cyprians Greek Orthodox
Primary School
THHTH CR7 ... 16 A1
St Davids College
WWKM BR4 ... 28 D1
St Davids School
PUR/KEN CR8 ... 45 F1
St Dunstans CE Primary
School CHEAM SM3 ... 32 A2
St Ebba's Hospital
HOR/WEW KT19 ... 30 A4
St Elpheges RC Primary School
WLGTN SM6 ... 35 E2
St Francis Catholic School
CTHM CR3 ... 59 H1
St Georges Hospital
TOOT SW17 ... 5 G2
St Giles School
SAND/SEL CR2 ... 35 H2
St Helier Hospital
CAR SM5 ... 23 E2
St James Medical Centre
CROY/NA CR0 ... 26 B1
St James the Great RC Primary
School THHTH CR7 ... 15 H1
St Johns CE Primary School
CROY/NA CR0 ... 27 H4
PGE/AN SE20 ... 9 G4
St John the Baptist CE Primary
School BMLY BR1 ... 11 E1
St Josephs Catholic Primary
School EPSOM KT18 ... 40 A4
St Josephs College
STRHM/NOR SW16 ... 7 H3
St Josephs RC Infant School
NRWD SE19 ... 8 A3
St Josephs RC Junior School
NRWD SE19 ... 8 A3
St Leonards CE Primary School
STRHM/NOR SW16 ... 6 D2
St Lukes CE Primary School
WNWD SE27 ... 8 A2
St Lukes School
THHTH CR7 ... 15 G3
St Marks CE Primary School
SNWD SE25 ... 17 E3
St Marks Primary School
MTCM CR4 ... 13 H1
St Martins CE Junior School
EPSOM KT18 ... 40 B5
St Marys Catholic Infant School
CROY/NA CR0 ... 2 E1
St Marys High School
CROY/NA CR0 ... 26 A2
St Marys Infant School
CAR SM5 ... 23 G5
St Marys RC Infant School
CAR SM5 ... 33 H1
St Marys RC Primary School
BECK BR3 ... 11 E4
WIM/MER SW19 ... 4 C4
St Michaels Sydenham CE
Primary School SYD SE26 ... 10 A1
St Nicholas Centre
SUT SM1 ... 32 D1
St Nicholas School
PUR/KEN CR8 ... 45 G3
St Peter & Paul CE Infant
School CTHM CR3 ... 58 C5
St Peters Primary School
SAND/SEL CR2 ... 36 B2
St Phillips Infant School
SYD SE26 ... 9 F1
St Philomenas Catholic High
School CAR SM5 ... 33 G1
St Raphaels Hospice
WPK KT4 ... 21 H3
St Thomas Becket RC
Primary School
SNWD SE25 ... 17 E5
St Thomas of Canterbury
Primary School
MTCM CR4 ... 14 A2
Sanderstead Junior School
SAND/SEL CR2 ... 36 B4
Saxon Business Centre
WIM/MER SW19 ... 13 E1
Sayer Clinic
CROY/NA CR0 ... 25 F5
Seaton House School
BELMT SM2 ... 33 F5
Secombe Centre
SUT SM1 ... 32 D2
Sedgehill School
CAT SE6 ... 10 D2

Selhurst High School for Boys
CROY/NA CR0 ... 16 B5
The Selhurst Medical Centre
SNWD SE25 ... 16 C5
Sellincourt School
TOOT SW17 ... 5 G3
Selsdon Community Centre
SAND/SEL CR2 ... 37 F5
Selsdon High School
SAND/SEL CR2 ... 37 H3
Selsdon Park Hotel & Golf
Course SAND/SEL CR2 ... 47 G1
Selsdon Primary School
SAND/SEL CR2 ... 37 G4
Selsdon Road Industrial Estate
SAND/SEL CR2 ... 36 B3
Shawley Primary School
EPSOM KT18 ... 50 C3
Sherwood Park School
WLGTN SM6 ... 24 D4
Sherwood School
MTCM CR4 ... 14 C3
Shirley Clinic
CROY/NA CR0 ... 27 G2
Shirley High School
CROY/NA CR0 ... 27 H4
Shirley Oaks Hospital
CROY/NA CR0 ... 27 G1
Shirley Park Golf Club
CROY/NA CR0 ... 27 F3
Shirley Wanderers RFC
WWKM BR4 ... 29 E5
Shortlands Golf Club
HAYES BR2 ... 11 G5
Shotfield Health Clinic
WLGTN SM6 ... 34 B2
Silver Wing Industrial Estate
CROY/NA CR0 ... 35 F2
Singlegate Primary School
WIM/MER SW19 ... 5 F4
Sloane Hospital
BECK BR3 ... 11 F5
Smallwood Primary School
TOOT SW17 ... 5 F1
Smitham Primary School
COUL/CHIP CR5 ... 53 G1
South Croydon Medical Centre
SAND/SEL CR2 ... 36 A3
South Croydon Sports Club
CROY/NA CR0 ... 36 C1
South Lewisham Health Centre
CAT SE6 ... 11 E1
South London Crematorium
MTCM CR4 ... 14 C1
South London Tamil School
CROY/NA CR0 ... 26 A1
South Norwood Country Park
SNWD SE25 ... 17 G3
South Norwood Hill Medical
Centre SNWD SE25 ... 16 C1
South Norwood Medical
Centre SNWD SE25 ... 16 C3
South Norwood Pools &
Fitness Centre SNWD SE25 ... 17 E4
South Norwood Primary
School SNWD SE25 ... 17 E4
South Park Hotel
SAND/SEL CR2 ... 3 G7
South Thames College
TOOT SW17 ... 5 G2
Sparrow Farm Community
Junior School EW KT17 ... 31 F1
Spitfire Business Park
CROY/NA CR0 ... 35 G2
Spring Park Primary School
CROY/NA CR0 ... 28 C4
Spurgeon's College
SNWD SE25 ... 16 C1
SS Peter & Paul RC Primary
School MTCM CR4 ... 13 H3
Stafford Cross Business Park
CROY/NA CR0 ... 35 F1
Stanford Primary School
STRHM/NOR SW16 ... 6 D5
Stanley Park High School
CAR SM5 ... 34 A2
Stanley Park Primary School
CAR SM5 ... 33 H3
Stanley Technical High School
SNWD SE25 ... 16 D2
Stanton Square Industrial
Estate SYD SE26 ... 10 B1
Stewart Fleming Primary
School PGE/AN SE20 ... 17 G2
Stirling Way Industrial Estates
CROY/NA CR0 ... 25 E1
Stoneleigh First School
EW KT17 ... 21 F5
Stowford College
BELMT SM2 ... 33 E3
Streatham & Croydon RFC
THHTH CR7 ... 15 G4
Streatham Ice Rink
STRHM/NOR SW16 ... 7 E2
Streatham Modern School
STRHM/NOR SW16 ... 7 E3
Streatham Park Cemetery
MTCM CR4 ... 14 C1
Streatham Swimming Pool
STRHM/NOR SW16 ... 7 E2
Streatham Vale Sports Club
STRHM/NOR SW16 ... 6 C4
Sunnydown School
CTHM CR3 ... 59 H1
Sunnyhill Primary School
STRHM/NOR SW16 ... 7 F1
Surrey Business Park
EW KT17 ... 40 C1
Surrey Institute of Art & Design
HOR/WEW KT19 ... 40 C2
Surrey National Golf Club
CTHM CR3 ... 58 D3

Sutton Alternative Health
Centre SUT SM1 ... 32 D1
Sutton Arena
CAR SM5 ... 23 F1
Sutton Bowling Club
BELMT SM2 ... 32 C4
Sutton Cemetery
CHEAM SM3 ... 22 B3
Sutton College of Learning
for Adults SUT SM1 ... 32 D1
Sutton General Hospital
BELMT SM2 ... 32 D5
Sutton Grammar School for
Boys SUT SM1 ... 33 E1
Sutton High Junior School
SUT SM1 ... 32 D2
Sutton High School for Girls
SUT SM1 ... 32 C2
Sutton Superbowl
SUT SM1 ... 32 D1
Sutton United FC
SUT SM1 ... 22 C5
Sutton West Centre
SUT SM1 ... 32 C1
Sydenham High Junior School
SYD SE26 ... 9 F1
Sydenham High School Sports
Ground CAT SE6 ... 10 C2
Sydenham High Senior School
SYD SE26 ... 9 F2
Taberner House
CROY/NA CR0 ... 2 D4
Tait Road Industrial Estate
CROY/NA CR0 ... 16 C5
Tamworth Manor High School
STRHM/NOR SW16 ... 14 D2
Tandem Centre
WIM/MER SW19 ... 5 F5
Tattenham Health Centre
EPSOM KT18 ... 50 B3
Thatched House Hotel
SUT SM1 ... 32 B2
Theatre Centre
BECK BR3 ... 18 D1
The Theatre on the Hill
CTHM CR3 ... 59 G2
Therapia Trading Estate
CROY/NA CR0 ... 24 D1
Thomas More Catholic School
PUR/KEN CR8 ... 35 F5
Thornton Heath Health Centre
THHTH CR7 ... 16 A3
Thornton Heath Pools &
Fitness Centre
THHTH CR7 ... 16 A3
Thornton Road Industrial
Estate CROY/NA CR0 ... 15 E5
Times Square Shopping
Centre SUT SM1 ... 32 D1
Tollgate Primary School
CROY/NA CR0 ... 17 G5
Tooting Bec Athletics Track
TOOT SW17 ... 6 B1
Tooting Leisure Centre
TOOT SW17 ... 5 F1
Tooting & Mitcham United
Football Club MTCM CR4 ... 6 A5
Tower Industrial Estate
SNWD SE25 ... 17 E3
Trident Business Centre
TOOT SW17 ... 5 H2
Trinity School
CROY/NA CR0 ... 27 G3
Tudor Lodge School
PUR/KEN CR8 ... 35 E5
Tweeddale Primary School
CAR SM5 ... 23 F1
Two Bridges Business Park
SAND/SEL CR2 ... 36 B2
UCI Cinema
SUT SM1 ... 32 D1
The Ullswater Business Park
COUL/CHIP CR5 ... 54 A1
Ullswater Trading Estate
COUL/CHIP CR5 ... 54 A1
Unicorn Primary School
BECK BR3 ... 18 D4
University College for the
Creative Arts at Epsom
EPSOM KT18 ... 40 B4
Valley Primary School
HAYES BR2 ... 19 H1
Vestry Hall
MTCM CR4 ... 13 H2
Victor Seymour Infant School
CAR SM5 ... 23 H4
Virgo Fidelis Convent Schools
NRWD SE19 ... 8 A3
Vue Cinema
CROY/NA CR0 ... 25 F3
Vulcan Business Centre
CROY/NA CR0 ... 39 G4
Waddon Clinic
CROY/NA CR0 ... 35 G1
Waddon Infant School
CROY/NA CR0 ... 35 G1
Wallace Fields County Infant
School EW KT17 ... 41 E3
Wallace Fields Junior School
EW KT17 ... 41 E2
Wallington County Grammar
School WLGTN SM6 ... 24 B4
Wallington High School for
Girls WLGTN SM6 ... 34 B4
Wandle Trading Estate
MTCM CR4 ... 23 H1
Wandle Valley School
CAR SM5 ... 23 G1
Warehouse Theatre
CROY/NA CR0 ... 2 E3
Warlingham Park School
WARL CR6 ... 57 G1

**Warlingham RFC & John Fisher**
**Sports Club**
*WARL* CR6 .................................56 B1
**Warlingham School**
*WARL* CR6 .................................56 B1
**Warlingham Sports Club**
*WARL* CR6 .................................56 D2
**War Memorial Sports Ground**
*SUT* SM1 ..................................23 G5
**Warren Mead Infant School**
*BNSTD* SM7 ...............................41 G5
**Warren Mead Junior School**
*BNSTD* SM7 ...............................41 H5
**Watergate School**
*CAT* SE6 ...................................10 D2
**Watermeads High School**
*MRDN* SM4 ................................13 F5
**Wattenden Primary School**
*PUR/KEN* CR8 ............................54 D2
**Westbourne Primary School**
*SUT* SM1 ..................................22 C4
**Westcroft Leisure Centre**
*CAR* SM5 ..................................24 A5
**West Dene School**
*PUR/KEN* CR8 ............................45 F3

**West Ewell Infant School**
*HOR/WEW* KT19 .........................30 B1
**West Thornton Primary School**
*CROY/NA* CR0 ............................25 F1
**West Wickham Swimming**
**Baths** *WWKM* BR4 ...................29 E2
**Westwood Language College**
**for Girls**
*NRWD* SE19 ................................8 A4
**Whitehorse Manor Primary**
**School** *THHTH* CR7 ..................16 B4
**Whitgift School**
*SAND/SEL* CR2 ...........................36 A1
**Whitgift Shopping Centre**
*CROY/NA* CR0 ............................2 D2
**Whyteleafe Business Village**
*CTHM* CR3 .................................55 H2
**Whyteleafe FC**
*CTHM* CR3 .................................55 H4
**Whyteleafe School**
*CTHM* CR3 .................................55 H3
**Wickham Court School**
*WWKM* BR4 ...............................29 F5
**Wickham Theatre**
*WWKM* BR4 ...............................29 F4

**Wide Way Health Clinic**
*MTCM* CR4 .................................14 D2
**William Morris Primary School**
*MTCM* CR4 .................................14 D2
**Willington School**
*WIM/MER* SW19 ..........................4 B3
**Willow Business Centre**
*MTCM* CR4 .................................13 H4
**Wilson's School**
*WLGTN* SM6 ...............................35 E2
**Wimbledon Chase Primary**
**School** *RYNPK* SW20 .................4 A5
**Wimbledon (Gap Road)**
**Cemetery**
*WIM/MER* SW19 ..........................4 D1
**Wimbledon High School**
*WIM/MER* SW19 ..........................4 A3
**Wimbledon House School**
*WIM/MER* SW19 ..........................4 B5
**Wimbledon Magistrates Court**
*WIM/MER* SW19 ..........................4 C3
**Wimbledon Recreation Centre**
*WIM/MER* SW19 ..........................4 D3
**Wimbledon School of Art**
*WIM/MER* SW19 ..........................4 A5

*WIM/MER* SW19 ..........................4 C4
**Wimbledon Stadium**
*WIM/MER* SW19 ..........................4 D1
**Wimbledon Theatre**
*WIM/MER* SW19 ..........................4 C4
**Windmill Trading Estate**
*MTCM* CR4 .................................14 C4
**Winterbourne Infant School**
*THHTH* CR7 ................................15 G3
**Woldingham Golf Club**
*CTHM* CR5 .................................56 D5
**Woldingham School**
*CTHM* CR3 .................................61 E5
**Wolsey Junior School**
*CROY/NA* CR0 ............................39 F3
**Woodbrook School**
*BECK* BR3 ..................................10 B5
**Woodcote High School**
*PUR/KEN* CR8 ............................44 D3
**Woodcote Park Golf Club**
*COUL/CHIP* CR5 .........................44 C4
**Woodcotes Primary School**
*COUL/CHIP* CR5 .........................44 D4
**Woodlea Primary School**
*CTHM* CR3 .................................61 F2

**Woodmansterne Primary**
**School** *BNSTD* SM7 ..................43
*STRHM/NOR* SW16 ......................6
**Woodmansterne Sports Club**
*BNSTD* SM7 ...............................43
**Woodside Health Centre**
*SNWD* SE25 ...............................17
**Woodside Infant School**
*CROY/NA* CR0 ............................27
**Worsley Bridge Junior School**
*BECK* BR3 ..................................10
**Wrencote**
*CROY/NA* CR0 ............................2

## Acknowledgements

Schools address data provided by Education Direct.

Petrol station information supplied by Johnsons

One-way street data provided by © Tele Atlas N.V. Tele Atlas

Garden centre information provided by

Garden Centre Association  Britains best garden centres

Wyevale Garden Centres

The statement on the front cover of this atlas is sourced, selected and quoted
from a reader comment and feedback form received in 2004

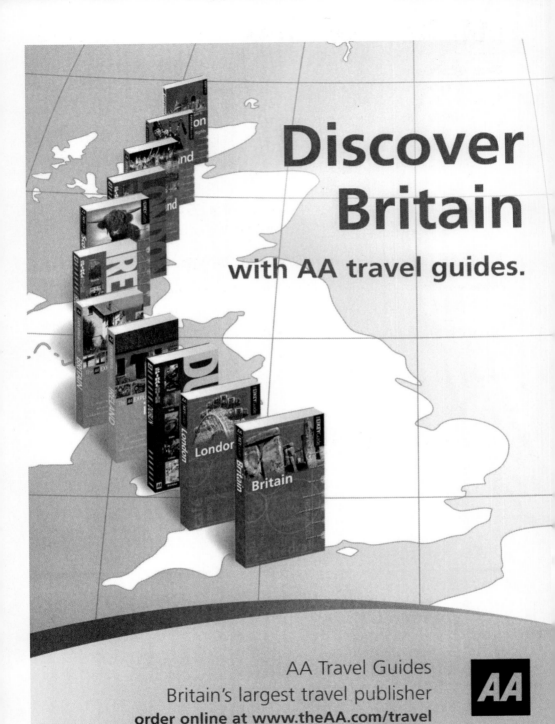

# Discover Britain

## with AA travel guides.

AA Travel Guides
Britain's largest travel publisher
**order online at www.theAA.com/travel**

**AA**

# **AA** **Street by Street** QUESTIONNAIRE

**Dear Atlas User**
**Your comments, opinions and recommendations are very important to us.**
**So please help us to improve our street atlases by taking a few minutes**
**to complete this simple questionnaire.**

You do not need a stamp (unless posted outside the UK). If you do not want to remove this page from your street atlas, then photocopy it or write your answers on a plain sheet of paper.

**Send to: Marketing Assistant, AA Publishing, 14th Floor Fanum House,**
**FREEPOST SCE 4598, Basingstoke RG21 4GY**

## ABOUT THE ATLAS...

**Please state which city / town / county street atlas you bought:**

_____
_____

**Where did you buy the atlas?** (City, Town, County)

_____

**For what purpose?** (please tick all applicable)

**To use in your own local area** ☐    **To use on business or at work** ☐

**Visiting a strange place** ☐    **In the car** ☐    **On foot** ☐

**Other** (please state)

_____

**Have you ever used any street atlases other than AA Street by Street?**

**Yes** ☐    **No** ☐

**If so, which ones?**

_____

**Is there any aspect of our street atlases that could be improved?**
(Please continue on a separate sheet if necessary)

_____
_____
_____
_____
_____
_____

**Please list the features you found most useful:**

_____

_____

**Please list the features you found least useful:**

_____

_____

_____

## LOCAL KNOWLEDGE...

Local knowledge is invaluable. Whilst every attempt has been made to make the information contained in this atlas as accurate as possible, should you notice any inaccuracies, please detail them below (if necessary, use a blank piece of paper) or e-mail us at *streetbystreet@theAA.com*

_____

_____

_____

## ABOUT YOU...

**Name (Mr/Mrs/Ms)** _____

**Address** _____

                                          **Postcode** _____

**Daytime tel no** _____

**E-mail address** _____

**Which age group are you in?**

Under 25 ☐   25-34 ☐   35-44 ☐   45-54 ☐   55-64 ☐   65+ ☐

**Are you an AA member?**   YES ☐   NO ☐

**Do you have Internet access?**   YES ☐   NO ☐

Thank you for taking the time to complete this questionnaire. Please send it to us as soon as possible, and remember, you do not need a stamp (unless posted outside the UK).

We may use information we hold about you to, telephone or email you about other products and services offered by the AA, we do NOT disclose this information to third parties.

Please tick here if you do not wish to hear about products and services from the AA. ☐

ML167y